Places of Silence,
Journeys of Freedom

Penn Studies in Contemporary American Fiction

Emory Elliott, Series Editor

A complete list of books in the series is available from the publisher.

Places of Silence, Journeys of Freedom

The Fiction of Paule Marshall

Eugenia C. DeLamotte

PENN

University of Pennsylvania Press

Philadelphia

10 9 8 7 6 5 4 3 2 1

Published by
University of Pennsylvania Press
Philadelphia, Pennsylvania 19104-4011

Library of Congress Cataloging-in-Publication Data

DeLamotte, Eugenia C.
  Places of silence, journeys of freedom : the fiction of Paule
Marshall / Eugenia C. DeLamotte.
      p.   cm. — (Penn studies in contemporary American fiction)
  Includes bibliographical references and index.
  ISBN 0-8122-3437-5 (alk. paper)
  1. Marshall, Paule, 1929– — Criticism and interpretation.
2. Women and literature — United States — History — 20th century.
3. Caribbean Area — In literature.   4. Afro-Americans in literature.
I. Title.   II. Series.
PS3563.A7223Z63   1998
813'.54 — dc21   97-47580
                                                              CIP

For Carl, Paul, and Mark

Contents

Acknowledgments

The encouragement of Henry Louis Gates Jr. enabled me to begin this book; funding from a grant by the American Council of Learned Societies in 1995 enabled me to complete it. In between, many colleagues, friends, and students contributed to the theoretical basis for my argument and to specific readings of Paule Marshall's work. I am especially grateful for conversations with Emily Chamberlain, Tris Laughter, Jacques Lezra, Susanne Wofford, and Kevin Quashie, and for the support, over the years, of Warner Berthoff, Franklin Burroughs, Ronald Bush, Nancy Gutierrez, Jean O'Barr, Elizabeth McKinsey, and Mary Rothschild.

More than anything else I have written, this book is rooted in my experiences as a teacher. Students in my African-American literature course at Bowdoin College contributed a great deal to the way I read *The Chosen Place, the Timeless People*; in particular I would like to thank Elizabeth Brimmer, who was working out her conception of Marshall's technique of "pentimento" for a senior thesis on that novel at the same time I was developing my ideas about superimposition and double exposure in Marshall's works as a whole. Students in women's studies courses at Duke University enriched my understanding of women's power in *Brown Girl, Brownstones* as well as of African-American feminist theory more generally. At Arizona State University, students in a seminar on Paule Marshall contributed immeasurably to my readings of all her novels, as well as to my sense of her vital importance and power as a writer. I would like especially to thank Jenita Landrum, whose comments in that class and whose painting of herself and her son against the backdrop of an urban landscape enhanced my understanding of *Daughters*.

I owe a special debt to the Carolina Friends School students in my feminist theory and African-American literature courses for their insights into *Brown Girl, Brownstones*, and for insights into other literature that enabled me to read Paule Marshall in new ways. In this regard I would especially like to thank Douala Dennis, and Weusi Chapman for his essay on the first mirror-scene in *Brown Girl.*

Finally, I would like to thank my family — Carl Gardner, Paul De-Lamotte Gardner, and Mark DeLamotte Gardner — for their patience, love, and support.

Introduction: The Double Visions of Paule Marshall's Art

Progressive art can assist people to learn not only about the objective forces at work in the society in which they live, but also about the intensely social character of their interior lives.

— Angela Davis, *Women, Culture, and Politics*

The argument of this book, like its title, is twofold: Paule Marshall's work makes an important contribution to feminism by means of a technique that makes an equally important contribution to narrative art. Her importance for feminism derives from her exploration of a crucial set of issues that coalesce around the question of silence and voice. These include the relationship between women's power and their dispossession; the significance, for that relationship, of the interpenetration of the social, political, and economic worlds with the world of the psyche; the role played in that relationship by the interlinked oppressions of race, class, gender, nationality. Her importance for narrative art derives from the mode of superimposition she has developed for representing, as if in double exposure, the simultaneities these categories imply.

As Marshall has emphasized many times in interviews, her women characters are "centers of power" (DeVeaux 71), "not victims" (Bröck, "Interview" 194). It is equally clear that their power in general is bound up with their power of voice.[1] "I'm concerned about letting them speak their piece," she said in 1979, "letting them be central figures, actors, *activists* in fiction rather than just backdrop or background figures ..." (DeVeaux 71). At the same time, her novels are complicated studies of the mechanisms whereby oppressive hierarchies disempower women through silence, and of the ways in which that silence works in turn to sustain and reproduce oppression. It is in this context that she represents women's agency, and it is in the context of their agency that she represents their oppression.[2]

The silences on which oppressive hierarchies depend take many forms, most of which play a major role in Marshall's novels. Foremost are the silences around which hegemonic discourse is constructed: all the speech and thought it cannot accommodate but must contain walled up, invisible, at its core.[3] This silence is especially at issue in *Daughters*, which raises the question of voice specifically in the context of coercive discourses, but each of the earlier novels studies at least one of its aspects. This fundamental silence is reinforced by particular acts of silencing. Among them are direct suppressions of voice through physical, economic, social, political, and cultural intimidation and through denial of access to the means by which dominant ideologies are promulgated: publication, news media, government, educational curricula. At the psychological level, these more overt acts of suppression replicate themselves in self-silencing — oppression internalized as repression. This silencing closes certain voices out of the space they should occupy in internal dialogue just as, at the political and economic level, the voices of the oppressed are barred from the centers of power.

Systems of domination also appropriate voices, creating silence that seems to be speech. One such silence is produced by a censored mode of "hearing" that translates the speech of the dispossessed into the terms of hegemonic discourse, discarding anything that discourse cannot voice. What is lost in this simultaneous translation is difference. "We used to have these long discussions on the race problem," Mrs. Benton says of her housekeeper Ettie in *Brown Girl, Brownstones*, "and she always agreed with me" (288–89). Another silence disguised as speech is the ventriloquism whereby an oppressor actually speaks in the voice of the oppressed, as when Jay Johnson, striking "hard, punishing little blows" to his hand, rails against "these Negroes" for not working hard enough (*Praisesong for the Widow* 134–35). Another is an act of appropriation whereby the voice of the oppressed, through its very opposition, comes to circle the oppressor angrily, unceasingly — not in a liberatory, self-defining way but as if mesmerized, obsessed, fixated in a helpless orbit around a stronger center of gravity that pulls the speaker away from affinities with other members of the dominated group. In Marshall's novels this appropriation takes the form of "runaway" monologues associated with imagery of a plunge down a hill, stampede, self-destruction, suicide.

A more complicated act of appropriation takes place through the designation of representative voices to speak at the center of power for other voices that center excludes. The appropriation occurs when the representative voice, by the very fact of its insinuation into the discourse of power, is constrained either to speak its concerns in a language that has no words for them or to speak no language at all.[4] In Marshall's novels this kind of silence is associated with the putative democracies of a post-colonial world in which those consigned to silence by the hegemonic discourse, which is still the discourse of colonialism, are offered only a putative voice. *Daughters* in particular is concerned with this voice, and with the gendering of its silences, but there are versions of it in the earlier novels as well.

All these silences are forms of doubleness:[5] that of hegemonic discourse divorced from but sustained by the silence it masks, of ventriloquism and other forms of appropriation in which one voice colonizes another, of the colonized mind (the doubleness of repression), of those constrained to "wear the mask" of silence. There is also the doubleness of the possessed voice struggling to free itself through a speech that only binds it more strongly to the oppressor. And there is the doubled doubleness of the dispossessed voice assigned to speak for another such voice in a language that is working, all the while, to recolonize the speaker. Paule Marshall's novels are extraordinarily complex explorations of these kinds of silence and doubleness, which as she presents them are all versions of each other.

The silences that sustain oppressive hierarchies are silences of dispossession. Whether such hierarchies can be subverted thus depends in important ways on the outcome of each struggle to possess the voices of the dispossessed. As bell hooks says, for the oppressed,

true speaking is not solely an expression of creative power; it is an act of resistance, a political gesture that challenges politics of domination that would render us nameless and voiceless. . . . Moving from silence into speech is for the oppressed, the colonized, the exploited, and those who stand and struggle side by side a gesture of defiance that heals, that makes new life and new growth possible. It is that act of speech, of "talking back," that is no mere gesture of empty words, that is the expression of our movement from object to subject—the liberated voice. (*Talking Back* 8–9)

All of Paule Marshall's novels trace a heroine's journey from the silence of oppression to the self-possessed voice of liberation.[6] But women's power and their dispossession interact in an interplay more complex than a simple identification of silence with oppression might suggest. In Marshall's novels, one hint of this complexity is the fact that silence, like other aspects of the life of the oppressed, can be used as a form of power. Such is the case in *The Chosen Place, the Timeless People*, which depicts silence as a sign of dispossession but also of resistance—of defiant self-possession. *Daughters* represents the relation between silence and the power of the dominated in an even more complicated way, as the heroine's mother silently dispatches her daughter on a mission to free an oppositional voice by silencing an appropriated one, that of her father, the M.P. who no longer speaks for his constituents.

Just as silence can be made into a form of power, so can doubleness. The many dualities of Paule Marshall's novels are a special locus of her interest in the interplay between women's agency and oppression, which has always to do, in her work, with women's struggle for an individual autonomy strong enough to support a significant connection with a broader, collective struggle for independence. Thus the titles of the first three novels are plays on various kinds of doubleness, each having two terms that have elements of connectedness but also of opposition. *Brown Girl, Brownstones*: a girl reflected by and reflecting her world, but not identical with it; part of it but also a single individual pitted against its collective conformities, battling alone the "army" of brownstones but then, at the end, finding her identity in the community as well as in opposition to it. *The Chosen Place, the Timeless People*: a place (singular) and its people (plural) — unity and diversity; a place "chosen" by Western powers for subjection but by history, fate, and its own people for resistance. *Praisesong for the Widow*: praisesongs evoking joy, celebration, and collective ritual; widowhood evoking sorrow and solitude but also Avey's chance to recover a self that is something other than her husband's "twin"; the double meaning of a praisesong in honor of the widow and a praisesong for the widow to sing.

The single word *Daughters* breaks with this tradition of double titles in one sense but in another provides its fitting culmination, a resolution toward which all the novels have been tending. For the single word is plural, and it refers at the same time to several women and to one in particular: a heroine both cursed and blessed with a penchant for "seeing double" (290). Ursa's tendency to see "everything superimposed on everything else" (333) as if in "a series of double exposures" (332) is expressed in the singularity of her dual existence as U.S. citizen and West Indian. All by herself she is the plural *daughters* of the title: a West Indian daughter and an American daughter; a man's daughter and a woman's daughter; daughter of a middle-class American woman and, metaphorically, of a working-class Third World woman; daughter of a wife and, metaphorically, of a mistress. Ursa's many dualities make up what Avey would call "a certain distance of the mind and heart" (*Praisesong* 139): a consciousness derived from being present in two places remote from each other; an *achieved* doubleness of which she is creator rather than victim. This kind of doubleness yields unities instead of disunities, like the double visions of the author herself, who has said that she thinks of her work as "a kind of bridge that joins the two great wings of the black diaspora in this part of the world" (Dance 14).[7]

The double vision Ursa describes is a good metaphor for the narrative technique that is the second focus of this study: a technique of super-imposition or "double exposure." Through this technique Paule Marshall has explored the relationship between women's power and their dispossession, the "social character of the interior life,"[8] the mutually shaping oppressions of race/class/gender, and the question of women's voice.

As her early short story "Brooklyn" (1961) makes clear, Marshall began exploring these issues in the 1950s, long before they emerged in the foreground of modern feminist inquiry. Nowhere is her art of double vision more evident than at the climax of this story, in which the image of a woman's powerlessness beneath a man's gaze becomes, beneath Paule Marshall's gaze, a simultaneous image of her power. Alone with her professor at his country house, wearing the bathing suit he invited her to bring so that he might "very much enjoy" the "sight" (37) of her swimming in the lake at his country place, his eyes following her as she walks out into the water, Miss Williams is in one sense a picture of complete dispossession. Nothing in Berman's domain is hers; just before she walks toward the water she refers to the lake as "yours," contrasting it with the lake near her far away home in the South. The lake, so emphatically described as Berman's, not Miss Williams's, is nonetheless "dark and serious-looking" like her, and she seems "a pale gold naiad," its spirit, "her eyes reflecting its somber autumnal tone and her body as supple as the birches" (43). Such imagery, conflating woman's nature with Nature itself, is imbued with the potential to be what Simone de Beauvoir demonstrated it so often to be in the (white) male literary imagination: an assigning of woman to the status of object. In this role, woman-as-Nature is an object either to be possessed, as in images of men conquering virgin territory, or to be eluded, as in stories such as that of Hylas and the water nymphs, in which her allure signifies a man's potential descent to the condition of being an object himself, through the plunge from transcendence into immanence (de Beauvoir, chaps. 9–11).

The identification of Miss Williams with the lake suggests the many levels of revisioning Paule Marshall is engaged in here. In her story, the woman's unity with nature becomes an image not of her status as object, but of her defiance of a potentially objectifying gaze: "She walked slowly into the water, unaware, it seemed, of the sudden passion in his gaze, or perhaps uncaring . . ." (43). Berman has tried subtly to coerce this dark woman he wants to "possess" into the dark body of water they both regard as his. But as she swims far out into it, Berman, in Marshall's imagery, turns out no more to possess this piece of his private property than he is able to "possess" (34) the woman he wanted to entrap in this colonized space. Miss Williams escapes Berman's power by choosing consciously the way in which she will occupy the space he has tried to assign her, remaking its symbolism so that, instead of becoming an image of the woman whose body Berman would like to claim, it becomes an image of her self-possession, her claiming of her own body and her own destiny. Instead of subsuming her as a natural part of Berman's domain, Miss Williams's pale golden oneness with the lake moves her out beyond his sphere of influence:

> . . . and as she walked she held out her arms in what seemed a gesture of invocation . . . her head was bent as if she listened for a voice beneath the water's murmurous surface. When the ground gave way she still seemed to be walking and listening, her arms outstretched. The water reached her waist, her small breasts, her shoulders. She lifted her head once, breathed deeply and disappeared.
> She stayed down for a long time and when her white cap finally broke the water some distance out, Max Berman felt strangely stranded and deprived. (43)

In this story as in Marshall's later works, the issues of multiple oppressions, women's power and powerlessness, and the personal as the political coalesce around the question of voice. Miss Williams seems to gain her power in a ritual invocation of the "voice" beneath the water, a voice with which she connects herself in her long, deep swim away from Berman and which is as beyond his power to hear as she is beyond him when she emerges. This listening plunge into the depths of a voice beyond Berman's power is the symbolic counterpart of her self-decolonization through speech at the climax of the story. Formerly shy and silent, having never spoken a word in class before Berman approached her, Miss Williams attains her formidable self-possession by accepting his invitation with the subversive intent of speaking her mind at the end of the visit. It is this self-possession that enables her to appropriate with the power of her body the image of the body he has fantasized about appropriating. Berman can look at her — she allows him the "sight" he anticipated–but her new self-possession renders his look impotent. At the end she reverses the roles by turning her "clear, cold gaze" on him like a mirror in which "He saw himself for what he was," before delivering the speech she has prepared: "In a way you did me a favor. You let me know how you and most of the people like you — see me. . . . I can do something now! I can begin. . . . Look how I came all the way up here to tell you this to your face. . . . That's all I came for. . . . You can drive me to the station now" (46–47).

Miss Williams's speech is presented as the climax of a power struggle between two individuals, but that picture is from the beginning superimposed on a broader picture of oppressive hierarchies beyond the narrow circle of this one personal encounter. In Miss Williams, Berman sees "the host of black women whose bodies had been despoiled to make her" (34). Behind Berman, similarly, Miss Williams seems to glimpse "a legion of old men with sere flesh and lonely eyes" (38), and Berman's half-guilty, self-consciously racist excitement by the "host of black women" ("He would not only possess her but them also" 46) conflates the two characters' encounter with all the encounters of race and gender domination in its background. Race is what gives Berman his most immediate power to strike Miss Williams dumb, as she later reveals: "Ever since I can remember my parents were always telling me, 'Stay away from white folks. . . . Don't go near them'" (46). But Marshall shows the power of race as bound up with the powers of gender and class. Miss Williams's parents had tried to make class work in her favor by teaching her, as Zora Neale Hurston's character Mis' Turner would say, to "class off" (*Eyes* 210) on the basis of color. As a result, self-possession for Miss Williams has to this point consisted of retreat "to a remote region within herself" (33). Her brief speech is a glimpse into the way the race, class, and gender relations of her society have worked to construct the drama of that resolutely interior life, with its climax in self-suppression: "I didn't marry the man I wanted to because he was dark" (47). The act of speech, however, changes that drama significantly — not by restoring what was lost (Miss Williams still searches wistfully in the darkness for the man's face), but by ridding her inner world of the confusion, fear, and shame (47) that colonized it. Miss Williams is Marshall's first representation of the dynamic whereby social, political, and economic realities give shape to psychological reality, which may in turn externalize itself in an act of self-decolonization that works to decolonize social, political, and economic spaces.[9]

The history behind "Brooklyn," which Marshall started writing in 1952 after an experience of sexual harassment and finally published almost a decade later,[10] is mirrored in the story itself. Miss Williams liberates herself from an oppressed silence, "coming to voice," to use bell hooks's term (*Talking Back* 12), by decolonizing the intended site of her domination and thereby decolonizing herself. In the same way Paule Marshall, by voicing her experience — for which, as she points out, there was not even a word in 1952 — took possession of the place of her dispossession, transforming it into one of the first sites of her power as an artist. For it is the protagonist's writing that her professor tries to make the occasion of his sexual domination, offering to comment more fully on her exceptionally good essay on Gide if she will come to his summer home. His move for power over her body is disguised, ironically, as a compliment to her power of voice as a writer. The moment in which Miss Williams sees through the disguise makes even more clear the conflation of the move to appropriate her body with the move to appropriate her voice, which vanishes into stunned silence as she catches his drift (37–38). This superimposing of the struggle for control of Miss Williams's voice and the struggle for control of her body provides the logic of the metaphor in which her swim to freedom is rendered as a deep merging with a voice beneath the water. The image links her refusal of Berman's physical control with her recovery of the voice she lost in their first encounter. It also pictures her individual strength as linked to an immersion in another voice that is both hers, as the "spirit of the lake" (43), and a source of power beyond her, with which she unites herself by listening. Marshall has often said that her own career as a writer derives from the Barbadian women's voices to which she listened so intently as a child in her mother's kitchen.[11]

The "favor" Max Berman did Miss Williams was to let her know *how he saw her.* That, we can assume, is the "favor" Paule Marshall's professor did for her as a writer. The primary double exposure here, that is, is a function of the way the narrative is focalized through Max Berman. It is through his power-gaze that Marshall portrays Miss Williams for the reader, but the author's vision of the events recorded through her character's eyes is always implicit. The author, herself the original object of the gaze, appropriates it as a lens through which to look at the power of the woman and back, self-reflexively, at the real powerlessness in which the man's power move — really an attempt to "snatch" the woman's power for himself (46) — is grounded. On the first evening of class, Berman tried in his mind's eye to capture Miss Williams as an object of art, imagining her as a Gauguin nude (32–33). His imagination, in other words, tries to render her as static, already fixed on the canvas, colonized by the artist's eye, eternally available for sensuous contemplation. It is, in fact, Miss Williams's role as art that is at issue in this story, and in more ways than one. At its climax she calls on the man who has been staring at her all these months to "look" at something different: the journey that his student, whose anger had been at first "trapped inside her" as "mute, paralyzing rage" (38), has made in order to speak her mind. "Look how I came all the way up here," she says, "to tell you this to your face" (47).

Paule Marshall wrote early in her career of her intention of creating a new kind of African-American woman character ("The Negro Woman in Literature" 1966). Miss Williams's journey to liberate herself from an objectifying art by speaking her mind is the very process of Marshall's self-liberation as the creator of a feminist art that sets women at the center, as subjects. "Only as subjects can we speak," bell hooks says. "As objects we remain voiceless — our beings defined and interpreted by others" (*Talking Back* 12). To set up an image of a young African-American woman in a bathing suit, walking in front of an older white man who is fantasizing about her sexually, a man invested with many kinds of authority to "define and interpret" her — and at the same time to make readers see this as a picture of the woman as subject rather than object: this is the essence of Paule Marshall's feminist angle of double vision.

At its most fundamental, double vision is the capacity to remember.

Ursa sees everything as a set of double exposures because she does not forget Triunion when she is in the United States, or Dresden in World War II when she sees Harlem in the 1980s, or the slave rebel leader Congo Jane when she talks with her friend Mae Ryland, a political organizer in New Jersey. Powerlessness in the world Paule Marshall portrays is always loss, and the loss in the background of every other is the loss of memory that creates the kind of negative, destructive doubleness only a creative doubleness can redeem. At the core of that destructive doubleness are lost voices: the voices forgotten at the centers of power from which they are kept separate, the voices forgotten at the core of the psyche, the capacity for speech that must be forgotten for one voice to appropriate another. If the fundamental loss is loss of memory, then the most fundamental opposite of loss is recognition: literally re-*cognition*, a reknowing, in which unities among people, forgotten or denied, are acknowledged. The journey of freedom begins with this "rescue of memory" and becomes a reclaiming of speech: one woman speaking both as an individual and in a voice larger than hers, in which she has immersed herself by listening deeply—a collective voice to which she is heir and which she transmits as a legacy. Paule Marshall's art resonates with the power of that voice.

Chapter 1
"The Mother's Voice"

Years ago, on an island that was only a green node in a vast sea, the mother had been a girl who had danced till she had fainted once, and she, Selina, had been nothing to her. Suddenly she yearned to know the mother then, in her innocence. Above all, she longed to understand the mother, for she knew, obscurely, that she would never really understand anything until she did.

— *Brown Girl, Brownstones*

1

"In order to perpetuate itself," Audre Lorde says, "every oppression must corrupt or distort those various sources of power within the culture of the oppressed that can provide energy for change" ("Uses of the Erotic" 53). The voices of two mothers epitomize those contested sources of power in Paule Marshall's first novel. At the heart of the contest is Silla, whose voice lights Selina's childhood world in "dazzling pyrotechnic display" (304), yet whose loss of voice at the workplace is the central experience of silence in the book. The significance of that loss is implicit in Florrie's admonition, "Talk yuh talk, Silla! Be-Jees, in this white-man world you got to take yuh mouth and make a gun" (70). Silla's talk is a bold assertion of Black womanhood "in this white-man world," yet as her daughter comes of age she recognizes in that voice the signs of a tragic metamorphosis — the corruption or distortion of a woman's power. Selina can "never really understand anything" until she acquires the ability to see through this transformation that has distanced Silla from her husband, her past, and the self her voice in so many ways affirms. She acquires this ability in an encounter with the second mother, the white Mrs. Benton, whose viciously polite deployment of voice against Selina, an enactment of the power to silence, catalyzes an explosive sequence of double visions. Through the transparent distortions of this white mother's racist narrative about a Black mother, Selina is able to glimpse her own mother clearly for the first time, and consequently herself.

Throughout the novel, the primary medium for Marshall's study of women's voice and women's power is a technique of superimposition that allows her to present the simultaneities at the heart of her feminist vision and that operates by means of a conflation of the methods of realism with the methods of allegory.[1] By means of this technique, she develops the brownstone simultaneously as a realistic setting that conveys the social texture of Selina's world and an allegorical setting that renders, through those same realistic details, the life of her psyche. The house, to borrow Henry James's phrase, is "the very atmosphere of the mind"[2] — Selina's mind — but the mind seen as a social, political, and economic space as well as a psychological one. Through this double exposure Marshall represents at the same time what Angela Davis would call the "objective forces at work in the society" in which Selina lives and the ways they come to be reflected, as well as resisted, in the "interior" life they work to shape. One of the major forces that Marshall studies in this way is the combination of race, class, and gender oppression, internalized through a molding of desire that also molds self-regard. Like all Marshall's novels, *Brown Girl* renders this process metaphorically as a process of silencing, for the re-presentation of external political and economic forces internally, in the psyche, is a voicing of oppressive ideologies that silences other, internal voices.[3] Marshall charts this process in two of the earliest scenes in the novel, Silla and Deighton's encounter in the kitchen and Selina's daydreamy descent of the grand staircase. They are set, appropriately, in those spaces of the brownstone that allegorize most starkly the roles of race, gender, and class in the external/internal power relations the novel portrays.

Lorde's comment refers specifically to "the erotic as a considered source of power and information within our lives" ("Uses of the Erotic" 53). In the world of the brownstones, the primary means by which an oppressive economic system exploits, reshapes, and appropriates "those various sources of power within the culture of the oppressed that can provide energy for change" is through materialism, which the novel depicts as a displacement or corruption of erotic desire. This displacement is linked to the process by which the voices of the dispossessed, as embodiments of their power, get appropriated or silenced. The first scene in the kitchen between Deighton and Silla reveals that the brownstone itself, as the object of Silla's impassioned desire to "buy house," is at the core of this displacement. From the beginning of that scene, the difference between their relationships to the "whiteness" of the kitchen, emphasized four times in the first three sentences, predicts their failure to transcend their different relations to an economic system in which Silla is working desperately to make this white place hers and Deighton dreams of "land home."

Kitchens are traditionally a locus of women's power, but the gendered nature of this particular space is in tension with the fact that it is racialized as white.[4] Silla augments the power she would ordinarily have here by assimilating it to the power of this "whiteness," amid which she stands "easily," even as Deighton pauses "uneasily" at the door. Unlike her, he is "shaken as always" by "the antiseptic white furniture and enameled white walls" (22). Despite this difference between them, the scene opens with their voices in concert—laughing, intimate—and with the possibility of lovemaking later: "He might find the words tonight to bring trust again to her eyes; his hands might arouse that full and awesome passion they once had . . ." (23). But the "burst of passion" is suppressed as Deighton, having incriminated himself with a "lame" excuse for going out on the town, breathes Silla's name: "This time her reply was to plunge her hand into the chicken she was cleaning and with one savage wrench lay the viscid clay-yellow entrails into the sink" (24). Standing in for Silla's "reply," the disemboweling of the chicken is all the more startling as the climax to a scene in which words and touch have been so intimately related. Deighton imagines finding the right words as he imagines finding the right touch; the intimate small talk is part of the atmosphere of upwelling passion. The image of organs being wrenched out of a body tropes silence as the evisceration of desire. The metaphor is fundamental to Marshall's representation of Silla's power and its metamorphoses.

The image of evisceration reiterates, more starkly, the loss portrayed in the novel's first description of Silla "striding home under the trees," her presence like a wintry blight on the lush summer landscape, her lips "set in a permanent protest against life" (16). Silla's somber transformation of the landscape and her impending transformation of the atmosphere of the house close the first chapter. The sense of her self-suppression is intensified by the opening of chapter 2, when immediately, like the inevitable return of the repressed, everything her American dream has brought under such rigorous control unfolds in the person of Suggie, cooking a sensuously described Barbadian meal and sitting afterwards in a sexual pose, "With a languorous gaze," hands resting "on the inside of her open thighs" (18). Suggie's open eroticism is fused with her relationship to her past, a Barbadian landscape her meal conjures up. With its "soft-sloping hills" and "susurrant sea of sugar cane" (18), this sensuous landscape establishes the room Silla so grudgingly rents to her unassimilated tenant, if only for a moment, as the "green node in a vast sea" (145) where Silla, as Selina eventually learns, once danced so passionately that she fainted: the island, and the self, she has tried to leave behind.

The house has long been an allegorical device for representing the self in its varying aspects. Often a single dwelling represents the body (for example, the House of Alma in *The Faerie Queene*), or a particular moral quality (for example, the Cave of Mammon). Rooms or levels of a house, together with its architectural details (porches, stairs, balconies) may correspond to physical features of the body, mental and spiritual faculties, or both.[5] The brownstone is such a place. As the anaphora of the title suggests, at the most basic level the house is Selina's body, whose crucial signifying mark in "this white-man world" is its color. At the same time, the facade of the brownstone, attached to a long line of other exteriors as if it were one in a sequence of mirror images or part of "an army massed at attention" (3), is also a representation of the Barbadian-American community whose strategy of assimilation, "buying house," has been its first line of defense against that white world.

Specific physical analogies between Silla and the house in the opening chapter portray her identity in particular, as well as the collective woman's identity she represents, as the milieu in which her daughter must search for self-definition.[6] The house is thus an image of the oneness of Selina's individual self — even her physical self, her body — and the collective self within which it is situated. It is an image, in fact, *of that situation* of the individual self within the collective self. The individual self Paule Marshall represents is also situated in opposition to this collective self — at war with it, even at war with its war. But the fact that the community contains the individual, *is* the individual and vice versa, means that this opposition is inevitably self-opposition. Our first glimpse of Selina is of a self in exactly this situation, at the same moment "hurl[ing] herself forward" and "reach[ing] back," injured by the "contradiction of her movement" (4–5). And appropriately, in terms of the allegorical architecture of the house, the setting for this self-conflict is its transition point — the stairway that connects the various levels of the house, which represent the various social, economic, and cultural aspects of Selina's world and their place, in turn, in her psyche. Each of these places has an explicit relationship to voice and silence.

At the foundation of the house-as-psyche is a mother-place, Silla's basement kitchen, dedicated to hard work and assimilation and a sense of women's collective strength, which is voiced again and again in the "dazzling pyrotechnic display[s]" of the Barbadian mothers' verbal art. If it is a foundational site of women's power, however, the early encounter there between Deighton and Silla establishes it also as the site of the distortion of that power through the evisceration of desire. Appropriately then, it eventually becomes the site of Silla's work as a writer: the distortion of her powers of voice as she forges letters in Deighton's name to win the "war" between them over what they should want most — land home, or a house in the United States. And the presence of this war in Silla's kitchen reveals the extent to which her power has been appropriated by forces outside the brownstone, through an intrusion of the external World War into the very sources of desire in the psyche.

Nearby is Selina and Ina's room, which when we first encounter it is a site of emerging adolescent womanhood, mysteries of blood and heat that Selina, the child-sister, cannot yet grasp. Upstairs is a father-place, Deighton's sunroom, the site of a diffused sensuality, warmth, and love of life that constitute a power of resistance to the assimilation evoked by Silla's belligerently white kitchen. On the top floor is Suggie's room, site of mature womanly sexuality associated with the same unassimilable Barbadian self represented in the father-place. And finally, next to Suggie's room at the back of the house is the place highest in the social and cultural hierarchy of Selina's childhood psyche. This locus of colonial power is the sickroom of the dying white servant Miss Mary, with her endless stories of the brownstone's glorious past. Under her influence Selina internalizes the myth of a gracious white life that her family's intrusion has sadly displaced. For Selina, one of the salient characteristics of this lost, superior world was its "mild" white voices (5): "Never a hard word spoken. . . . They wus none as happy as them . . ." (79).

The resonance of these voices in Selina's imagination is crucial to her experience of the psychological and economic power relations the house doubly embodies. Miss Mary's room is a kind of last colonial outpost in the brownstone, source of an ideology of white supremacy that places upper-class whites at the center of what is important and implicitly denigrates the Barbadian voices—including, by implication, Selina's—that are slowly taking possession of the house. Miss Mary's voice gains power to colonize Selina's psyche not only because it advertises so seductively its value as a white voice, but also because this voice she positions in Selina's inner world is itself an enactment of internalized oppression. Miss Mary does not tell her own story; she tells, as if it were her story, the story of the family for whom she was a servant. It is for the value of their superior life that she speaks, a life that would have been predicated on a view of hers as inferior.[7] The irony is underscored by the fact that, in particular, she voices the superiority *of their voices*.

Miss Mary's room is thus a place of silence in a number of senses, all of which point to the equation of the colonized voice and the silenced voice. Selina is silenced there not only because she listens, enthralled and silent, to the old white myths, but also because the myths valorize her silence and make her wish to silence the Barbadian voices of her family as well. Further, Miss Mary's endless talk is itself a version of silence, a ventriloquism whereby she speaks not only against the class interests of her audience but against her own. And when, much later, Miss Mary can no longer speak, she relies on the young woman Selina, in a further act of ventriloquizing, to tell the old stories she learned by heart as a child.

"Tom . . ." It was a dry rasp after a long struggle.
"Him so tall and strong with a smile for everyone," Selina said.
"Aye."
All afternoon they whispered together, the old woman's eyes, buried in a web of wrinkles but still alert, urging her on, and Selina filling in the words and feeling vaguely happy. (201)

In this later scene, Miss Mary's deathroom is a place of silence for Selina not because Selina does not speak there, but because the words she speaks are not her own. When Silla bursts into this room to try to reclaim her daughter by talking the old woman to death and exorcising the house of its white past, the allegorical function of the room is fused with its realistic function to illuminate the "intensely social character" of the interior life. From the beginning of this confrontation the focus is on Miss Mary's magnetic pull on Selina. "What it tis you does find here?" Silla demands, then turns the force of a corresponding question on Miss Mary: "But why you wun dead, nuh? . . . What it tis you waiting on? Tell me. You can't take this old house with you. It belong to me now. . . . And I gon get you out yet" (202–3). Silla's external war against white hegemony in the brownstone manifests itself in this scene as simultaneously a psychomachia — an allegorical battle for, or within, a soul.[8] Her attack on Miss Mary is part of her economic strategy to gain full ownership of the house, but it is also an interior cultural war that pits the white colonized voice against the Barbadian voice in Selina's psyche. Silla wins in two ways. She does, in essence, get Miss Mary out; the explosion of her Black voice in the white woman's room marks her competitor's "defeat" (203), which is at the same time psychological and economic.

With the logic of allegory, Miss Mary's sickroom, the greatest threat to Selina's psychological health, is located at the opposite pole of the house from the kitchen, site of Selina's spiritual nourishment in the collective voice of the Barbadian mothers. But that collective voice as Silla embodies it is not confined to the kitchen. In the opening character expositions, which are at the same time the descriptions of the disparate, competing spaces in the brownstone, Silla's voice introduces everyone. Metaphorically, her voice ranges over the house as she comments on Suggie, Miss Mary, Deighton (17, 19, 21). Indeed, this omnipresence of Silla's voice is a crucial element in the description of the house. Amidst these vastly different spaces, Silla's voice is everywhere, the one integrating element in Selina's as-yet-unintegrated psyche.

In one of the most telling paradoxes of the novel, we encounter the power of that voice first through its absence, as Selina stands on the upper landing of the staircase, reveling in the silence of the house.[9] All the voices in the house are silent, but "above all" the mother's: "Above all, it was a silence which came when the mother was at work" (5). In this scene that introduces "the mother's voice" through its absence,[10] we see how important is the role played by Miss Mary's voice in the construction of Selina's racial, class, and gender identity. In the absence of Silla's voice and the model of Black womanhood it signifies, other voices take over: the "mild voices" of the white ghosts Miss Mary conjured up, imploring her "to give them a little life" (5). What Selina gives them, for a moment, is her own life, allowing them to embody themselves in her as she throws her head back, lifts her "imaginary gown," and sweeps gracefully down the stairs in an eminently recognizable, stereotypical construction of upper-class white womanhood. So potent is the force of this construction in the development of Selina's interior life that she loses her race as she loses her solitude, feeling herself "no longer a dark girl . . . but one of them" — only to confront herself in the mirror as definitively and hopelessly something else. She is not "one of them" at all, but a little brown disheveled girl, "something vulgar in a holy place. The room was theirs, she knew . . ." (6).

This first of several mirror scenes that mark the stages in Selina's progress to womanhood reveals white ideology in the very process of shaping her self-image, as the "mild" beneficent voices unleashed by Miss Mary work to construct her, seducing her into using her own brown body to give them "life." This psychological victory over Selina is at the same time part of an economic battle, because it is the same as seducing her into seeing the brownstone, a fiercely contested economic space, as rightfully "theirs." The ghosts cannot live without her: among other things, the scene pictures a Black girl's body as the site of the construction of white women's identity. This is the process Chela Sandoval describes in a model delineating four categories of power inhabited by white men, white women, men of color, and women of color. In this hierarchy white women, "othered" by white men and feeling "the pain of objectification," attempt to "construct a solid sense of 'self' through the objectification of people of color," a process repeated, further down the scale, by men of color. Women of color, "the final 'other' in a complex of power moves," thus become "the crucial category against which all the other categories are provided their particular meanings and privileges" (64). The end of the scene, the shattering vision in the mirror, is a picture of a brown girl providing other categories with their meanings and privileges, not just by being othered but by seeing herself as Other.

"The room was theirs" puts the finishing touch on Marshall's picture, in the opening chapter, of the interpenetration of the economic world and the world of the psyche. The ownership of the house is inextricably bound up with Selina's ownership of her own body and with the colonization of her mind, in which at least one room, clearly, is "theirs." Selina's struggle for a sense of place in a room that is "theirs" evokes much of the allegorical resonance of the connection between the brown house and the brown body to which the title calls attention. Barbadians live in this house but do not yet own it; the tyranny of the house as an object of desire, the tension and urgency with which Silla's "fierce idolatry" of the brownstone is fraught (4), express the self-dissociation this Barbadian-American version of the American dream entails. Silla's presence is an important counterbalance to Miss Mary's view of things. But Selina's later recognition that Silla must have seen reflected in her children's faces "her own despised color" (293) shows that in subtle ways Silla, buying house, has been buying into this same ideology of white supremacy that animates Miss Mary's dying moments. This later image of Silla seeing herself as a despised Other in the mirror of her children's faces explains why, although the silence of the house in the mother's absence left Selina open to the destructive influence of the white voices, the mother's return had a similar effect. Anticipating her chastising voice, Selina rushed back to the mirror and again saw herself as something unacceptable: "Suddenly in one swift pure movement she was in front of the mirror, struggling out of her shorts and tugging at her matted braids" (16). These images of the child before the mirror — twice, both times self-alienated by an internalized voice that makes her Other to herself — picture the construction of gender, race, and class as by definition a fundamental source of doubleness in the life of a Barbadian-American girl. As the title of the novel suggests, Selina must shape her identity in a world that purports to resemble her. But the brownstone is full of white "ghost shapes" (6) and the very mirror in which she sees herself reflects them: "The floor-to-ceiling mirror retained their faces as the silence did their voices" (5).

2

"Mirror . . . faces . . . silence . . . voices." Some similar conjunction of silence, voices, and a mirror emerges at each stage of Selina's progress toward maturity, as Marshall sets questions of identity, again and again, in the context of the question of voice. Forces outside the heroine reproduce themselves internally as oppressive voices that not only shape the heroine's view of herself on the private stage of the psyche but, as the word "retained" implies, actually inhere in that view. The mirror image of herself as a "vulgar" brown child contains their faces just as the silence, which has been established as especially the mother's silence but is also Selina's, contains their voices. It is not merely that white voices silence hers or that her supposed ugliness sets off their beauty; her identity as they define it is, as in Sandoval's model, *constitutive* of their identity. The image of ghosts takes on its full meaning here. As in a story of ghosts who cannot return from the dead without inhabiting a living body, her identity is being used to construct someone else's. The same logic is at work later when Selina's vision of herself in the "mirror" of Mrs. Benton's eyes is conjoined with her fear that such people intend "to rob her of her substance and her self" (289).

At a deeper level than Miss Mary's room and the parlor, however, Silla's kitchen offers the potential for a self-image associated with a voice that can exorcise the seductive white voices of ghosts. But this Black mother's voice is not immediately accessible to Selina; she must contend for it against the mother herself. The paradox of this contest for the mother's voice against the mother's voice is illuminated in bell hooks's description of a world like Silla's kitchen, the "world of woman speech" she grew up in as an African-American child. In that world "There was no 'calling' for talking girls." A girl was to listen, or "talk a talk that was itself a silence," not "talk back" and "create [her] own speech." Yet in this very atmosphere of "the sharing of speech and recognition" among women, hooks says, "I made speech my birthright—and the right to voice, to authorship, a privilege I would not be denied" (*Talking Back* 6–7). In her visit to the factory to talk back to Silla and in her temporary victory in their dispute on the trolley ride home, Selina claims her birthright, in bell hooks's terms, by "talking back."

The setting of this mother-daughter drama outside the brownstone says a great deal about the way the novel, while operating on one plane as an intensely psychological, symbolic account of the "interior life," is always also looking, at the same time, at the "objective forces" at work outside that life, and the ways they impinge on it. Selina's confrontation with her mother is set in one of the central places of silence in the novel, the factory that is Silla's workplace during World War II. This setting, together with the trolley ride home through a kind of Vanity Fair that is both a surreal landscape of desire and a painfully realistic picture of class in America, places the whole issue of Selina's voice in the context of a larger question. Outside the family, outside the brownstone (and, we realize, at the same time translated into a different form inside it), what are the forces of silence? Who or what has the real voice in the economic, social, and political world? The answers depicted in this narrative sequence resonate through every other scene in the novel to suggest ways in which the roles of voice and silence inside the family, inside the brownstone, even inside the mind of Selina, replicate the external economic and political drama of the United States during the war.

The centrality of voice and silence to this drama as Marshall portrays it is overwhelmingly clear in her description of the factory, which associates power with voice, and powerlessness with silence. The "deluge of noise" that drowns Selina as she enters is, literally, a type of domination, by a "machine-mass" that assimilates the workers to itself (98–99). The description of their "mechanical gestures . . . as if somewhere in that huge building someone controlled their every motion by pushing a button" climaxes in a dramatically brief sentence: "And no one talked." Their silence recalls another work scene: "Like the men loading the trailer trucks in the streets, they performed a pantomime role in a drama in which only the machines had a voice" (99).

This is the first of many pictures in Marshall's novels that identify the exploitation of labor with an imposition of silence. Like the other such pictures, it is a complicated one, and the paradoxes of Selina's own new found eloquence in the scene that follows, when she lays claim to her mother's legacy of strong speech at the very moment she is challenging her values, indeed defying her whole way of life, underscore the paradox of the mother's experience in the factory. For Selina's quietly defiant speech takes its force from the contradictions implicit in the image of Silla in this place of silence, which, like all the places of silence Marshall represents, is both an intensely colonized space and a site of resistance. Although she is one of the "small insignificant shapes" whose movements seem dictated by some button-pusher in another part of the building, Silla performs her "pantomime" with awe-inspiring dignity, handling the lathe deftly, standing with "the same transient calm" she often has as she stands over the stove in her kitchen, her "formidable force" alone a match for the power of the machines (99–100).

The setting of her achievement, the picture of "white and colored" workers together (99), evokes all the issues of racial discrimination that arose in American factories in World War II, as the urgency of the war effort dictated temporary but nonetheless dramatic shifts in employment patterns. "When I first came," Silla tells Selina later, "they wun put me to work on the lathe. Just because your skin black some these white people does think you can't function like them. But when they finally decide to try me out I had already learn it by watching the others" (102). Silla may look like an insignificant actor in a pantomime, performing mechanical movements as if she were part of the machine itself, but her very deftness is an act of insubordination in the context of the power behind the machines. Similarly, to work here inside the machine-voice, she must suspend the power of speech that is so much the measure of her self-hood, yet even here her individual act of creation can be heard for an instant above the din: "The whine of her lathe lifted thinly above the roar as the metal whirled into shape" (99–100). But yet again, even as the vision of her mother's power overwhelms Selina with her own "effrontery" in coming here to talk back to her, the woman who relieves Silla takes her place "without interrupting the cycle" (100). Whatever resistance the workers' skill may represent in their individual lives, in a larger context it only makes them efficient, interchangeable parts of the system of levers and wheels.[11]

The image of Silla as part of a machine is not confined to the factory scene; her machine role, with all its accumulated references to her silencing by an external hegemonic power and her ironic attempt to resist that power by affiliating herself with it, intrudes as well into the family. It does so most dramatically in the scene of the buying spree, in which Silla and Deighton's private war over the issue of the house versus the land comes to its climax.[12] Marshall portrays subtly the differences in the gendering of Deighton's and Silla's ambitions,[13] using their different relations to the "machine age," as Silla calls it, to explore the way that gendering is colored by the very different positions the hegemonic power structure assigns them and the way, in turn, that structure gives form to what happens on the private stage of their family drama inside the brownstone. For the war between the sexes as it is played out in the brownstone is not merely a parallel to the World War raging outside; it is the interior version of that war. The denouement of the domestic war reveals this most clearly, as Silla's voice announcing Deighton's suicide speaks together with the voice of the radio announcer: "While Silla read them the cable, the radio announced the war's end . . ." (185). The superimposition of voices — the interior voice of the mother in the brownstone and the exterior voice of political reality coming into the brownstone through the radio — pictures objective forces outside the family playing themselves out in the conflicts of the family's interior life.

This is particularly evident in the spree scene, the climax of the domestic war. Underlying the scene, to begin with, is the difference between Silla's relation to the war machine and Deighton's. Silla scorned Selina's objection that the machine got her hands dirty: "I tell yuh, to make your way in this world you got to dirty more than yuh hands sometime . . ." (102–3). The reference to dirtying more than your hands is presumably an allusion to the way Silla has dirtied her soul by stealing her husband's land in Barbados to "buy house" in America. Indeed, as Kimberly W. Benston points out, the image cluster associated with machinery is related to "the prevalent theme of 'the plan' — or *machination*, as 'the plan' becomes in the hands of Silla" (68). It is logical that in Silla's subsequent victory over Deighton the image of Silla as a machine returns, because her ability to be part of the "machine age" and get a little dirt on her hands is necessary for her assimilation as a factory worker, which in turn is necessary to the success of her assimilation into the society where she plans to "buy house" and settle down without returning, as Deighton wants to do, to Barbados.

These differences in their relation to the machine age, again, express their different relations to themselves, and in particular the way those relations are gendered. Selina's father, although he works at a mattress factory, aspires to another, more individualized kind of work, studying his accounting manuals or practicing his trumpet at home, alone, in an attempt to define himself *as an individual* through some new employment. "That's the way a man does do things!" he says (85), gesturing magnificently with the golden trumpet. His friend Seifert responds with pitying incredulity to Deighton's rejection of buying house as the avenue to success: "How else a man your color gon get ahead? . . . Boyce, mahn . . . you can know all the accounting there is, these people still not gon have you up in their fancy office and pulling down the same money as them . . ." (39). What other men in his community recognize is the futility of Deighton's trying to assert his manhood in a territory white men have already appropriated and where, therefore, he cannot possibly count as a man. Percy Challenor typifies the alternative strategy of buying house, the one avenue of power the white world has left open to him. The version of manhood he plays out in that house is a rigorously patriarchal one. It is defined not, as Deighton's version of manhood was to have been, by self-empowerment in an external, integrated public world through some extraordinary individual achievement but, in a homogeneous interior world, by his ability to subject the women in his family to his authority. His power is expressed most dramatically in his power over their voices. One "hard look" from him is capable of silencing his wife (55), and he silences his daughter in an even more final way. Puzzled by Selina's insistence that she tell her what *she* wants rather than prefacing every sentence with "My father says," Beryl replies simply, "I don't understand. . . . I say the same thing he says" (197). In Percy Challenor's brownstone, this is the way a man does do things.

The issue of "manhood" in *Brown Girl* is a complicated one. On the one hand, the images of "unmanning" as a metaphor for dispossession and colonization tend to reinscribe in certain ways the patriarchal ideology that is implicitly criticized in the picture of Percy Challenor's relation to his family. On the other hand, the feminism that establishes women as "centers of power" in this novel involves an innovative inclusion of *women* in metaphors that describe colonization as a distortion of erotic power, through the portrayal of Silla as in certain senses unwomaned by the pressures of economic dispossession. It is this unwomaning that is represented in metaphors of Silla's assimilation to the war machines, whose usurping of the workers' voices at Silla's factory parallels her usurpation of Deighton's voice. Deighton's two defeats—losing the war of the sexes and being disabled by a machine—are metaphorically the same event. The machine force that silences the workers at Silla's factory, where "only the machines had a voice," epitomizes white hegemonic power outside the brownstone; at the same time it epitomizes destruction by Silla, who brings the machine force into the family with her relentless ambition to assimilate herself to the kind of power it represents. At the climax of the shopping-spree scene, that outside power's distortion of Silla's erotic powers is revealed in a horrifyingly mechanical, parodic image of love-making as she smashes the golden trumpet, symbol of Deighton's attempt to find a kind of work that "a man does do": "Repeatedly Silla's body rose and dropped in a threshing rhythm, the trumpet struck. She might have been a cane-cutter wielding a golden machete through the ripened cane or a piston rising and plunging in its cylinder" (130–31).

In neither of these images is Silla a power; she is only an instrument of power. Cutting canes as a child she was the member of a brutally supervised work-team; working in the factory she fits into the war effort like another interchangeable part. Indeed Silla, wielding her excoriating voice in this scene as she wields the trumpet, is no more the victor than Deighton, with his falsely carefree voice ("Woman, it insured. . . . Another one coming from where that come" 131). The clue to the real victory is in Deighton's description of his unaccustomed welcome in the stores: "Lady-folks, money does talk sweet enough in this man country" (124). What talks in this scene is not Silla or Deighton but money; what defeats both of them is the economic power that has the real voice. Indeed, as Deighton left for town with the check early in the day, and his "blithe voice," which assumes such a fleeting importance in these scenes surrounding the sale of the land, disappeared, "the silence gradually became as stark-white as the kitchen" (121). The whiteness of this kitchen associates Silla's final victory over Deighton with his more general defeat in his confrontations with the white world. At the same time, the whiteness of the silence suggests that in the end, Silla's final victory over Deighton's "blithe voice" is really a victory of the white world over both of them, as the America to which she wants to belong divorces her from her homeland and from him.

Silla and Deighton's defeat by the power of money to "talk" in this white-man world is a distortion of the powers of the oppressed, most specifically their erotic power, through an appropriation of their voices. Revealed first in the transformation of their bedroom at night into a place of "savage words. . . . voices raging in the dark" (51), it climaxes with Deighton's use of "a few words and thing in the night" to seduce Silla into giving him the check to cash by himself (121). The conjunction of "words" and "thing" resonates tragically with the earlier scene in which Deighton's words failed to arouse Silla's passion. This time they succeed, but in the service of a power beyond them: in the service not of love but of the exterior war that has worked its way into the interior of the brownstone, into the most intimate space of their relationship.

In *Feminist Theory from Margin to Center*, bell hooks distinguishes between "power as domination and control over others and power that is creative and life-affirming" (84).[14] The distinction is useful here, because the metamorphosis that brings about the tragedy of Silla and Deighton is a metamorphosis of the latter kind of power into the former. In terms of the gender issues the novel explores, one of the most interesting aspects of this transformation is that it is the same process whereby Silla becomes a woman writer. After the first scene in the kitchen, Silla and Deighton are never again represented in quiet, intimate talk; instead of sharing her voice with him, mingling it with his to affirm the erotic power of their relationship, Silla uses her voice as an instrument of power-over, usurping Deighton's voice in a consummate act of ventriloquism by forging letters in his name to sell his land. At one level, this picture of Silla secretly engaged in her single-minded task of forgery is an image of a woman who, in an illicit act of self-empowerment, by appropriating a voice that should have been a man's—was, in fact, a man's—becomes a writer. There are suggestions here of Sandra Gilbert and Susan Gubar's thesis about women's appropriation of the "pen" as an act of rebellion, and indeed Silla writing secretly at night is a kind of madwoman in the basement.[15] Here, however, the interplay between the gendering of this illicit act of authorship and its racializing, or nationalizing, opens a window on the dimensions of the woman writer's dilemma that Gilbert and Gubar's first exploration largely ignored.

Silla's authorship in the basement is bound up with her authority throughout the house, which is an expression of her formidable power. But the form her authorship takes, a war on her husband, also expresses the distortion of that power by the economic forces that warp her desire. Ironically, what Silla does in her final betrayal of Deighton to the immigration authorities is to take her voice "and make a gun" to use on her own husband, in collaboration with a quintessential representative of authority in the "white-man world." It is therefore only logical that the policeman's voice should displace hers in the very midst of her collusion: "All right, all right, lady. I'm asking the questions, not you" (181).

Silla's status as a woman writer is thus complicated by the ways in which her power, enacted throughout the novel primarily in the form of her power of voice, comes to be appropriated by the very "white-man world" against which she has tried to use her mouth as a weapon. The appropriation is not without connection to her own philosophy of power: "No, nobody wun admit it, but people got a right to claw their way to the top and those on top got a right to scuffle to stay there" (225). As Silla's pronouncement reveals, there is no essential difference between her conception of power and the conception animating the hegemonic power structure that is her ultimate antagonist. This absence in her philosophy of what bell hooks would call "an oppositional world view" (*Feminist Theory* 163) is exactly what lays her voice open to colonization. Silla is in one sense Gilbert and Gubar's rebellious woman writer, a portrait of the explosive potential harbored in a woman quietly writing at her kitchen table after her family is bed. The image captures all the rebellion of such an act, but it also captures its dangerous potential for being subverted. Silla exercises her creative power by writing, just as she exercises it elsewhere by speaking.[16] But her purpose affirms the hegemonic concept of power as domination, and that affirmation opens her voice to the powers that finally appropriate it.

3

Against this portrait of a woman writer's power colonized, Marshall sets the artist figure of Selina. Her "coming to voice," in bell hooks's term, is an act of rebellion, but not directly against white patriarchy as in Gilbert and Gubar's model. Selina rebels first against the metamorphosis that the white power structure has wrought in her mother[17] and, second, against that power structure directly. She confronts it directly, however, not in the person of a white patriarch but of a white *mother*, whose effort to entrap Selina in her benevolent racist matriarchy is an overt effort to appropriate her voice. The settings for these two acts of rebellion, the trolley ride home from the factory and Mrs. Benton's sitting room after Selina's dance recital, raise questions of voice and ventriloquism through allusions to the theater. The first contest pits the power of Selina's solitary voice against the allure of a landscape of stage settings, icons of the desires that have helped to distort Silla's power. Selina's task is to voice, against these mute representations, an alternative conception of desire that will be liberatory rather than imprisoning, self-generated rather than dictated by outside forces. She does so in a brief access of eloquence that sparks Silla's recognition of her emerging womanhood. In the second contest, which marks Selina's final coming of age, it is Selina's deepest desires for herself as an emerging artist that are under attack, as an aging, would-have-been "tragedienne" stages a desperate one-woman show designed to undermine the younger performer's ambitions. Selina's struggles in these two spaces for a liberated voice in which to defy the Black mother and the white mother come to be unexpectedly related at a critical juncture of the second battle, when the story of Mrs. Benton's housekeeper Ettie, a silenced Black mother, comes into focus behind the contest for possession of Selina's voice.

Notable in both the trolley ride and the battle with Mrs. Benton is the way Paule Marshall explores issues of power through women's power struggles *with each other*, a choice she makes even more explicitly, and with further-reaching consequences, in her second novel, which "embod[ies] the whole power struggle of the world" in women characters (DeVeaux 126). Although the global resonance of the conflict between Merle and Harriet in *The Chosen Place* is wider and more explicitly political, Selina's battle with the white mother raises some of the same issues. In particular, it represents the ways in which patriarchal power comes to be superimposed on women's power, fashioning it into self-contradictory forms. And it raises the question of what kinds of double vision, or powers of voice, are necessary for self-defense against that adulterated power. In the trolley scene Selina succeeds in talking back to the Black mother; in the drawing-room scene, the white mother wins temporarily, in an ambiguous victory that encapsulates almost every form of silencing by means of which white power sustains and reproduces itself in the world Paule Marshall's novels portray. Despite that, however, Selina arrives, through the very experience of being silenced so absolutely, at another kind of victory. A new access of perception, this victory is in one sense the boon Miss Williams wrested from her encounter with Max Berman — the vision of exactly how those who regard her as Other see her. In another sense it is an ability, derived from this new double vision, to hear "the mother's voice" in a new way.

The setting for Selina's verbal combat with Silla, the trolley ride home from the factory, depicts Selina's "coming to voice" as both a journey with and battle against her mother, played out against a backdrop of contested images of desire. As the trolley passes from darkness into a shopping area, "the dazzling window displays [flash] by like stage settings" (103) — an image connecting them with the "pantomime" performed by the factory workers in a "drama" they do not control (99). This drama is the American dream, apotheosized in a "manikin bride gaz[ing] pietistically into the night, the white gown foaming around her like a white sea" (103). The lifeless bride in her stage setting foreshadows yet another pantomime drama, the wedding at which the desires of 'Gatha Steed's daughter, compared to Iphigenia at Aulis, will be sacrificed to her mother's ideal of "playing white" (142). The white bride dressed in white, with her lost, abstracted, saintly gaze — assimilated to nature in the image of the sea but at the same time artificial, lifeless — is the very icon of white womanly desire in the culture into which the Barbadians have transplanted themselves.[18] The iterated whiteness of the image evokes Silla's kitchen, the whiteness with which she is so much at ease; the strange oxymoron of "manikin bride" marks contradiction as the essence of this alien, alluring, uncanny icon to which mothers such as Silla and 'Gatha have offered up their daughters. In response to it, Silla talks of the dresses she will buy for her daughters to wear to 'Gatha Steed's daughter's wedding: "I tell you, there's one thing 'bout money. It can buy you anything you see there in those store windows" (103). Selina's quietly eloquent back talk in response constitutes a kind of victory not just over Silla but over the power of the ideology the whole drama of the capitalist landscape is designed to sell:

> "Some people don't care about those things in the store windows." . . .
> "But what you talking? What kind of people is they?"
> "Ordinary people."
> "What they does care 'bout then?"
> "Other things."
> "Like what?"
> "I dunno. Things they don't get in stores. I dunno."
> "I bet you don know." The mother turned away, then swung back. "What kind of things is they, Miss Know-it-all?"
> "I said I didn't know." Selina tried to avoid the mother's eyes, but there was no place to hide and finally she blurted out, "Well, take 'Gatha Steed. She could buy her daughter that pretty gown in the store window but she can't buy any love there so her daughter would marry the boy from home and stop all the fuss." (103–4)

Selina's small triumph here comes as a result of having forced her way into her mother's discourse of desire, opening a space there for talk about what people really "want" — a space wider than the fixed artificial stage settings of the store windows, little theatrical presentations of desire as consumer capitalism fashions it: white. Initially her eloquence defeats Silla; later Silla recoups her losses with a laugh that echoes back to Selina as she follows her silently home through the "winter scene" of Chauncey Street after a snowfall (106). Selina is silent, but the way Silla's echoing laugh assimilates her voice to the white-dominated landscape suggests that she, not Selina, is the loser.

Brown Girl is dedicated to Paule Marshall's mother, of whose eloquence in the kitchen she has spoken often and eloquently — "every opportunity I get,"[19] she says — as the source of her voice as a writer. The novel itself, however, seems to represent a process more complicated than the one she has described in her essays and interviews. The story the novel tells is not a straightforward account of a young woman writer "coming to voice" by laying claim to her mother's legacy of voice. It is the story of the risks the claiming of that legacy entails, in a struggle that requires not only speaking truth to white power but also talking back to the mother herself. Selina eventually comes to artistic maturity by choosing a silent medium of self-expression, dance. But she is initially portrayed as a writer in the making, a poet wandering through the brownstone trying out her lines aloud. Even after she has left poetry behind, the continued emphasis on her voice reveals her dancing as a displaced version of writing. The displacement is most evident in the encounter with Mrs. Benton. For in this thinly veiled autobiographical portrait of the writer as a young woman,[20] the crisis in Selina's vocation as an aspiring dancer does not occur in the form of stage fright or physical incapacity. It is really a young writer's crisis, in the form of a contest of voice with a white mother whose effort to halt Selina's career as a dancer takes the form of an attempt to silence her.

Selina approaches this place of silence by way of her solo in her dance club's recital, the birth-to-death cycle in which she first comes into her own as an artist. After the recital she accompanies the rest of the girls, all white, to the chorus member Margaret's apartment on the upper East Side, where Mrs. Benton summons her for a private interview in response to Margaret's description of her "catharsis" during Selina's dance. Another way of putting this is to say that Selina approaches this place of silence by doing something her lover warned her against when she first joined the club: forgetting "what they can't ever seem to forget" (255). But later, when Selina tries to decide "What had brought her to this place," she settles on quite a different answer: "the part of her which had long hated her for her blackness" (289).

This analysis establishes a subtle link between that early place of silence in Selina's childhood, Miss Mary's room, and Mrs. Benton's. At the symbolic level of the novel, that is, the necessity for Selina's battle with Mrs. Benton is established by the presence, *in her own psyche*, of a colonized voice for which Mrs. Benton speaks—a voice that aims, like Miss Mary's earlier, at silencing Selina's other, uncolonized Barbadian-American voice. Like Miss Mary's, this mother's voice is the obverse of Silla's, but the description of it "flurrying like a cold wind" (288), suggesting not only winter but a snow flurry, also ominously recalls the wintry form into which Silla's voice was assimilated in the scene on Chauncey Street. It is not surprising, then, that the figures of Shakespeare and Joseph Conrad and the Greek dramatists should hover behind this confrontation, emblems of a white male legacy of voice that, deployed in certain ways, poses a threat to the Black woman writer's voice embodied in Silla and Selina.

The word that triggers Selina's invitation into the white mother's inner sanctum sets the contest between Mrs. Benton and Selina precisely in the context of a contested space of art, white art, that Selina has invaded.

Although Margaret's abilities as a dancer are ostensibly at issue, Mrs. Benton's defense of this space establishes the white daughter's *voice* as a major part of what is being contested by means of the contest over Selina's voice:

> "The birth-to-death cycle, Mother, and I had . . ."
> "I know, dear. A catharsis." (286)

Silence as a tool for reproducing hierarchy is quite literally an issue here, as Mrs. Benton tries to repossess her progeny by controlling her speech, which has escaped its proper limits with her choice of the classical word "catharsis" to describe a young African-American woman's art. Mrs. Benton's exasperated dismissal of the word vibrates with the hostility that literary critics have reserved through the centuries for errors of decorum — which have always, since Aristotle defined the proper subjects of tragedy, been identical with transgressions against class boundaries. Dramas that produce catharses are supposed to center upon heroic figures of the upper classes; otherwise there is no height from which the central character may fall. "Well, my dear, how does it feel to be the star of the show?" Mrs. Benton asks, and Selina unwisely answers, "A little like the real ones. Very high up" (285–86). Bringing Selina down from the high place to which Margaret's word "catharsis" has assigned her is Mrs. Benton's goal as, in an ever-so-genteel display of racism, she talks with animated false interest in a coercive pretense at conversation. Her long pseudodialogue with Selina, really a monologue, the solo performance with which she attempts to displace Selina's solo performance, becomes a "contest of strength" in which speaking is the key to victory. To her horror, Selina finds herself silent: not simply because she cannot bring herself to talk back but because the woman's chilling voice, as it closes in on her victim, is circling in on the subject of Barbadian women's voices themselves, trying to assimilate them to her own.

The issue here, as in other critical scenes in Paule Marshall's novels, boils down to the question of who will possess the voices of the dispossessed. In her struggle for this prize, Mrs. Benton plays on Selina's debased status in almost every hierarchy the two of them embody: race, class, age, nationality, North-versus-South, and even — despite the fact that Mrs. Benton is also a woman — gender. Gender, in fact, is Mrs. Benton's first point of attack: "All girls want to dance or act or write at some stage. I fancied myself a great tragedienne after I played Lady Macbeth freshman year . . ." (286). Mrs. Benton's use of gender to wage her war against Selina's desire to be a dancer illustrates the subtlety of Marshall's study here of the racializing and class inflection of gender issues and the gendering of race and class issues. In Mrs. Benton, Marshall shows a white woman's commitment to racism as inextricably woven together with a sexism that oppresses her as well, but that she is willing to invoke, nonetheless, to help shore up her race and class positions. Sexism here is Mrs. Benton's first line of defense against the possibility that the lives of Black women might have something to do with hers. "All girls" have these sorts of ambitions — a phrase that works at undoing the commonality it implies between Selina and Mrs. Benton by marking these ambitions as *only* common: meaningless, trivial, and, most importantly, destined to come to nothing. These ambitions do not define a girl as exceptional; on the contrary, they define her as commonplace and destined to lead the commonplace life of a woman. Why? The answer, surely, lies in the word "girls": the answer is gender. Mrs. Benton was once an ambitious "girl," too — a point of unity between her and Selina. But the unity is insignificant, because the ambitions of a girl are insignificant. And if the word "girl" seemed to ally her with Selina, her next use of the word, to describe "a girl who did our cleaning" (287), is a disavowal of that kinship, a reminder of the word's specialized overtones when a Black "girl" is in question. Mrs. Benton makes a point of calling attention to the insulting word: "Oh, she wasn't a girl, of course. We just call them that. It's a terrible habit" (287). The disclaimer is a reminder that Selina will never be able to look back on the days when she was a "girl" in quite the same complacent way Mrs. Benton does, for in racist discourse she will never stop being one. The word functions as a pivot for the modulation from the ostensibly raceless gender issue of "girls" overreaching themselves to the question of Selina's proper place as a "girl" of color. Mrs. Benton was a girl, but she was not and never will be a "girl" in this other sense that impinges on Selina's possibilities as a young artist. Mrs. Benton underscores the difference with her delicate choice of pronouns, "we" and "them," which leaves Selina out of the picture entirely. "We" are white; "they" — adult women of color — are "girls." In this discourse of power there is no signifier for Selina.

Mrs. Benton's modulation from an implicit gender issue to an explicit racial issue shows a great deal about the success of Paule Marshall's choice of a private scene of conversation between two women as an embodiment of power principles. The white mother's cultivated chit chat about her role as Lady Macbeth ("For a long time she talked of this..." [286]) establishes the private domain in which she is receiving "the star of the show" as a literary and cultural space, a scene of elegant women's conversation. The privacy of the domestic space is important; implicitly, Mrs. Benton has retired from the public life she might have had as an actress. And implicitly, Selina should retire, too — not only to domestic life, perhaps, but even, Mrs. Benton's word "girls" suggests, to domestic service. In keeping with this implication, when the "other words" that have "loomed behind" the cultivated talk in the sitting room burst through (286), this private cultural space is unmasked as a social, economic, and political arena, in which Mrs. Benton is engaged in a desperate, but deceptive, defense of an interlocking system of oppressive hierarchies.

The desperation reveals itself in the lack of transition between the two parts of Mrs. Benton's monologue. "Abruptly" halting her long reminiscence about having "fancied myself a great tragedienne" — the ostensibly self-deprecating narrative intended instead to deprecate whatever ambitions Selina may have — Mrs. Benton moves, as if by compulsion, into a series of questions about Selina's life, aimed at getting her to say she has a West Indian background:

> Her lively voice became preoccupied. Other words loomed behind it and finally she could no longer resist them and asked abruptly, "Where do you live, dear, uptown?"
> "No, Brooklyn."
> "Oh? Have you lived there long?"
> "I was born there."
> "How nice. . . . Not your parents, I don't suppose."
> "No." (286–87)

The compulsion driving this interrogation comes from "behind" Mrs. Benton's voice, from something else that (pre)occupies — pre-inhabits — it. That she speaks for something larger than herself is subtly evident in the extent to which her oppression of Selina involves a distortion of her own self-image. For the perversity of her line of questioning lies not only in its general racism but in its specific attempt to obscure the most striking point of unity between her and Selina. As Cherríe Moraga says, "it is not really difference the oppressor fears so much as similarity" (56). Because Mrs. Benton too was a young artist devoted to her craft, she must work doubly hard to show that Selina's background, far from having an important connection with hers, is, literally, foreign to it: "Not your parents, I don't suppose." It is at this point that Selina senses an "inquisition," "a contest of strength" in which an unwise answer will give her hostess the "advantage" (287). After being as evasive as possible, however, she must finally say the words the woman intends her to say: "The West Indies" (287).

Margaret's mother responds to these words, Selina's first defeat, by sitting back, "triumphant," and moving into her falsely fond reminiscence about the West Indian "girl" Ettie: "We were all crazy about her. . . . She was so ambitious for her son, I remember. She wanted him to be a dentist. He was very bright, it seems" (288). This is a coldly simple outsider's version of the whole world Paule Marshall has portrayed with such loving complexity throughout the book. Ettie's meticulous housekeeping was a proud effort to pay for her son's professional education; the white mother's little summary aims to strip that effort of dignity. "He was very bright, it seems." The calculated final phrase, "it seems," is a device for establishing distance, because it is used to describe things a speaker knows of only at second hand — things that may not exist at all. In the white mother's world, a black mother's child has no reality: that is the point she is making to Selina, who has been portrayed throughout the novel as so very much a Black mother's child. In the account of Ettie the whole world of Selina is seen, or rather not seen at all, through the narrow window of a white woman's fleeting memory, recounted with just barely polite false interest.

Mrs. Benton is repeatedly described in images of attack and assault, and words are her weapons. Silla's words are often described, too, in images of attack: they impale (24), ensnare (46), swing like punches in a boxing match (44), "rip" like the beaks of "ominous birds" (75). What Marshall describes in Mrs. Benton's words, however, is not just an isolated, individual act of speech; they belong to a discourse. Silla's words are not merely individual either; they are repeatedly described as collective. But Florrie's picture of Silla's mouth as a gun is an image of a solitary act of self-defense, whereas what Mrs. Benton's monologue embodies is a *system* of power relationships. As Mrs. Benton's speech becomes more and more coercive, its role as a private, individual enactment of a broader hegemonic discourse becomes more and more clear. It becomes more clear, too, that her goal is to subsume Selina into this discourse, as she "race[s] on" through a self-serving account of her visit to the dying Ettie, then into a "confidential whisper" about dishonest Black people who, "poor things," just haven't had "the proper training and education" (288). The "confidential whisper" is a move to assimilate Selina to the white mother's side, an invitation for her to isolate herself in a vision of herself as unique and other members of her race as indeed Other. At the same time, Mrs. Benton tries to appropriate the role of representative voice for these Others: "You can't help your color. It's just a lack of the proper training and education. I have to keep telling some of my friends that. Oh, I'm a real fighter when I get started!" (288). It is true, at least, that she is a fighter. Having bullied Selina into saying next to nothing, Mrs. Benton praises her for being so well spoken — a move to detach her voice from those other, allegedly less articulate voices for which Mrs. Benton has taken it upon herself to speak among her white friends. "Your race needs more smart young people like you. Ettie used to say the same thing. We used to have these long discussions on the race problem and she always agreed with me. It was so amusing to hear her say things in that delightful West Indian accent" (288–89). It is easy to see, from the way the white woman has coerced Selina into excruciating silence or into speaking only what she wants to hear, how these "long discussions" must have worked. Even without Mrs. Benton's coercive style of monologue, the power positions themselves would have worked to silence Ettie.

It is an eminently recognizable public discourse that Mrs. Benton brings so privately to bear on Selina, and her desperate effort to wall Selina up, silent, at the center of their supposed dialogue repeats on a smaller scale the construction of that hegemonic discourse itself around a silent core. The hallmarks of this particular form of white liberal discourse of racial equality that shaped much of the debate about civil rights in the late 1940s and 1950s are everywhere in her speech. The first such mark is its exclusion of the voices of those it describes even when the subject is the voices themselves. The second is its method of establishing Euro-American as the norm and African-American as Other by accenting the "exceptional" quality of Black achievements. Finally, this discourse is recognizable for the way it transposes into class prejudice the racial prejudice it disavows. The displacement is manifest in Mrs. Benton's words "proper training and education" and in her obvious hope that Selina will turn out to be from a poorer part of town.

Mrs. Benton traps Selina in this discourse by forcing her into a position in which she will lose if she speaks the wrong word but will also lose if she is silent. Having backed her into this corner, she then plays a final trump card by inviting her, not to give her opinion, but to "say something in that delightful West Indian accent for us!" (289). It is Ettie's accent—that is, Silla's accent—for which Mrs. Benton is calling so enthusiastically. Selina is invited to speak in the mother's voice, but stripped of its power. "Say something"—anything will do, because only the accent will signify. All that matters is that Selina's voice fix her, when she speaks, in her proper place in the hierarchies of North and South, rich and poor, white and Black, women and "girls."

Mrs. Benton's secure position in these hierarchies depends on maintaining her position in the discourse that sustains and reproduces them, which depends in turn on keeping its silent core from exploding into speech. But the hierarchy of gender complicates her relationship to that silence. Once again Moraga's perception is relevant: "it is not really difference the oppressor fears so much as similarity" (56). Mrs. Benton's obsessive monologue is at one level a desperate, elaborate evasion, by way of race and class, of kinship with Selina on the basis of gender. Like Selina, she was once an ambitious performer, a role she has obviously given up in the course of taking on the position of mother in a wealthy but downwardly mobile family. Something, we do not know what, went wrong with her career plans; the slightly contemptuous edge to her old-fashioned word "tragedienne" calls attention to her gender as a possible factor in the tragedy. We may also infer that this would-be Lady Macbeth, aspiring to power through manipulation of her husband's power, has failed due to the husband's failure to maintain his status. The room in which she struggles so desperately to prove her superiority to Selina is located in a once opulent building, poised ominously between a "decrepit row of tenements" and a modern high-rise (283).

The silence at the core of Mrs. Benton's monologue — the refusal to speak seriously of her own aspirations as a young woman — keeps Selina, and the high seriousness of *her* artistic ambitions, safely apart from Mrs. Benton, in a space circumscribed as Other. This space, to which Selina is consigned by virtue of her position as a West Indian, is therefore in an important sense the same space as that to which Mrs. Benton's youthful ability to take herself seriously as an actor has been consigned. The space of Selina's oppression is the space of Mrs. Benton's self-suppression, or perhaps repression, since it seems she has lost touch completely with her youthful aspirations. This is a preliminary version of the space that, in Paule Marshall's second novel, is at the same time First World repression and Third World oppression and is allegorized in the "chosen place" of Bournehills. To both situations James Baldwin's perception is relevant: "[W]hatever white people do not know about Negroes reveals, precisely and inexorably, what they do not know about themselves" (*The Fire Next Time* 44). Paule Marshall's renderings of this truth have always to do with voice. Mrs. Benton is her first portrait of the way in which oppression by means of the white silencing of Black voices is also a repression of self-knowledge. As Selina recognizes after she escapes this place of silence, "Her dark face must be confused in their minds with what they feared most: with the night, symbol of their ancient fears, which seethed with sin and harbored violence, which spawned the beast in its fen; with the heart of darkness within them and all its horror and fascination" (291).

What such white fears of dark people amount to is a power move aimed at appropriating their bodies as signifiers in an internal, psychological discourse that denies them anything more than symbolic reality. The allusion to Conrad, even as it pays homage to one of the young Paule Marshall's literary heroes,[21] reclaims the brown body of her heroine, a young woman writer-dancer, from symbolic colonization. The logic of the displacement whereby the dancer's crisis of vocation becomes a crisis not of body but of voice becomes clear in this passage. For Paule Marshall, the grown up "brown girl" as a young writer, the process of coming to voice is bound up with the struggle to reclaim a woman's brown body as her own signifier, not someone else's.

The question of whom Selina's body will signify evokes the mirror scene in the parlor, with its representation of a brown girl's identity constructed in such a way as to construct a white woman's identity. It is not surprising, then, that Selina sees her reflection in Mrs. Benton's eyes as she saw her reflection in the white people's parlor mirror long ago after vainly imagining herself, for a moment, "one of them" (5). "Those eyes were a well-lighted mirror in which, for the first time, Selina truly saw—with a sharp and shattering clarity—the full meaning of her black skin. . . . What had brought her to this place? to this shattering knowledge? And obscurely she knew: the part of her which had long hated her for her blackness and thus begrudged her each small success like the one tonight . . ." (289).

From the angle of realism, Selina's question, "What had brought her to this place?" perhaps implies questions about her motives in joining an all-white dance club, or celebrating so unwarily with this group of white people in such a white milieu. But it is a central question, always, in allegory, a mode in which settings appear out of nowhere in correspondence to the spiritual, moral, and emotional "place" at which the hero/ine has arrived. How did Bunyan's hero Christian come to be in the Slough of Despond? Why did the Red Crosse Knight find himself in the Castle of Despair so soon after visiting the House of Pride? As Angus Fletcher says, "Allegory is structured according to ritualistic necessity . . ." (150). Selina sees her spiritual progress as having led, of necessity, to Mrs. Benton's room, which is thus explicitly allegorized in this passage as a part of Selina herself. The unity this allegory implies has a two-edged irony. Mrs. Benton's racism, her desperate effort to establish Selina as foreign to her, can have its deepest triumph only if what Mrs. Benton represents is "part of" Selina—but Selina's recognition of the unity is Mrs. Benton's defeat. The "part of her which had long hated her for her blackness" is the part that made her long to be one of the supposedly genteel white people of whose mild voices Miss Mary told her. Mrs. Benton's "confidential whisper," intended to draw her into a cozy unity with her oppressor, recalls the earlier scene with Miss Mary: "All afternoon they whispered together" (201). A well-practiced ventriloquist, Margaret's mother is another version of that dying woman to whose stories Selina listened and for whom, when Miss Mary needed a younger voice to tell the old white myths, Selina spoke. Now, however, Selina, grown up—and indeed this moment is her coming of age—refuses to collaborate. She rejects the self-divisive unity with her oppressor into which Miss Mary lured her and Mrs. Benton tries to tempt her—the longing to be "one of them" that she experienced on the stairs as a child. And this rejection is the same as claiming another, different unity,[22] so that as she emerges from the subway back into the landscape of Brooklyn, it is suddenly her true, interior landscape for the first time: "She was one with Miss Thompson. . . . One with the whores, the flashy men, and the blues rising sacredly above the plain of neon lights and ruined houses. . . . And she was one with them: the mother and the Bajan women, who had lived each day what she had come to know" (292–93).[23]

In the aftermath of her encounter with the white mother, Selina gains a capacity for seeing double. She sees the many other places of silence behind the one she has just escaped; she sees through the story of Ettie what Silla's experiences must have been in white women's houses. The core of Selina's new double vision of her life as part of others is in her new re-visioning, and re-hearing, of the mother in her memory. Remembering all the scenes like that at the close of Chapter 1, she sees again the mother returning home, but this time with "the day's humiliations" in the background of her grim figure. She hears her voice again, but now against the background of her silence at work. She sees herself not only in her mother, but in all "the Bajan women."

These new powers of double vision are prepared for by her meditations on the ways in which her face reflected in the vacant store window is both her true self and, to whites who only see its color, not herself at all. Having rubbed off the layers of illusion created by the dirt on the window and the stage makeup on her face, she sees in this reflection, "clearly for the first time," that other illusion of the heart of darkness: "the image which the woman — and the ones like the woman — saw when they looked at her" (291). This image, she realizes, confusing "Her dark face . . . with what they feared most . . . had the shape and form of her face but was not really her face" (291).[24] There is a significant difference between this scene and Selina's vision of herself in the parlor mirror after falling prey to Miss Mary's ghost voices. In the earlier scene her illusions of being white were shattered, but not the illusions that being white was better. Now Selina is disturbed by something quite different: the recognition of the image of herself-as-Other *as an illusion*.[25] Even so, this face with the shape of her face is indestructible. She strikes out at it but it remains, "gazing at her with her own enraged and tearful aspect" (291). Even her own face is powerless against the false reflection of it. As her "feverish face strik[es] the cold one" she cries "because their idea of her was only an illusion, yet so powerful that it would stalk her down the years, confront her in each mirror and from the safe circle of their eyes, surprise her even in the gleaming surface of a table. . . . She cried because, like all her kinsmen, she must somehow prevent it from destroying her inside and find a way for her real face to emerge" (291).

4

"The woman — and the ones like the woman"; "like all her kinsmen. . . ." No act in Paule Marshall's work occurs outside a system in which individuals speak and act not only as themselves but, knowingly or unknowingly, in concert with others. This is not to say that Marshall is a determinist; in her works the individual will is a source of tremendous strength. But in the world she portrays, part of that strength, the power-to, comes from a recognition of unity, just as the oppressor's power-over comes from a rejection of certain unities. In Selina's childhood fantasy she had thought herself "one of" the whites, and was rudely "put in her place," as Margaret's mother would no doubt envision it, by a glimpse of her face in a mirror. Now she affirms her place in the collective identity of Black women: "she was one with them." And yet it is true, after all, that she is "one with" all humanity, as her dance — the birth-to-death cycle that all people perform — affirmed. That is part of the significance of her encounter, together with her white friend Margaret, with the white mother who is also in a sense one of Selina's progenitors in the distant past of the Caribbean. This progenitor seeks to deny the unity between her black and white daughters, exiling Selina from the sisterhood she has celebrated by her membership in the dance club. The act of division is at the same time the white mother's denial of her own unity with the Black mother, Ettie, ambitious for her son just as the white mother is ambitious for her daughter.

These unities create the most important superimposition at work here, the double vision of the encounter with the white mother as also an encounter with the Black mother. The double exposure enables Selina to see the realities of her mother's life for the first time, bridging in her imagination the gap between herself and Silla. Her sudden insight into the meaning of "the mother's voice" she has loved and feared since childhood is also a recognition of her place in a community of women: "And she was one with . . . the mother and the Bajan women, who had lived each day what she had come to know" (292–93).[26] Selina's journey of freedom begins with this recognition, liberating her, paradoxically, to leave the mother whose voice she now understands so well.

The passages describing Selina's anagnorisis have the rhythm of closure, but the narrative sequence that follows suggests something else. What comes next in Selina's life is a week of recurrent nightmare, a kind of terrifying re-visioning that unlocks the Gothic terror of the earlier, seemingly unterrifying experience of possession by white ghosts. In a "parlor," Selina wanders "familiarly amid the ornate Victorian furnishings": a dream-superimposition in which the brownstone, her own house, is also Mrs. Benton's ornate apartment. Suddenly she hears footsteps outside — a classic Gothic convention, which is followed, conventionally, by the heroine's terrifying realization that an intruder is approaching. Selina's revelation is different: what she realizes, as terror seizes her, is that *she* is "an intruder" in what is obviously supposed to be her own house (298). Having searched frantically for a window, "a second door or a closet," she plunges into an "open grand piano, tearing a way through the wires" into the street, where the pursuers give the chase over to a "huge, silent, swift" beast (298). From this beast, "a low-slung, dark-furred animal with eyes as innocent as a child's," she narrowly escapes, having almost given in: "Some perverse part of her suddenly wanted surrender more than escape, and thought with pleasure of the claws ripping the last breath from her throat . . ." (298). As another of Marshall's characters likes to quote, "At any moment the beast may spring."

Selina's escape through the piano literalizes such expressions as "She used music as an escape from her problems" or "The piano was her escape," with music standing in for Selina's own art of dance. The moment bears a striking resemblance to a Gothic nightmare recounted by Henry James in his autobiography. At first he is "defending himself, in terror, against the attempt of someone to break into his room," then suddenly he defies the nameless intruder by forcing the door open himself and pursuing the pursuer, who flees until he is a mere spot in the distance. James, triumphant, realizes that he is in the beautiful Galerie d'Apollon in the Luxembourg Palace. I have suggested elsewhere that this dream is a perfect image of the final Gothic escape, which is the writer's own escape through the door that opens from the haunted mind into the palace of art (*Perils of the Night* 144–45). But the art and the artist in James's dream were white, and the contrast between James's Gothic nightmare and Selina's is one answer to the question "What difference does difference make?" when the person escaping across the artist's threshold of maturity is a woman of color.

James escaped his perils of the night through his entry into a public palace of art, and that was that. But Selina's escape through art brings no such closure. The room in which she wanders "familiarly" turns out, like that room so long ago, to be "theirs"; the grand piano represents an art associated with another class and race; it cannot offer the ease of escape that such an art offered to James. Her escape through art, in fact, is exactly what triggers the spring of the beast, just as her triumph as a young dancer inspired Mrs. Benton's attack of racism. The beast is clearly an alien Other, intent on consuming Selina's "substance and her self." The leg wound it gives Selina before she escapes, for example, is an obvious analogue to the leg wound Miss Thompson got in her struggle with the white rapists. But with its dark color and eyes innocent as a child's the beast is also partly Selina. Indeed we may deduce from her longing to surrender that it is, in addition to being an external force, "the part of her which had long hated her for her blackness."[27]

That part of Selina embodied in the "silent" beast is linked not only to the white colonizing voice that lured her into a "confidential whisper" in

Miss Mary's room but also to a part of Silla, standing easily in her white kitchen or laughing derisively in the "cold light" of Chauncey Street after a snowfall. Silla disapproves of Selina's dancing as thoroughly as Mrs. Benton. Yet Silla has another self, evoked by old Mr. Braithwaite when Silla declines his invitation to dance: "You don does dance! You must think I forget how you used to be wucking up yourself every Sat'dy night when the Brumlee Band played on the pasture. You must think I forget how I see you dance once till you fall out for dead right there on the grass. You must think I forget, but, girl, I ain forget" (144). Silla laughingly responds, "But Mr. Braithwaite, how you does remember so good?" — a question to which he replies in a line that could be the epigraph to any of Paule Marshall's novels: "How you can forget the past, mahn? You does try but it's here today and there waiting for you tomorrow" (145).

Brown Girl, Brownstones ends with a complex image of the past in which the house plays its final role as a double rendering of social and psychological space — a role intimately linked to the question of silence, voice, and power. The perspective for this final double vision is an outside, exterior perspective, in keeping with Selina's departure from the world of her childhood. Having made her plans to sail for "the islands," she wanders, as a form of leave-taking, through a landscape of "ravaged brownstones" that are no longer silent and closed, as they would once have been at this hour — not "drawn within the darkness of themselves" (309). In a metonymic suggestion of Selina's emergence from the womb of Silla's psyche and from the closed-in life centered on the drama of her family, these brownstones are open to the outside world: "Now, the roomers' tangled lives spilled out the open windows, and the staccato beat of Spanish voices, the frenzied sensuous music joined the warm canorous Negro sounds to glut the air. As she passed, a man — silhouetted against a room where everything seemed poised for flight — burst into a fiercely sad song in Spanish" (309). The surrealist image of the contents of a room "poised for flight" brings to its climax the picture of interiors in the process of exteriorizing themselves. In this process voices, in particular, are pictured as bursting outward, uncontained. That Selina herself is in a sense "poised for flight" links these voices to hers; their newness in this environment, and their foreignness to Selina, enhance the sense they convey of possibilities — of an opening out of the interior of the brownstones into the larger world.[28] But this opening out, at its most extreme, is also devastating destruction — the "vast waste" of demolished brownstones to which the man's song leads Selina. Here "A solitary wall stood perversely amid the rubble, a stoop still imposed its massive grandeur, a carved oak staircase led only to the night sky" (309). The staircase at the beginning of Selina's story led up to Miss Mary's and Suggie's rooms and down to the parlor that was irrevocably someone else's. At the end of the book—which is yet again the beginning of Selina's story—the staircase leads up and out into the unknown dark. Neither Miss Mary's colonized and colonizing space nor Suggie's particular version of an unassimilated space exists any longer. What remains looks from one angle like ruin and from another like hope.

Similarly, from one angle the architectural fragments are monuments to the power of the Barbadians who made these lost houses theirs; like them, they persist despite the forces brought to bear against them. From another, they are defeat: "For it was like seeing the bodies of all the people she had ever known broken, all the familiar voices that had ever sounded in those high-ceilinged rooms shattered—and the pieces piled into this giant cairn of stone and silence" (310). Silla's power was a voice that could "split the serenity of the house." In the image of the brownstones reduced to "cairns" the silence of the house is the silence of Barbadian voices that are themselves "shattered," and the wrecked houses are themselves broken bodies. Already in Selina's mind the "monolithic shapes" of the new city project are occupied with "life moving in an oppressive round within those uniformly painted walls" (310). The sheer monumentality of the "oppressive" life being constructed here for the poor suggests the anonymous, almost unopposable economic and social forces at work in this final metamorphosis of Selina's childhood world: the same forces that brought about Silla and Deighton's tragedy through the corruption and distortion of a woman's power. Like all such pictures in the novel, this landscape of economic change is also a picture of psychological change. It is as if, at the end of the novel, the "shattering clarity" of Selina's hard-won inner vision had finally to be literalized in the shattering of the whole architecture of her childhood world. And that devastation is troped, in turn—in the climax of the house-body allegory—as a breaking of loved ones' bodies that is also a final, devastating silencing of their voices.

The paradoxes here—of freedom and loss, ruin and strength—are heightened, in a corresponding paradox, by the affirmation of doubleness symbolized in Selina's ritual division of the two silver bangles she has worn since birth. She keeps one as she turns her back on this scene, tossing the other behind her onto the heap of rubble, where it makes "A frail sound in that utter silence" (310). The final image is one of a dancer—a woman expressing herself in a ritualized gesture.[29] But the final context in which this gesture is presented—the opposition of "frail sound" to "utter silence"—suggests once more that the art at issue here is a writer's art, drawing its strength from the mother's voice, articulating itself finally in the space of the mother's silence.

Silla's voice was the most immediate power in Selina's childhood world. Selina, having begun as a poet, grows up to claim dancing, instead, as her own form of self-expression. But that choice brings her back, full circle, to the mother: a different, younger, unsuspected mother who once danced till she fainted, "Years ago, on an island" (145). *Brown Girl* ends with Selina's return, as it were, to her mother's silenced past, the "green node in a vast sea." For even in breaking free of the world of brownstones, symbol of the Barbadian women's identity that overwhelmed her as a child, she goes off to look for her own separate identity in the mother's deep sources of selfhood. This journey is her final, paradoxical response to the contradictions of the mother's voice. Selina is "one with" other Black women in the mother's battle. But her journey is a way of saying as well, in the words of the *Freedom Charter* bell hooks quotes in *Talking Back*, "Our struggle is also a struggle of memory against forgetting" (4).

Chapter 2
Losses and Recognitions
Allegorical Realism in *The Chosen Place, the Timeless People*

The root of oppression is loss of memory.

— Paula Gunn Allen

1

The shift in settings from the old allegorical topos of the house to another traditional allegorical setting, the island, announces the vastly broadened scope of Paule Marshall's feminist inquiry in *The Chosen Place, the Timeless People* (1969). Much more than *Brown Girl, Brownstones*, this second novel superimposes a realistic world and a spiritualized, allegorical space to portray "the intensely social character" of the interior life. Described with stark, sunlit precision in densely novelistic detail and at the same time rendered as a dreamy, elusive psychological landscape, Bourne Island becomes a trope for the interpenetration of the social, political, and economic worlds with the world of the psyche. It is on the plane of this setting — the realm where oppression in the external, novelistic world of "objective forces" represents itself, re-presents itself, as repression in the interior world — that the struggle of memory against forgetting takes place. At issue is the global drama of imperialism as it plays itself out on each private individual stage: the drama of imperialism in the mind; the linked possibilities for psychological and political transformation.[1]

Even more than her rendering of the brownstone, Marshall's rendering of Bourne Island overlays pictures of economic, political, and historical forces on pictures of psychological experience.[2] This general technique works by means of more specific superimpositions involving the primary setting of the novel and a sequence of embedded settings that are places of silence. The resulting double exposure conflates a white First World character's symbolic landscape of the mind with an African-Caribbean character's realistic landscape of economic and political dispossession. Bourne Island thereby becomes a simultaneously psychological and political landscape in which the split between the First and Third Worlds, portrayed as a self-division deriving from forgotten or rejected unities, is replicated in the self-divisions of Merle and Harriet and manifested for both of them as versions of silence. The narrative superimpositions culminate in a set of double exposures of whiteness and blackness that constitute a double revisioning, through these two women who "embody the whole power struggle of the world,"[3] of Conrad's heart of darkness.

What Audre Lorde called "the transformation of silence into language and action" is the central drama of this revisioning. But this is not to say that the novel identifies silence exclusively with powerlessness and voice with power. Transformation is not only a central theme of the novel; it is one of the central modes of superimposition by which Marshall's narrative proceeds. By means of it, her double images of dispossession and power, tragedy and hope, picture the triumphant self-possession of the dispossessed, their ability to make even the signs of their powerlessness signify their power. One of these signs is silence. Whereas silence is almost always associated with powerlessness and loss in *Brown Girl*, here it plays a more complex role through self-decolonizations that decolonize economic and political spaces, sometimes through speech, sometimes by turning silence into a mode of resistance rather than defeat.

The superimposition of Bourne Island as a real place and a dreamlike symbol for the psyche begins in the juxtaposition of two views of the landscape from an airplane. The first is Vere's as, with a worker's "practiced eye," he sorts the fields of sugarcane into new and ready to harvest.[4] But what Vere sees most clearly in this landscape are places hidden from view: Cane Vale sugar factory where his uncle was "crushed to death" by the rollers, and Spiretown, where his mother "died giving birth to him" (14). Drawn in memory to these scenes of his past, Vere senses the landscape claiming him irrevocably.

Harriet's view, like Vere's, is linked to memory—but also to a loss of memory whose roots are entwined with the forms of oppression Vere discerns so clearly in the landscape beneath them. Seeing the mild green side of the island for the first time, Harriet inadvertently lets a memory of childhood "slip" past her customary "guard." Having caught an unwilling glimpse of her repressed past, she immediately catches sight of Bournehills, the region inhabitants of the more prosperous side try to forget: "she wondered . . . how an island as small as this could sustain such a dangerous division. To add to matters. . . . Because of the shadows

Bournehills scarcely seemed a physical place to her, but some mysterious and obscured region of the mind which ordinary consciousness did not dare admit to light" (21). Similarly, when Lyle touches her arm she perceives his blackness as "some dark and unknown part of herself which had suddenly, for the first ever, surfaced, appearing like stigmata or an ugly black-and-blue mark at the place he had touched" (96–97). As David Carroll points out in a study of Achebe, Conrad's African landscape, devoid of internal meaning, is there "to provide a convenient background for the anguish and self-questioning of the introverted European characters. 'There were moments,' says Marlow, 'when one's past came back to one' " (2).[5] Looking down on Bournehills from the air — a perspective from which, to her, the people look "minute and insignificant and black" (22), and the landscape looks like her own psyche — Harriet has one of these "moments," fearing the plane will take her "back to the past which she had always sought to avoid" (21).

But in Marshall's subversion of the "heart of darkness" trope, what confronts the First World characters in Bournehills is not just a repressed interior past projected from their tormented psyches onto the blank screen of an unknown place; it is that place in reality, as the people who live there know it. Thus Harriet's vague suspicion that the most oppressed part of the island is the repressed shadow side of her dangerously divided mind is right, but in a sense she is never able to comprehend. Marshall limns the true connection between Harriet's psyche and Bournehills by positioning Harriet's symbolic view of the island in the context of Vere's realistic one. Harriet's sensation of being borne against her control into the past ironically echoes his feelings of a fated, inescapable return. Prominent in the landscape he sees are actual, exterior places of exploitation and death. The past Harriet fears confronting is an interior reservoir of memories about her family and her first marriage to Andrew Westerman, whose work on nuclear weapons left her infertile. But the past that Vere senses claiming him is also her past, because her family business is rooted in the slave trade in which the history of Cane Vale Factory began. Further, her business is now affiliated, through the United Corporation of America, with Kingsley and Sons, owners of the sugar industry that consumes Bourne Island's agriculture and necessitates the import of dried salted cod — a staple of Bourne Island's inadequate diet, Harriet's original fortune, and Unicor's profits. From Harriet's point of view the landscape is a fearful objective correlative of her buried interior reality, signifying her inner dramas but lacking any significance of its own. To Vere, a native son returning from an exploitative labor scheme in the United States, Bournehills is a real, not a symbolic world, a landscape of poverty and work, not of metaphors for the psyche.

Marshall's own symbolic system conflates both views from the airplane.

A fusion of allegory and realism, Bourne Island functions as a private psychological terrain shaped by the historical forces it represents simultaneously—an image of the political and economic configuration of a society configuring the interior life. Bournehills, which Harriet has never seen, is as literally her history as it is Vere's, and the identity of repression and oppression in both histories is mirrored in the divided landscape. Bourne Island's geographical division into prosperity and poverty reflects a class system sustained by a repression that has cost the wealthier inhabitants their memories of slavery and drawn them into such an intense identification with their colonial masters that they see people like Vere as "brutes" (59). The island's "dangerous division" is thus a microcosmic version of the larger schizophrenia that enables the First World, including Harriet, to exploit the Third World without recognizing any personal connection to the lives that sustain its own. Furthermore, the "ravaged" landscape of Bournehills (21), depleted of self-sustenance by centuries of export agriculture, is the legacy bequeathed by such people as Harriet's slave-trading ancestor: the shadow side of the "modest inheritance" (39) she enjoys. The reason for the divided landscape is the reason for her economic security, and the island's self-division is her self-division, because its oppressed side—the past that reaches out to claim Vere—is politically and economically her repressed past. Indeed, at the symbolic level the divided landscape of Bourne Island stands, among much else, for the moral schizophrenia that sustains Harriet's blindness to this identity of Vere's history and hers: for the self-division that enables the First World to see the Third World in abstract terms as a symbol for its heart of darkness but not in concrete terms as a victim of the evil that "darkness" supposedly represents.

Through her portrait of the work of silence in Harriet's psychology, Marshall examines the First World's self-distancing from the Third World, a process in which Third World voices are, as in some perverse simultaneous translation, rendered as silence. A carefully cultivated system of silencing enables Harriet to maintain her sense of the unreality of Bournehills even in her personal encounters with its people, to whom she listens as if she were the onstage "spectator" of a play (171). The image evokes not only her mystified distance from a drama in which she actually participates, but her real economic relation—as a consumer—to people she sees as acting for her benefit. The same relation is expressed in Harriet's deliberate deafness to the Bournehills sea, whose "roar of outrage and grief" (172) speaks her historical connection to Bournehills people. Its sound is "like that of the combined voices of the drowned raised in a loud unceasing lament—all those, the nine million and more it is said, who in their enforced exile, their Diaspora, had gone down between this point and the homeland lying out of sight to the east" (106).

In an image that reinforces the connection between Harriet's personal psychological repressions and the oppression of which the sea speaks, the first time she hears this voice of the drowned it calls up her past by evoking a recurrent nightmare from her last year with Andrew Westerman: after an explosion, a mushroom cloud rising "in the final silence" (39), and her hand "guiding Andrew's on the lever" (107). In this memory the personal and political are already inseparable manifestations of each other, through the double image of the private, gender-related suffering a man of her own race and nationality caused her and her complicity, because of those same factors, in the more widely oppressive power structure that "Wester[n]man" represents. The description of the wave that evokes the memory "gathering force and power and speed across the entire breadth of the Middle Passage," then exploding like a "depth charge" (106), further superimposes on this double image the history of slavery, from which Harriet still profits, and the history of modern warfare, in which she is implicated through her connection with a company that sells munitions. The setting of Bourne Island repeatedly evokes such memories in the First World characters—memories in which an intimate personal past is identical with a broader political history.

A series of embedded settings, places of silence and stasis, further superimposes these two versions of the past. "Once a great wrong is done," the epigraph says, "it never dies." The places of silence in this novel are places of "great wrong": exploitative workplaces;[6] domestic spaces where understanding has failed; repressed regions of the mind associated with pain suffered or inflicted; Bournehills itself in a set of images portraying its inhabitants as silent, static, timeless, like ghosts of the slaves. And in a series of apocalyptic allusions, there is the place all the rest foreshadow, the world in "the final silence" after nuclear annihilation (39). The action of the novel moves through a sequence of these places in such a way that their superimposition reveals a double psychological and historical pattern of loss at the heart of relations between the First and Third Worlds: for the oppressed, a loss of connection with their past, their work, each other, and themselves; for the oppressors, a loss of any sense that the lives they exploit are connected to theirs. The two faces of this pattern of loss are oppression in the "objective" realm of historical forces and repression in the realm of the characters' "interior lives." In both realms, the opposite of these losses is the recognition of forgotten unities through a "rescue" of memory.[7]

An attempt at such a rescue is at issue in the first place of silence associated with Merle, the workplace from which she has recently been dismissed as the novel opens. Breaking the colonized silence in which she was expected to participate as a history teacher, Merle's lessons on Cuffee Ned, like the annual Bournehills carnival pageant celebrating his slave revolt, were a political "struggle . . . against forgetting." Outside the workplace her talk often performs the same function, in scathingly accurate analyses that reveal how cogent her apparently verbose speech can be.[8] But even as Merle voices her "historical awareness" (Nazareth 116) in a struggle against forgetting, in her private life the obsessive talk is also a struggle against memory—a kind of silence, a substitute for confronting her tragic personal history. She "never, but never" speaks directly of this history (116), although it is the psychological counterpart of the more public history to which she is always giving voice. Only when she can voice her knowledge of their connection, and move from her "standstill" despite it, can she be free.[9]

In subtle ways the second place of silence in the novel, Sugar's nightclub, resembles Merle's classroom. Here too, oppression and repression are two faces of the same reality and, as in the colonized classroom with its official version of "history," silence is disguised as something else. This disguise is part of a larger mystification in which the great wrong the nightclub represents is ironically masked as a ceremony of reconciliation: a wild dance in which people of all colors and nationalities seem to have merged into "one body, the inseparable parts of a whole" (81). Despite this apparent unity, the nightclub, "divided . . . between great areas of shadow and light" (92), is an image in miniature of Bourne Island, with its "dangerous division" between a more prosperous side and an impoverished side whose hills are filled with shadows even at midday (21). An "arena the size of the world" (92), the club, like the island, is a microcosm in which some people buy and others are sold. Indeed, in the rusted manacles of the cellar beneath the frenetic noise of Sugar's is its silenced history as a barracoon. In the contrast between this foundation and the nightclub above it, the architecture allegorizes the nightclub's perverse representation of silence as voice and oppression as unity, exposing the true economic relations on which that representation is constructed. Full of strange objects its patrons have left behind, the club itself, like the cellar below, is a repository of lost, forgotten, and abandoned things. Even the music is "a lesser version of some richer, fuller sound" (80), symbolized by an ornate talking drum, cast aside, "waiting for a drummer to give it voice" (83).

The identity of oppression and repression, suggested in the presence of a rarely talked-about subterranean history and a silenced African drum, is reiterated in the person of Sugar himself. Barely moving or speaking, he embodies the silence, stasis, and disunity all the noise and motion conceal. Sugar is the middleman in much of the buying and selling, responding to patrons' whispered requests with the one word he is ever known to utter: "a deep, hoarse, thrilling 'Yeah!' " (84). He speaks nothing and everything; he is also, like the multiracial dancers who appear to be "one body" (81), all colors and no color — "a neutral, indeterminate beige (all the colors known to man might have come together and been canceled out in him . . .)" (83).

Sugar's contradictions are a key to the meaning of this place, whose surface gaiety hides the fact that it is a scene of recreation for only a small portion of the world. For the rest it is the most degrading of workplaces — for the hostesses and even for Sugar, who will sell anything but whose name identifies him with the chief commodity of the island. His name says that he, nominal proprietor, is just another object of transaction, "Signed, sealed, and delivered," as Merle later describes the whole island when its legislature prostitutes it to First World investors (209). A man of striking individuality whose face seems "without features" (84), named for a famous winner but resembling a body shrunken by victorious enemies (83), exploited as commodity but also doing the exploiter's work like the "banker in a gambling house where no one ever wins" (83), possibly West Indian but thought to be American, Sugar stands for the dislocations of the colonized mind, itself a superimposition of oppressor and oppressed.[10] In essence he is a yes-man — his only word is "Yeah!" (84) — but his eyes contemplate an infinite negation, "some nothingness that absorbed him totally" (84). Ironically, one function of this man who conceals his past and contemplates nothing is the task of memory. His club is a warehouse of "mementos" (82); on his walls are letters from former patrons asking that he "remember them" (83). If he is indeed a repository of history, he does not speak it; at his workplace he plays the role Merle was fired for not playing at hers.

Sugar is more than a mystery; he embodies the whole process of mystification that allows the First World to get away with turning Bourne Island's blood, as Merle says, to sugar water. The multinational recreation over which he presides, false unity cloaking a "violent combat" (92), epitomizes the developed world's abuse of Bourne Island as part of a commercial network that binds the world up like a children's ball of rubber bands twisted "around a toy marble" (37).[11] The logical end of this toying with the earth is prophesied in the first apocalyptic image of the novel. In the "phantasma of color" sweeping the dance floor is "a dark smoldering amber that one imagined could be found only at the heart of a conflagration that had consumed the world" (81). As in later instances of the motif, the image describes a world already destroyed, one in which the developed nations' potential for apocalyptic violence is not merely potential but a power already unleashed. The apocalypse in such images is both inconceivable future and history: history equally inconceivable to those who, having produced the destruction, misread their war on the Third World as a holiday dance — even a form of racial harmony.

By superimposing on the picture of Sugar's as a disguised place of

silence an image of the global apocalyptic struggle of which such workplaces are only a local manifestation, Marshall exposes the silence the
dispossessed suffer there as just one aspect of "the final silence" in which
the world's dangerous self-division into North and South will end. At the
same time, all her pictures of the oppressed superimpose a celebration of
their power on the portrayal of their exploitation. Sugar's one word may
be *yes*, but it is "deep, hoarse, thrilling . . . encompassing every emotion"
(84). Speaking their self-degrading script in mocking voices ("Touch me
here, touch me there . . ." 90), nearly mauling the patrons in the guise of
seduction, the hostesses resist even as they suffer the predation whose
broadest meaning is parodied in one of Sugar's "mementos": a stuffed
bald eagle with "blood-red" beak, its wings "casting their shadow over the
entire room" (82). Meanwhile the apparent unity of the dancers, preda-
tors and prey, is both an illusion masking their violently opposing interests and the reality of their unacknowledged common blood. Despite
their "combat," they are truly "inseparable parts" divisible only in the
fiction the First World's repression of history creates: the fiction that a
part is the whole and the rest of the world its shadow.

Merle, always speaking and withholding her truth at the same time, is a
fitting commentator on this noisy place of silence, talking obsessively as if
she were the Ancient Mariner recounting "some unspeakably inhuman
act" (89). The paradox implied in the description of Merle telling an
unspeakable story underscores the contradictions of her powerful voice,
which are at the heart of this novel just as those of Silla's voice were at the
heart of *Brown Girl*. Merle speaks unequivocally about the political and
economic history of the island and its consequences, including the psychological effects of colonialism. At the same time she is always telling,
but not directly, about something "unspeakabl[e]": those consequences
as they have played themselves out in her private life. Merle's monologues about Bourne Island's history speak publicly for other, silenced
voices, but they also camouflage a mute, more private history she must
speak in order to be free. Until then her self-consuming talk will be
suicidal, "the voice rushing pell-mell down the precipitous slope toward
its own destruction" (66).

bell hooks describes such talk: "[Black women's] speech, 'the right
speech of womanhood,' was often the soliloquy, the talking into thin air,
the talking to ears that do not hear you—the talk that is simply not
listened to" (*Talking Back* 6–7).

Within feminist circles, silence is often seen as the sexist "right speech of womanhood"—the sign of woman's submission to patriarchal authority. This emphasis
on woman's silence may be an accurate remembering of what has taken place in
the households of women from WASP backgrounds in the United States, but in
black communities (and diverse ethnic communities), women have not been

silent. . . . Certainly for black women, our struggle has not been to emerge from
silence into speech but to change the nature and direction of our speech, to make
a speech that compels listeners, one that is heard. (*Talking Back* 6)

The barriers to Merle's development of such a speech are evident in
the circumstances of her scathing demystification of Sugar's on the first
night of the Americans' arrival. Harriet and Allen are asleep during
Merle's harangue, Harriet back at her hotel and Allen right at Merle's
table. For them, Merle's words are silence. Saul, in contrast, hears more
than he would like, but he cannot allow himself to hear quite enough.
Inwardly acknowledging his lust for some of the women at Sugar's, he is
"willing . . . to confess his part in it all" (88–89), without seeing that
his complicity has to do not merely with his secret interior life but with
its social and economic character. For despite his tortured good inten-
tions, Saul is wedded — literally — to the money interests that impoverish
Bournehills. Without forgetting most of "his part" in its economic history, he could not be here. Correspondingly, he has closed off to memory
much of his personal history and thus of his capacity to feel, so that he
experiences Merle's political tirade in intensely personal terms, feeling it
as a fist pounding at his heart, "demanding that he open it again" (92).

Marshall's description of Sugar's culminates in a layering upon layering
of voices, dominated finally by a kind of voice-over intoned by Lyle Hutson, eminent barrister and member of the government's elite: " '*Arma
virumque cano,* / *Troiae qui primus ab oris . . .*' " (92). The irony is scathing,
for in Lyle's fancy school the *Aeneid*, epic of a heroic journey across the
seas to found a nation, was part of the British education that would have
blocked from view a journey more relevant to him: the journey of the
Middle Passage. His drunken resurrection of a language of empire is
really a silencing, just as the kind of history-teaching Merle was expected
to do in the still colonized school system was intended to bury the past.
The bitter ironies of Lyle's declamation gloss the ironies of Vereson
Walkes's name. He is the tragic hero, the *vir*, of Marshall's counterepic,
his death in the Whitmonday Race already foreshadowed by the image
of Merle's voice plunging as if by fate "down the precipitous slope to its
own destruction."[12]

The image of the precipitous slope links the tragedy of Vere and the
potential tragedy of Merle's voice to another place of silence in one of the
most brutally realistic scenes of the novel, the description of a morning in
the canefield. Marshall's relentless account of this "ordeal" (160) is striking for its almost physically oppressive detail, its tremendous compassion,
its stark anger, and its status as one of the few genuine descriptions of
work in an American novel.[13] It is striking, too, for Marshall's ability to
evoke the power of the oppressed even as she portrays their devastating

dispossession, a long history of exploitation compressed into the transformation of two workers in the space of a few hours. Stinger begins the
day "silent and absorbed," pressing his "assault" against canes "ranked
like an opposing army" up the steep hill, and giving a "low private grunt
of triumph" as each one falls. But as he continues he undergoes a dramatic change, his body seeming to shrink with age, his expressions of
triumph vanishing, his skin pierced by bits of chaff "like slivers of wood
driven into the flesh," his breathing labored like that of "a winded wres-
tler being slowly borne down in defeat" (160–62). The imagery depicts
this kind of labor as a violent assault on the workers: a military attack; a
form of torture (splinters driven into flesh); a war of attrition in which
silencing represents the sapping of life. The ultimate embodiment of this
distortion of human power is in the distortion of a woman's power — that
of Gwen, doubly burdened with her pregnancy and the two-hundred-
pound bales as she descends the precipitous slope. "Fallen silent" after
having joked all morning with the other women, concentrating all her
energies now on not falling in fact, she passes Saul, who sees her face,
"aged beyond recognition," and her eyes, with "the same slightly turned
up, fixed, flat stare that you find upon drawing back the lids of someone
asleep or dead" (163).

Marshall's use of Saul as a witness to the "ordeal" of the canefield is
part of the project of superimposing a novelistic Bournehills, a landscape
of exploited labor, on an allegorical Bournehills that functions as a landscape of the soul. In Bournehills Saul confronts the wrongs that are
actually, not merely in racist fantasies of self-encounter, the First World's
"heart of darkness." At the same time, for him as for Harriet, "Bournehills could have been a troubled region within himself to which he had
unwittingly returned" (100). As he walks the roads, episodes from his
past rise to confront him, especially those in which he wronged someone.
The contexts are personal, but the fact that past guilts surface as he walks
through this impoverished area points to his present complicity in the
great wrong done Bournehills' ancestors. And the landscape he encounters is disturbing precisely because it is not solely a projection of his
psyche, like Conrad's landscape, but is at the same time a real place, with
real people whose lives force him to confront the ignorance at the core of
his liberal sympathies. "I know how difficult it is for you living here," he
tells Merle at one point, to which she rightly replies, "No, you don't. . . .
You don't have a clue" (227).

Thus, despite his blinding "vision" after the visit to the canefield,
Saul continues to experience Bournehills as a place of "mystery" (216,
410), whose deepest message for him he cannot decipher despite all
his efforts. As Simone de Beauvoir pointed out, such mysteries depend
on objectification:

[T]here is mystery in the Black, the Yellow, in so far as they are considered absolutely as the inessential Other. It should be noted that the American citizen, who profoundly baffles the average European, is not, however, considered as being "mysterious": one states more modestly that one does not understand him. And similarly woman does not always "understand" man; but there is no such thing as a masculine mystery. The point is that rich America, and the male, are on the Master side and that Mystery belongs to the slave. (*The Second Sex* 293)

Saul's conviction that Bournehills holds some elusive secret is related to Bournehills' otherness for him, and to all that keeps him "on the Master side." As Merle says, "maybe deep down you don't really want to see" (390).

Saul's ambivalent sense of Bournehills' mystery makes it a place of silence for him. On the night of his first contact with the poorest people there, he makes a speech, but they, standing just out of range "like so many ghosts washed up by the sea," make no response (139). Like the African drum and the old barracoon, these people—the "timeless people" of Saul's "chosen place"—are the past, which, as Mr. Braithwaite told Silla, is "here today and there waiting for you tomorrow." Standing on the beach like ghosts—by implication the ghosts of the drowned slaves—they haunt Saul, seeming to regard him "from the other end of a long dimly lit corridor, whose distance was measurable both in space and time, and down which he was certain he would have to travel if he were ever to know them or they to know him" (137). Saul does have a long journey in front of him before he can truly meet these people to whom he is being introduced, but they seem immediately to know him and, especially, Harriet. "The masked smiles they gave her . . . held a profound recognition" (137).

Recognition is a crucial term in this novel, which has so much to do with knowing, not knowing, reknowing. Its opposite is loss, especially the loss of knowledge through repression. Memory is one of the things the poor of Bournehills have not lost, and memory alone provides the key to double vision. Thus the people of Bournehills recognize Harriet, reknowing her from long ago, but she has lost what she would need in order to recognize them: a sense of her past as a crucial part of their history. Keeping Bournehills a place of silence is crucial to sustaining her repression, just as keeping Selina silent was crucial to sustaining Mrs. Benton's. While Saul tries to hear what is behind Bournehills silences, Harriet tries to silence Bournehills voices by closing her mind to what little she hears. Her need for nonrecognition is both psychological and economic. At both levels, she has an investment in silence.

Harriet's experience of Bournehills' silence is different from Saul's partly because of the class position that commits her to internal silencing to evade the contradictions of her relationship with the people there, but also because of the disjunctions between her class status and her position as a woman. Marshall's complex study of the relationship between Harriet's class and gender is one more reminder of how often she has pioneered in areas that become central to feminist theory only much later. Her choice of dysphoria to represent the ironies of Harriet's position is particularly apt: "the terrifying feeling that her hands, no matter what she was holding in them, were empty" (450). As a hereditary member of the wealthiest class Harriet holds a great deal in her hands, even a great deal of power, but as a woman she finds "the better part of her in disuse" (44). Denied any official contribution to Saul's work on the island, she creates her own form of volunteer work, dispensing fruit juice and aspirin to the women and children who visit her at Merle's guesthouse. Going even further, she takes it upon herself to make an omelet for Gwen's malnourished children one afternoon before their mother returns from the canefield. Overcome by the children's hunger and a sense of her heroism, she breaks the eggs she has found inexplicably set aside in a bowl and begins strenuously to whip air into them, failing to notice the reaction of the oldest girl. As it turns out, Gwen saves her eggs to sell, and Brenda later receives the thrashing foreshadowed in an image that subtly conflates Harriet's efforts to help the child with an attack on her: at the first crack of an egg Brenda "uttered a near-soundless, quickly stifled cry of protest or dismay—it was impossible to tell, and then silently bowed her head. Harriet brought the fork down a second time" (177). As Harriet works in Gwen's kitchen, the sun on her hair gives it the appearance of "a bright helmet she had donned as part of some battle gear" (177). (Like Mrs. Benton, Harriet is quite a fighter when she gets started.) Afterward, pleased at what she regards as her victory, she fails to understand the children's quietly stoic reaction, not realizing that her fight was part of the battle against them.

Like Merle's classroom, Sugar's, and the canefield, many places of silence in this novel are workplaces, elaborations on the meaning of the silences associated with work in *Brown Girl*. The association is especially complex in *The Chosen Place* not only because the political context of the workplaces is broader, but because the kinds of work done by First and Third World characters are associated with two different but related kinds of silence. The scene of the omelet-making, together with its sequel and the implicit commentary it provides on Saul's work, is an example. In Gwen's kitchen, the experience of Brenda, "wanting to say something but not bold enough" (177), is one silence, recalling Selina's in her encounter with the white mother. The other silence is in Harriet's memory, which does not remind her that her inheritance comes partly from salted cod. In short, Harriet had already supplied food to Bourne Island long before she arrived with her fruit juice to try to remedy the deficit it created. Both of these silences point to the irony of her attempt to establish a connection with the children without making it possible for them to communicate their own needs, and without attending to the connection she already has with them: she profits from their hunger.

Saul reproves Harriet not for any of these reasons but for interfering with his work, and she responds by falling "bewildered, silent, crushed" (181). As this reaction indicates, one place of silence in the novel is Saul and Harriet's home, where Harriet in particular keeps many feelings to herself, and which is her workplace both as homemaker and unpaid assistant to Saul. Fearful at first of being useless during her stay in Bournehills, she has found work that is not even dignified by that name. Saul, insensitive to any of the issues involved, responded to her original worry with anger: "You've got a thing about this notion of being useless which really bothers the hell out of me" (49). It is this "thing" that expresses itself in Harriet's dysphoria.

Bournehills is Saul's workplace; he thinks it is not Harriet's. In that assumption, however, he is mistaken. Harriet's experience at Gwen's house, working with her back to the silent Brenda, is a symbol in miniature of Saul's experience on the job, doing his chosen work in Bournehills and unable all the while to read its silence correctly. But there is an even more disturbing connection between Harriet's experience of Brenda's silence and Saul's experience of Bournehills. The single member of his team whom he does not even regard as a worker, Harriet goes steadily, unobtrusively, about her essential project in Bournehills, the business of silence. Her foremost task is to be the way Saul fondly imagines her on the first night at Sugar's as he steels himself against Merle's angry voice: "He wanted to . . . walk . . . away from this woman. . . . He wanted the hotel room and Harriet, his rare find of a wife — poised, contained, beautifully self-assured . . ." (90–91). Harriet's work for Saul is the task of being "contained" — separate — of refusing the unities on which Saul's conscience, in the voice of Merle, insists. Although Harriet's repressions annoy Saul, he needs them. It is logical that he should be married to someone whose chief work is silence, because Harriet represents the silence at the heart of Saul's presence in Bournehills. She stands for the one critical fact omitted from Saul's genuinely caring, compassionate speech at Merle's party, which is that the funders of the development project, with their vested interest in the poverty of Bournehills, need for it to fail.

As Saul's workplace and Harriet's, Bournehills is a place of silence. As Stinger's workplace and Gwen's it is also a place of silence — the same place and the same silence, but seen from a different perspective. That perspective emerges again in two pictures of Cane Vale Factory. The first is the scene in which Ferguson, having nerved himself to warn the London office director that the rollers need repair, fails agonizingly to speak anything but the lines Sir John and the local Kingsley representative expect:

> Their eyes met . . . the little commanding lift to his head challenging Ferguson to speak, and Ferguson straining to do so, the veins and tendons that strung together his limbs standing out in a tangle beneath his skin in the effort. But no sound came. He stood silent. Behind his glasses his eyes were eloquent with the speech he was to have given, that he had rehearsed so often for Saul's benefit, but his lips were as if sewn together. His long pliant body that moved with such passion and force when he declaimed upon Cuffee Ned in the rumshop at night seemed a thing of stone, a dumb effigy of himself. . . . [Saul]. . . . felt the unspoken words choking Ferguson choking him. . . .
> "Well, I see you're still here, yes. How's it going?" It was Hinds addressing Ferguson. . . .
> And Ferguson, sounding unlike himself, answered, the words issuing in a rapid breathless burst from his constricted throat, "Fine, sir, thank you, sir." (221–22)

Ferguson's "sealed lips and stricken eyes" recall Gwen in the canefield and Brenda in the kitchen with Harriet. The conversation in which, "sounding unlike himself," he says only what Sir John expects to hear, speaking someone else's script, recalls the ventriloquism whereby Mrs. Benton hears her own ideas in the words of her employee Ettie. Like Gwen's dead eyes and Harriet's battle helmet, Sir John's "brisk military stride" and the images associated with him as he marches about "Like a general reviewing the matériel with which he wage[s] his war" (221) make even clearer the equation in *Brown Girl* of a war machine with an economic system destructive of human life. In this novel as in the first one, those who exploit labor seek to reduce workers to puppets, pantomimes in someone else's drama, ventriloquist's dolls. The "war" Sir John wages with the machines and products of this factory is in one sense simply the work that goes on there: an economic assault on the lives of Third World people. Further, the fact that the multinational network he represents produces weapons underlines the connection between the silencing of workers and "the final silence" Harriet imagined in her dream.

The double-exposed picture of a psychological compulsion to silence and a violent imperialistic assault that creates silence reappears, again in a representation of exploited labor, when the factory suddenly closes for the season before the smallholders have ground their canes. In an image magnifying that of Ferguson standing like "a thing of stone, a dumb effigy," the workers stand "Silent, impassive . . . caught in that stillness of body and gesture only people in Bournehills were capable of; which, at times . . . made them almost resemble statues . . ." (385). Inside, defying the "absolute" silence, Merle excoriates Saul, conjoining in one vision "the final silence" after the neutron bomb, the domestic place of silence central to her personal tragedy, and the silence of the workers "turned to stone" instead of "overrunning this place and burning it the hell down, or better yet, taking it over and running it themselves" (389). She curses Saul's technology, good only for destroying life with the neutron bomb: "The houses with the curtains at the windows like people are living in them but not a soul inside. . . . Oh, God, the silence! You can hear a pin drop the world over. Everybody gone. All the poor half-hungry people who never had a chance. The little children" (391). The image of a silent world, which filled her mind eight years ago when she returned to her flat in Leeds to find her husband and child gone, calls her memory to that scene:

"The baby's gone. Everything in place but both of them gone. Oh, how could he have done that to me? I see it, you hear, I see it. The whole world up in smoke and not a fire to be seen anywhere!"
　Her eyes were so filled with that apocalyptic vision, her words, re-echoing endless through the empty building, had made it so vivid, that Saul, struck dumb on the steps, could almost see that flameless fire raging between them on the platform. (391)

As in the image of the amber light at Sugar's, it is as if the apocalypse had already occurred. The silent factory foreshadows the global tragedy of the neutron bomb, and the cause of both silences is the same economic system. Merle's personal tragedy too is tied to these, rooted in her colonized relationship with the racist Englishwoman who deliberately destroyed her marriage.[14] Bourne Island's history as a colony made it easier to seduce Merle into a British drawing-room "empire" (328); her poverty, rooted in that history, made her lover's wealth an almost inescapable bond. The history of colonialism is the history of the First World's military imperialism, which Merle sees as leading to nuclear apocalypse. Harriet, in whose face Merle later recognizes the face of the Englishwoman, was responsible in a dream for that "final silence." The Englishwoman, Harriet's double, was responsible for the silence in the flat, which Merle imagined, in turn, as the silence Harriet dreamed she created with Andrew. In the factory, whose silence is explained by the same history, economics, and politics that explain Merle's personal tragedy, her vision of nuclear holocaust turns abruptly into a memory of the silent flat. The multiple superimpositions of the three silences express the connections among racism, colonialism, Caribbean history, the arms race, and Merle's "interior life" — her private experience of family and love. The deadly silence that ended her marriage was a personal failure of communication, but it was also an imperialistic assault on her freedom to shape her life as she chose.

In one of the novel's many paradoxes of power and powerlessness, it is not Saul but Merle's ability to recognize him that rescues both of them from the burning building she envisioned. Just as the flameless fire "reached up to snatch away her voice and consume her utterly, a faint light glimmered for an instant within the darkness that had engulfed her and she saw him . . . 'Saul, oh, Saul, take me out of this terrible place!' " (391). In the image of the fire, the threat to Merle's voice is the same as the threat to her existence. What can "snatch away her voice" can "consume her utterly." This is the equation Selina saw during her encounter with the white mother who tried, by robbing Selina of her voice, "to rob her of her substance and her self" (*Brown Girl* 289). Merle rightly perceives Saul, a white American, as part of this threat. But she also sees his individual identity, embedded though it is in the destructive power relations the fire represents. Both Merle and Saul are saved by her ability to do what Kingsley and Sons cannot do—to recognize, across the already raging fire of the apocalypse, the full—complex reality of a person whose different race and nationality have placed him on the other side of the "dangerous division" between North and South.

Merle stands "in Ferguson's place" on the platform (388), and the scene between her and Saul is a revealing variation on that played out earlier between Ferguson and Sir John. In the earlier scene Ferguson was silenced by the white man's power; here the white man, Saul, is "struck dumb" by his sense of powerlessness. There Hinds, profoundly "representative" of Kingsley and Sons, at first failed to see Ferguson, then failed to hear what Ferguson needed to say. Here Saul's very ability to see Merle's pain and hear the full meaning of her tirade means that he stands with her in a place of impotence. The powers with whom Saul's race, nationality, and profession ally him never intended his funds to right the fundamental wrong behind Bournehills' poverty. Thus as he has moved toward empathy with those dispossessed by that wrong—burned by the cane peel driven into Stinger's flesh, choked by Ferguson's silence, "struck dumb" like the workers in front of the silent factory—he has become in a sense dispossessed himself of the money he thought he controlled. In the earlier scene Ferguson could only say what he did not mean. Here Merle translates her vision so accurately into speech that her very power of representation nearly "consume[s]" both her voice and her. But the threat is not her voice; it is the destructive power her words describe so vividly. Merle's ability to keep speaking in the face of this power saves her, and Saul's capacity to be silenced by what she says saves *him* from being merely another "representative" of the First World. By calling Saul's name, Merle differentiates him as an individual capable of acting independently of all that the fire represents. He in turn proves that, despite his unwilling alliance with the powers that would silence

Merle even as she speaks of them, he has the individual power to hear her voice and act in response to it. By asking Saul to "take me out of this terrible place," Merle summons him to walk through the fire that divides them, and he does.

2

Three places of silence — the canefield, the factory, and Sugar's — typify the three kinds of labor Bourne Island performs for the First World: export agriculture, the industry related to it, and tourism, which Marshall represents as another version of export agriculture in which the lifeblood of the island's people is turned to its chief commodity. All the double exposures through which these places are represented come together with the starkest clarity in the starkest place of silence in the novel, the bedroom at Cassia House where Merle lies in a cataleptic trance after the factory closing. This room is profoundly interior; one could say, in fact, that it is the true "interior" of the island at which the explorer Saul finally arrives. It is specifically allegorized as Merle's psyche; Saul feels here as if he were "wandering through the chambers of her mind" (402). But it is at the same time an elaborate picture of the objective forces at work in Caribbean history, so that what Saul encounters there, unlike Marlow in his encounter with Kurtz, is precisely the social character of the interior life.

Labor, for example, appears in this scene in multiple guises, all related to silence and stasis. Most obviously, Merle's catatonia reenacts the suffering of the workers standing as if "turned to stone" (389).[15] With no way to translate her farseeing energies into action, she lies "numb," her "dead eyes" like Gwen's in the canefield. Merle's energies are ignored and Gwen's are exploited, with the same effect. Her catatonia is also the counterpart of Harriet's dysphoria; both are women "who had never found anything truly their own to do, no work that could have defined them" (437).

For the smallholders, the work they do that is more "truly their own" than their labor in the canefield or factory is raising their own canes to sell. The early factory closing shows how little dignity, or even how little reality, that work has in the eyes of Kingsley and Sons. As in the world of Margaret's mother, the silence imposed on the workers robs their labor, and threatens to rob them, "of . . . substance and self." Thus Sir John, for example, hardly sees the people in the factory at all, concentrating his attention on the products rather than the act of work. As the portrait of him reveals, one reason exploitive workplaces in this novel are places of silence is that part of the great wrong they do is to render labor invisible to those it profits. For the oppressed, by the same token, voice is related to sight. Gwen falls silent in the canefield and her eyes go dead; Ferguson's "stricken eyes" reflect his silence before Sir John. In the rumshop with Saul after the factory closing, "Staring with unseeing eyes," Ferguson speaks of his sense of responsibility for the roller breaking. "Cuffee woulda done different. He would've spoke up" (396–97). After a silence he speaks again, "his huge sheened eyes filled with the belief that sustained him: 'He's goin' come again. For all such as me, Cuffee's goin' come' " (397). On the way from the rumshop to Merle's, Saul's eyes hold "Ferguson's look. . . . screened by the same colorless opaque glaze that was designed to shut out both the world and the fact of himself" (398). Among the questions the novel addresses is that of vision: on the one hand what to look forward to — what there might be to envision; on the other, all there is to look away from — "the world and the fact of [one]self." Ferguson's eyes are "stricken" before Sir John, but afterwards he moves out of blind despair to prophecy, his eyes full of sustaining faith.

Merle's "dead" eyes as she sits numb in her room are like Ferguson's before his vision. She is also compared explicitly to Sugar, "staring, with his same flat quiet intensity, into all-absorbing nothingness" (399). At Sugar's, workers are items for sale. In Merle's room the most extreme treatment of workers as commodities is pictured in the diagram of a Bristol slaver with its human "cargo." Labor appears, too, in other art on Merle's walls. There are prints of slaves working in "deceptively pleasant" fields, and "beguiling scenes" of high tea, lawn tennis, a plover shoot, nightlong feasts (400) — colonial leisure created by colonized people's work. The prints silence history by falsifying the meaning of slave labor, effectively rendering it invisible, just as the official curriculum silenced the history Merle taught. The bed in which Merle lies is an ironic legacy from the planter Duncan Vaughan, famous for exploiting the Black women who worked for him: "It might well have been the bed in which old Vaughan had sired the forty-odd children . . ." (400). Merle's presence in this bed links her to those women, whose work of being sexually exploited recalls her colonized sexual relationship with the rich white woman who essentially bought her. In Merle's room the psychological and the political are one; her talcum powder and straightening iron, her half-unpacked trunk and the photograph of her lost family bespeak the same history as the Bristol slaver and the planter's bed. Here "the memorabilia of a lifetime — and of the time that reached beyond her small life") are jumbled together (401), because her private loss is inseparable from a broader, collective loss, just as her face reflects a "wide suffering — wide enough to include an entire history" (68). Thus Saul can finally see in this room, image of Merle's inner world, the meaning of Bournehills' apparent inability to change, which her catalepsy mirrors.

The conflation of the psyche with history is the key to his revelation in this interior of the island, the first of Marshall's revisionings of Conradian anagnorisis. In a fascinating reversal, the mysterious silence of Bournehills as Saul's objectified Other is suddenly revealed from another angle as Bournehills' subjective *resistance* to being Othered, as Saul finally sees the meaning, from Bournehills' own point of view, of its silent, static timelessness. The fact that this silent stasis is mirrored in Merle's catalepsy adds a remarkable dimension to the scene, a tour de force in which a woman who is from one angle a discarded "doll," inert on the bed where her foremothers were raped, paralyzed by a sense of impotence in the face of economic forces beyond her control, is revealed as after all the chief actor. For it is she who, by means of this whole tableau with herself at the center, succeeds in communicating through her silence the one clear insight Saul finally gains: that Bournehills, "at its deepest level," is like her room "a kind of museum" where the past is "still alive, a palpable presence beneath the everyday reality":

> And it would remain as such. . . . as a reminder — painful but necessary — that it was not yet over, only the forms had changed, and the real work was still to be done; and finally, as a memorial . . . to the figures bound to the millwheel in the print and to each other in the packed airless hold of the ship in the drawing.
> Only an act on the scale of Cuffee's could redeem them. And only then would Bournehills itself, its mission fulfilled, perhaps forgo that wounding past and take on the present, the future. But it would hold out until then, resisting, defying all efforts, all the halfway measures, including his, to reclaim it; refusing to settle for anything less than what Cuffee had demanded in his time. (402)

In this revelation Saul sees clearly what his "opaque" eyes tried to shut out earlier: "the world and the fact of himself." In the context of his empathy with Ferguson, the "fact of himself" is his speechless rage and powerlessness. But in another context the "fact of himself" is his complicity in the tragedy of the workers whom his own work, meaningless in the face of "the real work" yet to be done, cannot help. At Merle's bedside he experiences this same complicity and empathetic helplessness, as his past confronts him through a sudden memory of his first wife lying comatose as Merle is now, "the faces merging, becoming one, before his eyes" (399).

This double-exposed image of Saul mute and helpless at the bedside of two women he has loved and failed belongs to the novel's examination of power. This is so not only because both images evoke the helplessness of a single Euro-American in the face of the history his country has helped so forcibly to shape, but because in both cases the helpless spectator of the tragedy is also implicated in the system that has caused the suffering. His situation is reminiscent of Harriet feeling her hands empty no matter what they hold. Instead of empowering others, Saul has merely discovered his own powerlessness in the face of the powers with which his work inadvertently colludes.

Merle's silence and stasis during her breakdown resonate with descriptions of other characters, especially women: women who know the truth — who in a sense are the truth — but whose truth is contained in silence, their power exploited or stilled. Among them are Gwen, Brenda, and Vere's girlfriend silent with helpless resignation beneath his blows. And there is Carrington, the "last keep-miss" of Merle's planter-father (110), whose salient characteristic is her monumental silence. Guarding Merle's sickroom, she rises up "towering, maternal, and mute" as Saul approaches (398); as he leaves, he passes her asleep "on her chair outside the door, her chin fallen onto the great breasts that had been used, it seemed, to suckle the world" (403). Carrington is asleep, "mute," almost invisible to the white man who can barely distinguish her from the shadows. But she is there, an "inescapable force" (398).

The image sheds another light on Merle's cataleptic state, which looks so much like defeat. In one sense it is. Her speechlessness and deathlike look recall Gwen's eyes as she worked in the canefield; her stillness recalls Ferguson at work in the factory, his power of speech erased by Sir John's uninterested gaze. Like Ferguson in that scene and like the factory workers at the gate, she is a "dumb effigy" of herself, apparently incapable of action, voiceless. But Gwen in the canefield is not defeated; the next morning and the next — and so on despite the silence to which each day reduces her — she will be joking again with the other women. As in the image of Carrington, every image of Bournehills people as powerlessly immobile or silent has another side. Ferguson is a good example. Hinds's only perception of him is an obtuse recognition: "Well, I see you're still here, yes" (222). The comment has an irony the speaker cannot appreciate, for the military imagery associated with the factory tour shows Sir John and his hinds working to make sure the rest of the world will not be here for long. That Ferguson, despite his temporary defeat, is "still here" in the face of such destructive power bespeaks his extraordinary strength. By the same token, Marshall's double vision makes us see Merle in the bedroom at Cassia House not as the object of Saul's gaze but as the generator of his revelation: not the passive object of Saul's colonizing exploration of her mind and her island's history, not the blank screen onto which he can project his own grief and guilts, but an active resister, "still here" despite the slave ship, the fields, the planter's bed.

At the end of Njabulo Ndebele's novella *Fools*, a Black South African resists a white man's power by standing silent as the white man attacks him with a whip. "I wanted to scream," Zamani says later, "But my silence was my salvation . . ." (275). As the Boer reddens with frustration, averts his eyes, and seems "to grow smaller and smaller," a laughter wells up in

Zamani, "the beginning of the kind of laughter that seemed to explain everything." When it explodes, the white man's blows diminish, then stop: "I had crushed him with the sheer force of my presence. I was there, and would be there to the end of time: a perpetual symbol of his failure to have a world without me" (276). Like Ferguson, whom Hinds dimly recognizes as "still here," Carrington is one of these timeless people. So is Merle. Her sleeplike state looks like death; she might be a victim of that final "conflagration" foreshadowed at Sugar's or of the final silence she foresaw in her flat and Cane Vale Factory. But like Ferguson and Carrington, she is "still here." Indeed, Carrington and Merle are two faces of the same experience: Carrington who never speaks and whose motherhood of the world is unrecognized; Merle who eventually tells her story and goes off to Africa to reclaim her child, insisting that her motherhood — her entitlement to the future — be acknowledged. Early in the novel Marshall describes the sense Merle's eyes convey of "life persisting amid . . . nameless and irrevocable loss" (5). The life in Merle's eyes is the essence of Bournehills' "timeless people" — the source of their ability to hold out, "resisting, defying" (402), clinging to the past to ensure a future that takes full account of it. Their silence and stasis bespeak their determination to "be there to the end of time."

3

In *Fools*, the protagonist transforms a scene of oppression into an act of resistance, thereby claiming for himself and others like him the direction of South African history. In *The Chosen Place* a significant pattern of imagery and meaning is based on such transformations, which constitute another form of superimposition. At the end of the factory-closing scene, for example, the "flameless fire" of the neutron bomb threatens to "snatch away" Merle's voice. But her voice conjured up Saul's vision of the apocalypse in the first place, figuratively igniting the fire she said the workers should have lit. The same double vision informs the image of the workers standing silent like stone. From one angle their stasis looks like absolute powerlessness. From another, their power is active in the stasis itself, the stance of changelessness and timelessness that insists history be present — *makes* it be present — and looks forward with absolute assurance to the future. "Silent, impassive . . . they were all . . . caught in that stillness of body and gesture only people in Bournehills were capable of. . . . And today, more so than usual, their deep-set eyes appeared endowed with a two-fold vision: of not only being able to see backward in time . . . but . . . forward also. They knew, you were certain, what the future held and that, despite all they had undergone and had yet to endure, it was assured" (385).

In the subtle choice of words is Marshall's own "two-fold vision." The people are "caught," passively, in the stillness of which only they are "capable" — a word that turns the image around to reveal their stasis as a special form of power. The silence and stasis in this scene speak for the multiple losses of Bournehills people, but also for their resistance.[16] Such double images reveal the power of the oppressed to maintain control of their lives — to repossess in vision, through perpetual resistance at each moment of their dispossession, what is theirs.

Such transforming resistance is the core of the Bournehills carnival pageant that resurrects Cuffee Ned from the shadow world of Bournehills every year.[17] The drama of slave revolt pictures a historic moment of change, in which the experience of oppression turned into an act of resistance. Furthermore, the pageant translates the players' specific personal experiences of oppression into representations of political resistance, just as the players transform experiences of oppression into acts of resistance in their daily lives. The members of the band, for example, seem to have become the slaves they depict or to have "been them all along" (283). This transformation, like all the other images of Bournehills people as ghosts of the African slaves, asserts the identity of past and present. But here the double exposure is an act of power, not merely an inescapable circumstance. Deliberately claiming their past selves, superimposing them on the present in the form of the old slave costumes, the masquers implicitly invoke a revolutionary future by challenging the spectators to "act in some bold, retributive way that would both rescue their memory and indemnify their suffering" (283). Behind the implication that both actors and audience have been the African slaves "all along" is the question of how to transform the present into a future that acknowledges the past — how to act in a way that will "rescue . . . memory."

The interior/exterior nature of such a revolutionary act is manifest in the personal transformations through which the actors represent their political theme, in each case turning the signifiers of their oppression into signs of their resistance. In the canefield, for example, the exploitation of labor usurps workers' voices and stills their power, which nonetheless reasserts itself each morning. The carnival drama brings alive the transformative potential of that power as people such as Stinger and Gwen act out their loss, reclaiming their voices through a revision of the silence imposed on them. In the pageant, Gwen, reduced to silence by her work each day, presents the history of that silence by performing the slaves' silent march of exile. Armed with his billhook and dressed as Cuffee Ned, Stinger opens the pageant in his silent climb of Pyre Hill toward the sleeping white planter. A man who silently scales a hill for someone else's profit day after day now silently scales a hill to start a revolution. He who seems at the end of each day to be engaged in a losing wrestling match now wins the "locked struggle" with Percy Bryam (284). Stinger climbing "Pyre Hill" with his billhook transforms his daily work into defiance in the same way that he makes the billhook, symbol of his alienation during the daytime, into an instrument of oratory at night in the rumshop. In the canefield the billhook is in a sense the planter's weapon against Stinger. In the rumshop and more overtly in the pageant, it is his weapon against the planter.

Stinger's opponent is played by Ferguson, his nightly opponent in the rumshop debates about Cuffee Ned—mock battles that are never resolved but ensure that Bournehills continues to remember its history. In the struggle on the carnival float, this mock battle is transformed into another mock battle that has the same purpose. Ferguson's role requires him at first to feign sleep. But unlike his stony silence in the factory before Sir John, this silence and stasis are forms of self-expression—part of a collective art that speaks his mind. The pageant transforms his helpless silence at the factory into a silence that acts out his passionate historical memory.

What Audre Lorde calls "the transformation of silence into language and action" is thus the essence of the pageant, which culminates in the "fused voices" (286) of Bournehills people celebrating the unity Cuffee Ned established. In the drama, however, this transformation gets reversed. The song tells of Cuffee's eventual defeat; the voices fade; the dance slows to the march of exile again. Cuffee's fate is signified by a doll's head on the end of a pike—a fleeting, ironically macabre superimposition of the imagery of the Bournehills pageant on what might have seemed its polar opposite, the Parade of the Dolls. In counterpoint to the Bournehills pageant and the meaningful transformations it represents, in this pageant the central transformation is of a woman into an object. Here untransformed (indeed untransformable) silence and stasis are intended to invite admiration. The Parade of the Dolls is in a sense a victory over what Cuffee Ned represents. The white mask of the young woman at its center, topped by a golden blond wig, is the triumph of colonial values. Cuffee's defeat by colonial powers turned him into a static object for display. But the centerpiece of the doll pageant turns herself into such an object—or rather affirms, in the pageant, her acquiescence in the role she has been assigned. She wants to be what Ferguson became only against his will, a "dumb effigy." As Merle says, "they colonized our minds but good in this place" (129). The doll's head on a pike is an ironic revelation of the stasis, objectification, silence, and death that the Parade of the Dolls really signifies. What the onlookers objected to at the beginning of the Bournehills pageant was its repetition. Why dredge up this "old-time business" again and again, every year? The multiple, identical white dolls mirroring the doll-woman at their center are another sort of repetition, an image of the oppressed turned into mirrors of the colonizer's face—Frantz Fanon's "black skin, white masks." They are another version of the blank screen, the empty "interior" waiting to be peopled by the explorer's self-projections.

If the signs of oppression can be transformed into signs of resistance, there is always the danger of transformation in the other direction, as the repeated following of Cuffee's resurrection with his end as a doll's head on a pike makes clear. The repetitions of the pageant reflect the repetitions of history: the cycle of oppression, revolution, oppression. But then another transformation occurs, bringing this cycle to an end. The silence that intermittently overcomes the actors' voices, just as it overcomes the workers in the canefield each day, disappears. The story of alternating victory and defeat becomes a story of victory alone. The pageant—itself a journey through the streets—begins as the slaves' long march, ends at first with a return to that march, and finally breaks free of the cycle, transforming it into a single, liberating moment of history, which is the past but becomes the present and an intimation of the future.

This future is predicted most fully in the final "jump-up" at the Sports Oval, where people of all races, classes, and nationalities participate in a joyously transformed version of the mad, combative dance at Sugar's. The unity, however, will last only for the night. The next day the professionals will avoid the glance of clerks or carpenters they dance with now (302). The carnival itself is part of a cycle; life on Bourne Island returns to oppression, loss, separateness. Other images in the book evoke the same cycle. When Vere first returns to Bourne Island and the Americans first arrive there, for example, there is a moment at Cassia House when the circle of Merle, Vere, Allen, Saul, and Harriet resembles "the coming together of the members of a family who had been scattered to the four corners of the earth and changed almost beyond recognition . . . but the same still" (109–10). Recognition, the image implies, is still possible, if only briefly. "They might have been searching for each other for a long time, seeking completion. And they had met finally (although it was too late and could only last the moment) here on this desolate coast . . ." (110). After the carnival, book 4 begins with another gathering at Merle's house, this time to witness the blooms of the cassia tree, a seeming overnight miracle of light and fragrance. But within a week, "all the blossoms were down, the sharp salt wind sailing off with most of them before they could reach the ground" (346). The brief unity of the jump-up is like the transitory nature of the family reunion on the "desolate coast" and the cassia tree's brief flowering. And yet these transient moments are also images of "life persisting"—the persistent impulse toward the affirmation of unity, the persistent reemergence of the human family as "a

People." To recognize this kinship, even if only for a moment, is to attain the redemptive double vision that sees things whole.

In Vere, Merle, and Saul, the carnival inspires self-transformations that answer the transformations of the pageant. In Harriet and Allen, who cannot open themselves to unity, it provokes a recoiling into isolation. Marshall's initial focus is on Harriet, whose race, class, and gender give her a double status as oppressor and oppressed,[18] and hence a potential for transformation in several directions. She could move toward an affirmation of unity with the oppressed; she could side with the oppressor; or, alternatively, she could entrench herself more firmly in the detached position she has cultivated in all of her dealings with Bournehills people. Assuming she is going to "play carnival" (232) in a way different from the other women with whom she marches — that is, merely play at being a masquer, act like an actor — she is, in the pageant, literally in her customary position of onstage "spectator" (171). Here the irony is even stronger than before, because Harriet actually takes part in the play, and what the drama portrays is a history she does not recognize as hers.

The picture of Harriet marching with the same silver bracelets and Osnaburg dress that the Bournehills women wear literally imposed on her body establishes an intriguing double view of oppression. Harriet's class, nationality, and race give her extraordinary privileges, yet she is, like Gwen, Merle, and Leesy, a woman, and the carnival pulls her toward a different relationship with Bournehills women than she has had in the past. When a woman spectator calls out, "What, don't tell me you's a Bournehills, too, my lady?" Gwen answers for her — an interesting variation on the scenes in this and other Paule Marshall novels in which a white woman usurps a Black woman's voice. Here, in contrast to those scenes, the Black woman is legitimately giving voice to one of the white woman's unacknowledged truths. "How you mean!" Gwen shouts back. "Of course she's one of we." Harriet, "strangely enough," finds herself nodding in agreement (292).

Harriet experiences these feelings of kinship, however, in a self-dissociated way, as the phrase "strangely enough" suggests. She holds herself apart from her potential for recognition, and eventually her desire to reidentify herself with white people becomes so strong that she fantasizes about a drink she does not even like — a "supremely civilized" martini (293). Her attempt to break away toward the exclusive Cockerel Club fails, however, as the Twenty-sixth of July Guerrilla Band crashes into her "like one of those powerful Bournehills breakers" whose sound she has evaded (293). Gripped by "a revulsion and rage . . . almost sexual in its force" (295), moving in the opposite direction from her approach toward unity as "one of we," she is swept into the other transformation that has always been a potential for her. She becomes fully the oppressor, "lashing out" at the faces around her, "slapping savagely. . . . her hair, swinging . . . like a short whip" (296). Her inefficacy reflects the powerlessness that is part of her inferior position as a woman within the powerful class to which she belongs. As in Mrs. Benton's case, this scene calls to mind Chela Sandoval's analysis: "while white women are 'othered' by men and feel the pain of objectification, within this secondary category they can only construct a solid sense of 'self' through the objectification of people of color" (64). When Lyle Hutson and Dorothy Clough find Harriet slumped against a door like "the victim . . . of some casual crucifixion," she responds to Lyle with "rage and fear," refusing to take his hand and knowing that if she had the strength, she would strike him (297).

Harriet's collapse into racism during the carnival, like Mrs. Benton's racist assault on a young woman who so much resembles her, is not only a violent separation from other people; it is a perverse construction of self through self-estrangement. In Marshall's works the two separations are always simultaneous. Such is the unity among people that those who shut themselves off from others are inevitably repressing a part of themselves. Harriet does have a link with Bournehills; to deny it is to deny part of herself. The resulting self-dissociation is so nearly total that she responds to Lyle and Dorothy's concern in a voice she is not even conscious of projecting: "she heard her voice (it seemed to come from a great distance)" (297). Nor can she ever voice this experience: "how to speak of the terror that had seized her, or of the paroxysm of rage that had sent her hands slashing out like knives . . . ? How talk of this?" (299).

Harriet's encounter with the heart of darkness that is her "savagery" produces no true self-recognition because of her assumption of its unspeakable nature, which is tied to the necessity of her view of herself in this scene as a "stranger." A passage from one of the few white writers who have tried to "talk of this," Mab Segrest, is relevant to Harriet's condition:

What white women—and class-privileged women and Christian women—who are working on their privilege have to do is find a new basis for our identities because the sense of self we have been taught is based on lies. . . . I have found that for me and friends who work together this process has four stages. First, I am so racist, class-privileged, Christian that I don't even realize it but assume that I am naturally wonderful and superior. Then I begin to see the false status that I get from my race and class and Christian privilege. And as soon as I do, I begin to see lies everywhere and everywhere my own responsibility, my own complicity. As I begin to feel what slavery did to Black people, I look up and see—God, we killed the Indians too. Then I hit the third stage of intense self-hatred which is the reality beneath the false self-love all along. I think the reason why white women avoid their racism so much and can act so weird around women of color is because deep down we are afraid that this third level is all that there is. That we will end up stuck in despair and self-hatred and suicide. But I believe that underneath there is another level, a self that longs for wholeness and connection. (171–72)

Harriet perceives her racism as that of a stranger; not acknowledging the stranger as part of herself, she cannot risk "wholeness and connection" either internally or in her relationships. And indeed she ends in "despair and self-hatred and suicide."

In Vere, the *vir* of whom Marshall sings in her counterepic, there emerges a kind of transformation diametrically opposed to Harriet's. After it he is "barely recognizable" to his friend Allen (307), who lies alone at the end of carnival, hearing Vere and Milly behind the folding screen and imagining Vere, "his dark body rising and falling, advancing and retreating, like one of the powerful Bournehills waves they sometimes rode together in the early evening" (312). Vere, making love to a member of the guerrilla band, becomes a force of nature, like the mighty "river" of the carnival marchers who will alter the course of history. Allen, even as he brings himself to a climax simultaneous with Milly's, has lost him.

At the level of psychological realism, this loss is portrayed sympathetically, as Allen's unacknowledged love for Vere has been portrayed earlier. One of the most beautiful passages in the book is that in which Allen and Vere first go swimming together in the Bournehills sea, and Allen, "The next morning, and every morning thereafter . . . could be heard singing in the garden at dawn" (152). At the symbolic level, however, the loss of Vere, an expression of Allen's loss of heterosexually defined virility, is part of a limiting pattern of imagery in which heterosexual manhood and womanhood stand, as heterosexual "manhood" did in much Black Power rhetoric of the sixties, for an independent, decolonized selfhood. In this novel as in *Brown Girl*, Marshall, using a metaphor common to many writers on colonialism, sees First World racism as emasculating. Feminizing the metaphor in a way that builds on her portrayal of Silla's loss of contact with her full erotic powers, Marshall adds to the image of lost masculinity in Vere a female counterpart in Merle's relationship with her lesbian colonizer/lover, who made her unsure of whether she was "fish or fowl or what" until the uncolonized African man, Ketu, affirmed her womanhood (332), a category to which this novel assigns only a heterosexual meaning.

In *The Chosen Place*, that is, homosexuality—viewed as a defect, a loss of sexuality rather than a sexuality—becomes a metaphor for self-loss and for collective economic and political loss.[19] The revolutionary Elvita bursts with an energetic heterosexual womanhood that is emphasized again and again as an integral part of her guerrilla activism. Allen's lack of sexual interest in her is paralysis—a First World counterpart of the paralysis that elsewhere afflicts Ferguson, Merle, and the workers at the factory closing. The breaking of Allen's glasses, Freudian symbol of castration, suggests that all along Allen had made his observer status into a substitute for virility. The First World, that is, has also lost its *vir*—its strength, its manhood—by pretending to be an observer on the stage of the Third World's drama instead of acknowledging its role as a participant. At Sugar's, one of the final sounds onto which Lyle superimposes his declamation from the *Aeneid* makes this perfectly clear. As the scene becomes more and more pandemoniacal, the shrieks of the American men on the balcony reach "a new and terrifying high . . . like the cries of the lost and anguished ringing through an empty cosmos" (92). These men have been described earlier as pederasts who greet with "an ecstatic howl" a Bournehills man dancing in a ballet costume with "the instrument of his manhood dangling limp and perverted" beneath it (91). That the emasculated voice here is the colonizer's own is a clever reversal, but what is not at all reversed, but rather reinscribed, is the demonizing of homosexuality that plays its part, always, in bolstering the same sexism Marshall otherwise attacks so eloquently.

This imagery of sexuality defined in terms of heterosexual "manhood" and "womanhood," woven tightly, elaborately into the seamless unity of the book, is the tragic flaw of what otherwise surely is what it seems intended to have been, a great epic spanning the divisions of the globe. The problems this imagery introduces into the narrative are summed up in the paradoxes of the author's choice of a white lesbian to represent Western hegemony—paradoxes on which the narrative is itself silent. While in reality Merle's lover would have the power of race, class, and nationality on her side, her sexual orientation, no matter how those other privileges might enable her to manipulate it as a source of power in some contexts, would have to place her in other contexts as a member of an oppressed group. The narrative's silence about the oppressive realities of any lesbian's life, whatever her status with regard to other categories of privilege, is necessary to make the "metaphor" of homosexuality work.

That metaphor's centrality wanes and almost disappears in Marshall's work as time goes on. Most extensively present in *The Chosen Place*, it is foreshadowed in *Brown Girl* when Selina and Clive make love during the Barbadian Homeowners' meeting, its young members portrayed as "queers" typified in "that fairy" Julian Hurley (*Brown Girl* 229). But it has no counterpart in her later books. It is worth remembering that *The Chosen Place* was written between 1963 and 1968, a time when the rhetoric of "manhood" was a central ingredient of liberation movements, when African-American feminists were only beginning publicly to challenge the sexism implicit in that rhetoric (Marshall's expansion of the metaphor to include women's sexuality can be seen as part of that challenge), and before many progressive women and men on the Left who identified themselves as heterosexual had been called on to affirm coworkers' gay and lesbian sexualities as forthrightly as they were in the early seventies. *Praisesong for the Widow*, published in 1983, abandons the metaphor of homosexuality completely; indeed, Avey Johnson's lost sexuality is restored to her by an island woman's massage. And *Daughters*, although its outlook is as plainly heterosexual as that of *Praisesong*, leaves behind the metaphors of "manhood" and "womanhood" for a more complicated examination of Black men and women's political, sexual, and psychological partnerships, as well as focusing intensely on a relationship between two women that would certainly fit somewhere along Adrienne Rich's "lesbian continuum."

Nor is the perspective on virility in *The Chosen Place* a completely traditional heterosexist one. Vere falls prey to an insensitive version of manhood in his beating of his first girlfriend. And one reason he falls prey to the First World is that it appeals to him with a traditional image of masculinity,[20] tempting him to realize his manhood through the vicarious power of First World machines. The German-American car Vere soups up for the Whitmonday Race deludes him into the sense of controlling a power that really controls him. "It's the car make him feel he's a man" (347). Vere's true Third World manhood, as opposed to the First World illusion of manhood that finally destroys him, is expressed in the carnival in his bold eye, his newly powerful voice, and the strong sexuality of his union with the "guerrilla" Milly, who involves him afterward in political activism (347). He dances at the jump-up "as if laying claim to every square inch of ground he touched" (303). Through the transformations of the carnival, that is, he takes rightful possession of what the people of Bourne Island should lay claim to: their own land.

Vere lays claim to the future; Harriet's past lays claim to her. The carnival is a time of recovery, but as Milly tells Allen, "People are always losing things at carnival" (305). Allen and Harriet lose a great deal. Both end by hardly recognizing their own voices; so thorough is their internal division that it is as if they had ventriloquized themselves. The pageant ends with the self-integration of Bourne Island through the rescue of memory, but Harriet and Allen end with self-disintegration. In fact, both are described at one point as already dead: Allen like a "lifeless body" (310); Harriet like "the victim . . . of some casual crucifixion" (297).

In contrast with the vibrant coming-to-life of Bournehills people such as Vere, the latter image, especially, recalls a theme underlying the stories of *Soul Clap Hands and Sing*: "Perhaps in order for a person to live and know himself somebody else must die" (*Reena* 36).[21] Miss Williams is intrigued by Andre Gide's working out of this idea through the story of a man who (like Saul in *The Chosen Place*) "destroys his wife" in the process of "finding out what he is" (36); she proves its truth as she triumphs over

Berman, abandoning him to the darkness of old age and death as she enters into the full strength of her womanhood. The button worn by the heroine of "Barbados," as she dances in the moonlight with her young lover while the old man who wants her looks on enviously, makes the same point: "The Old Order Shall Pass" (*Reena* 65). If the people of Bournehills are to lay claim to what is theirs, what Harriet stands for must die just as surely as what Percy Bryam stood for. But Harriet is not attacked deliberately, as is Percy Bryam; her "crucifixion" on this Shrove Tuesday is "casual" — a minor concomitant of Cuffee Ned's resurrection. The youths do not intentionally hurt her; she and her ideas are simply irrelevant to their project and so get swept aside.[22] She refuses to change herself; she stands back from unity; therefore in the end she is cut off from the source of new life the guerrillas represent. Her crucifixion is really a self-defeat, one more forecast of her ultimate self-destruction.

At the other pole from Harriet and Allen are Merle and Saul, who overcome the temptation of self-concealment and silence by sharing "unspeakabl[e]" personal memories, recovered in their agonizing, cathartic conversation at Sugar's after the jump-up. In keeping with the importance of an affirmative heterosexuality in Marshall's pictures of self-decolonization in this novel, the climax of this rescue of memory through conversation is sexual, a conjunction of body and voice that points forward to more elaborate representations of voice as an attribute of body in the next two novels. Whereas Harriet's "sexual" feelings express themselves in cruelty and Allen's in solitary disconnectedness, Merle's and Saul's, like Vere's, are expressed through lovemaking as the culmination of the carnival. Their last carnival journey is toward "the house where Merle had boarded as a schoolgirl," which they reach as the sky turns "the color of the ashes that would be placed on the foreheads of the faithful later in the morning" (339). The reference to Ash Wednesday suggests the confessional nature of Merle and Saul's conversation and places their lovemaking in the context of ritual, just as Vere's lovemaking with Milly was described as a "rite" (310), in a bed "like an altar" (307). As the epigraph says, "Generations perform ceremonies of reconciliation but there is no end." Merle and Saul's ceremony of reconciliation, in the space between the carnival of Shrove Tuesday and the morning of Ash Wednesday, stops one cycle of great wrong for a moment just as the pageant of Cuffee Ned stopped for a moment the cycle of history.

4

Set against the images of silence and stasis that represent loss throughout *The Chosen Place* is the journey motif to which the carnival pageant belongs. Among the many journeys of the novel is the smallholders' cooperative transportation of canes after the factory closing, which in certain ways re-enacts the carnival journey. If it is not the fully revolutionary act Merle imagined (taking over the factory and running it themselves), it nonetheless successfully transforms stasis into action. At the other pole of the motif is the journey Vere makes. The first part of this journey is to America, where he counters his disappointing experience with fantasies of winning the Whitmonday Race back home. The second is his "inevitable" journey home (14) and then the race, in which the car he has rebuilt destroys him. "*Arma virumque cano. . . .*" Lyle's drunken declamation is Marshall's veiled, ironic commentary on the tragedy of Vere, a Bournehills man whose journey ends not in the salvation of his people or the founding of a new nation but in death. The image of Vere lying dead by the roadside is the logical extreme of all the others: Gwen with her "dead eyes" (163), Ferguson in his statuelike silence, the workers turned to effigies, Merle in a cataleptic trance. It shows the ultimate potential of the First World for destroying the Third World, not only through an overt imposition of power through "labor schemes" in both places, but more subtly through commodities that inspire the illusions of participation and power in people such as Vere. Marshall identifies such illusions directly with the illusion of gaining a voice. As Vere returns home each night from Milly's bed, the sound of his car is "like his voice speaking with a new impressive authority and force" (346). But the sound is deceptive. Not his voice at all, it belongs to a power inimical to his, as becomes clear when the car falls apart: "It was as if the Opel . . . while doing his bidding and permitting him to think he was making it over into his own image, to express him . . . had also at the same time been conspiring against him . . ." (366).[23] Vere's death, in other words, is no accident; it is a form of racial violence, as Harriet unwittingly recognizes in a double vision of Vere as Alberta's nephew, "*the one . . . who was found murdered at the bottom of the pond that time. It was as though her nephew was the one lying dead under the tree. . . . Or that it was both of them in one body*" (371).

This superimposition functions at the "objective" level to represent the global political and social content of Vere's tragedy. At the "subjective" level it delineates the interior version of that content in Harriet's psychology. White people's responsibility for Vere's death is as direct, Marshall implies, as in a lynching. And the will to power that responsibility betrays is, as in every other picture of the First World's deadly ambitions, suicidal: "The collapse . . . flowed perhaps out of a profoundly self-destructive impulse within the machine itself, and Vere, in foolishly allowing himself to be taken in by what he had believed was its promise of power, was simply a hapless victim" (367). But the double exposure that renders this truth for the reader is unintelligible to Harriet, even though her own mind produces it. Indeed her sense of the "odd" nature of the conjunction of images in her mind attests to its dangerous self-division, which does finally end in suicide.[24] Harriet sees everything but she sees nothing; her witless double vision of Vere as Alberta's nephew is thus a kind of obverse rendering of her moral schizophrenia.

Early in the novel, Vere's future is predicted — erroneously, as it turns out — in an image of a man already old at forty-five or fifty, playing dominoes and drinking rum "with pursed and trembling lips," the hollows under his eyes now "the repository of his dead dreams" (30). Vere's actual story is overlaid on this more predictable one, revealing his potential to make the deep-set patterns of Bournehills history mean something new. His carnival transformation and subsequent political involvement imply that he might "[lay] claim to" the land that is his (303), unlike the Lyle Hutsons who are busy selling it. He is also the center of the "family" reunion with Merle, Saul, Allen, and Harriet, his smile "a source of light and strength they could all draw upon" (109). This image of a restored heterosexual manhood as the center of a restored family is echoed, despite his tragedy, in the fact that Milly is pregnant when Vere dies. She stands over his body with her fist clutched protectively against the life inside her — another of the moments in which the tragedy of Bournehills and its hope for the future come together in a single image. Indeed the presence of the early, false description of Vere's tragic future suggests that even the actual tragedy that befalls him may be, at the symbolic level, no more accurate a description of his fate than the first one.

5

Most importantly, Vere's journey is balanced by that of Merle, the true protagonist of Marshall's epic, which offsets its theme of "arms and a man" with the countertheme of a woman and her struggle against a deadly economic, political, and cultural system of oppression epitomized in the arms race. From the beginning of the novel, Vere's journey away from this oppression and finally into its heart is set in counterpoint with Merle's. Chapter 2 begins with Vere's return from the United States to Bournehills; chapter 1 begins with Merle's abortive trip to the airport to pick up her American guests, which ends when she has to turn around because of the washed-out road that typifies Bournehills' stasis.

At the allegorical level, that is, we meet Merle in the middle way: not in a shadowy symbolic wood, however, but in the sunlit devastation of a landscape eroded by a very specific commercial venture. The terrain is at once her spiritual landscape and a locus of economic assault on those who work the land for other people's profit. The work they do on their own behalf is represented by the first laborers we meet, Mr. Douglin's road crew engaged in their Sisyphean task of repair. Each heavy rain washes out Westminster Low Road; each time the crew repairs it with the inferior materials Bournehills can afford, by a time-honored method that never works. The scene situates, in the whole *economic* context of Bournehills' place in the world, the *psychological* work Merle must do to move out of her personal crisis — a crisis later revealed to be intimately bound up with the history of imperialism.

Merle's personal crisis, like the economic crisis of Bournehills, is paralysis. "I've stopped dead in my tracks," she says later. "Paralyzed" (230). Stopped dead in the middle of her journey in the first chapter, Merle has to turn around and go back. But as she and Saul later agree, sometimes you have to go back in order to go forward (359, 468). Inspired by the carnival,[25] in her conversation at Sugar's with Saul she returns in memory to the story of her personal colonization. The defiant repetition of the Bournehills pageant against carnival rules is a means of resisting oppression by ensuring the return of the repressed. The fact that what has been repressed in this case, a slave revolt, is the history of resistance to oppression underlines the revolutionary nature of Bournehills' "struggle of memory against forgetting." Such resistance is a struggle against silence: against the public silencing of history, the private silencing of individual memories, and the silencing of the connections between the interior life and its social context. When Merle tells Saul her private history in the wake of the carnival pageant, she wins all of these struggles in a voicing of the past that comes to fruition in a triumphant encounter with the Englishwoman by proxy, as it were, in the person of Harriet. The confrontation in which Harriet offers Merle money to leave Bournehills after her affair with Saul catalyzes Merle's self-integration, a wholeness possible only for those who can see "the intensely social character of their interior lives."[26]

This capacity implies other kinds of double vision as well. It implies the ability to see different forms of oppression superimposed on one another; it also implies the ability to see the oppressor superimposed on the mind of the oppressed. Merle exercises both abilities when she sees fully the double exposure with which Harriet's appearance has confronted her all along. Recognizing in Harriet's face the Englishwoman's face, Merle begins laughing in an "anguished scream. . . . like a woman in labor with a stillborn child, who screams to rid herself of that dead weight" (439–40). Representing a civilization that "can no longer sustain life" (Keizs 74), infertile as a result of a nuclear arms race heading toward "mass suicide in which its creators would be the first to go" (39), Harriet herself, like the Englishwoman, is described here as a stillbirth. She seeks a securely colonial, maternalistic relation with Merle, but Merle, rebelling against the "face . . . attached . . . like an incubus to her mind" (440), refuses the role of child. Instead, recognizing herself as the mother, she struggles to deliver herself of the death she has entombed for so long. As she said of the drawing-room "empire," while it seemed the English-woman "was giving us so much" she was "draining our very substance" (329). One thinks of Carrington, mother whose breasts have been "used" to nurture the world (403). Colonial maternalism makes the receiver look like the giver so that the nursling — or rather the "incubus" — looks like the source of life. Recognizing this white incubus on her mind is Merle's counterversion of Conradian anagnorisis, her vision of the Black woman's burden: the white evil that First World imperialism has made her harbor in herself. Her laugh rejects Harriet, the Englishwoman, and all the others whom she has been forced to carry inside her, nurture, endow with life, endow with *her* life just as Bournehills has suckled the world that depletes it of the capacity to nourish itself.

Merle announces that she will "be right here" when Harriet comes back to Bournehills (442) — announces, in effect, Harriet's "failure to have a world without" her. After that, her laugh becomes "more a laugh and less the anguished scream. . . . She might have been delivered. . . . She entered the house and the suddenly free ringing laugh routed the stale silence in all the rooms and dim stone halls through which she passed, setting off echoes which found their way out to the veranda long after she had disappeared" (442). Like Zamani's laugh in *Fools*, Merle's laugh understands everything. In a metaphor of combat to answer those associated with the canefield and factory, the laugh "rout[s] the stale silence" of her house, proving her victorious over the "dead weight" of colonial history.

The confrontation between Merle and Harriet, drawn up "like two armies" (437), is the end to which the metaphors of war and combat have been leading: Stinger battling an army of canes; Sugar resembling a shrunken body, the spoil of war; the "flameless" apocalyptic fire in the factory; the apocalyptic flame at Sugar's; Harriet's "battle gear"; Sir John's "bombs and missiles" (221); Cuffee Ned's Revolt; the eagle with "blood-red" beak; the "violent combat" of the nightclub dance; the roar of the Bournehills sea that sounds like Wester[n]man's bomb; canes crushed in the factory with a sound like the "cry of someone being broken on a rack" (221) — the daily assault on Bournehills workers that Vere's uncle's death under the rollers only made for a moment more plain. The book is pervaded by these violent images, all of them, except the slave revolt, encapsulated in Harriet as a representative of First World military and economic power.

Marshall's decision "to embody the whole power struggle of the world" in women (DeVeaux 126), whose traditional role in novels is to embody private, psychological conflict, superimposes once again a picture of "objective social forces" on pictures of the interior life. At issue here in particular are the roles that social constructs of gender, race, and class play in the psyche. The contrast between the principles of power the two women represent, for example, shows what links them psychologically and socially in terms of gender and what separates them in terms of race. Harriet's power is rooted in white, male, First World domination of every-thing that is Other — including, in certain respects, herself. As a girl in that dominant world she was educated to be "little more than another attractive appointment" in a rich man's house (41). As a woman married to powerful men she has indulged in the kind of behind-the-scenes ma-nipulation that feminists beginning with Mary Wollstonecraft identified as a disguised form of powerlessness. On the other hand, her race and class give her a kind of power in the external world that Merle, who like her has a modest inheritance from her father, will never have. Even so, the power principle Merle represents gains ascendancy in this scene. It is a genuine power of womanhood rather than the vicarious power she knows she has also, like Harriet, tried to wield through men (437).

Merle's victory comes through her talk, an excoriating rejection of Harriet's attempt to make her behave like "the little colonial" (442). This speech is in one sense "the right speech of womanhood" that bell hooks says patriarchy assigns to Black women — "the talking into thin air, the talking to ears that do not hear you" (*Talking Back* 6) — because Harriet succeeds in closing her mind to it, once again turning a Black woman's speech into silence. The crucial audience for Merle's voice here, how-ever, is not white but Black, not Harriet but Merle, who speaks of Harriet in the third person, as if talking only to herself. And this talking back, for Merle's own benefit, is a release of her pent-up power. Merle triumphs by acting on her own behalf, apart from the "incubus" of white colonial power that has threatened to drain and corrupt her own. It is of this alien power, superimposed on her psyche, that she must deliver herself in the encounter with Harriet, its representative.

The double image of birth and death in this scene recalls one of the most ambiguous images of the novel: that of Gwen, apparently in the late stages of pregnancy and confident that the baby will come in its own time, but possibly carrying a tumor or stillbirth. Her ambiguous pregnancy, and the contrast between her "dead eyes" (163) and resilient spirit, say that what she bears may be either life or death. The image is of Bour nehills itself; it poses the question whether the people there can trans-form what they have borne for centuries — the "dead weight" of slavery — into the birth of something new, or whether all that they bear will over-come them as it overcomes Gwen when her eyes go dead.

The simile of Merle in labor recalls the image of Gwen pregnant with either death or life. The climax of the encounter between Merle and Harriet portrays the burden of Third World womanhood as both. What

Merle does is cast off one of these burdens by refusing to confuse a journey undertaken for Harriet's benefit with the journey she owes herself. Merle screams like a woman in labor struggling to "rid herself" of the "stillbirth" that is her wealthy white English patroness and her would-be patroness Harriet. Victorious at the end of that struggle, "She might have been delivered" (442). Having triumphed over Harriet, Merle — delivered of the death inside her, delivered of her enemies, but also "delivered" like a newborn child — gives birth to herself. By rejecting her false progeny and announcing she will "stay put" (441), Merle liberates herself, in a paradox akin to the freedom-through-stasis of Bournehills people, to travel to Africa and claim her daughter — her true progeny, her entitlement to the future.

Harriet, in contrast, moves in the direction suggested by the metaphor of the "dead weight," taking Saul's project down with her in the deliberate sabotage of the Bournehills project that only makes literal the metaphorical sabotage Saul's marriage to her implied all along. Appropriately, the scene of their final, most intimate domestic conflict is inaugurated by an apocalyptic image that casts that conflict in global terms: "The darkness came pouring into the house: smoke, it seemed, from the final conflagration set off by the departing sun atop Westminster" (450). As in the scenes of silence in Merle's flat in Leeds and her bedroom at Cassia House, this domestic interior is infused with political meanings. The "conflagration" prophesied in the mad scene at Sugar's was the logical outcome of the "combat" on the dance floor between rich and poor. By trying to destroy the Bournehills project, Harriet has finally entered that combat unambiguously. Initially it seems she has almost won, as Saul responds to her exercise of behind-the-scenes power with a stillness like that of a statue (449). But then the same unity with Bournehills expressed in his stonelike silence draws him out of it into Bournehills language: "[I]f I should find out that you and your blue-blooded friend on the board were in any way involved in what's happened. . . . It would be finish for us" (452). As he talks on, Saul comes increasingly to life and "a strange rigidity" comes over Harriet: "She had become the stone effigy now" (454). Leaving, he speaks even more strongly in the Bournehills idiom: "As I've heard people here say, you come like a stranger to me from now on" (455).

Saul's move out of silence into the voice of Bournehills is part of the same process whereby the experiences of the oppressed come to be physically imposed on him, expressed through his body in reversals of the process of colonization whereby the experience of the colonizer is imposed forcibly on the bodies of the oppressed. The most striking example of the latter process is Merle's earrings, replicas of statues on Westminster Abbey, given her by the Englishwoman because Merle told her about

Westminster Hill back home. The image of her face framed by these other faces, which she wears in her flesh, describes the imposition of Eurocentric culture and its canons of value quite literally upon the bodies of African peoples, just as names like "Westminster" have been imposed on the land that should belong to the people of Bournehills. The statues imposed on her, mute images of white culture, trope the silence and stasis imposed on her by all that they represent. For these reasons, Saul's removal of the earrings when they make love is a counterpart of the moving of Bournehills voices into him.

The repressive personal silence into which Harriet finally retreats, contrasted with the quickening voice of Bournehills, is conflated at the end with the "final silence" of nuclear annihilation: an apocalyptic self-disintegration, at once political and psychological, that is rooted in her refusal to acknowledge the unities that are the First and Third Worlds' shared economic history. These unities, which have steadily become her Nemesis, overtake her in the scene that presents Marshall's climactic revision of the heart-of-darkness theme. Resembling in her last conflict with Saul a "stone effigy" (454), then sitting alone through the night like one "asleep with her eyes open" (457), Harriet has become what she and the powers she represents succeed, but only intermittently, in making the people of Bournehills. In Marshall's world, the fundamental unities Harriet denies mean that to silence and immobilize someone else is to do the same to oneself; to exercise destructive power is suicide. During Harriet's vigil, the woman who worked as a housekeeper for her family, of whom she has thought with increasing unease since Bournehills first jolted her memory, once again surfaces from that interior place of silence to which Harriet succeeded for so long in relegating her. Alberta Lee Grant's persistent resurgence despite the oppression and repression designed to subdue her—a private counterpart in Harriet's life to Cuffee's yearly resurrection on Bourne Island—culminates as Harriet remembers refusing to send a toy to Alberta's nieces and nephews. Obsessed with recalling what it was, she struggles to make her mind "offer up its secret" (458). But for all her possessive clinging to the toy, Harriet has lost it; her habit of repression keeps it from her just as her childish act of oppression kept it from Alberta. This example of the oppressive exercise of power over others as self-repressive and defeating leads logically to the only image the search for the toy brings to Harriet's mind: her old dream of nuclear holocaust, "that mass suicide in which its creators would be the first to go" (39).

Marshall's final revisioning of Conrad's heart of darkness now emerges in two extraordinary images of blackness and whiteness superimposed. In the first, Harriet imagines Andrew leaving on her a mark like that she imagined when Lyle touched her, except that now it becomes a stain spreading over her whole body (458). To Harriet black is a symbol of evil; as a child she thought the fairies had turned Alberta black to punish her for naughtiness (458). Her vision of herself as black expresses her sudden, unevadable recognition that she has been implicated in a struggle for power (458–59). Harriet sees this truth "in the spreading stain" that brings her hidden depths "surging to the surface" (458). The scene is an interesting conjoining of Selina's recognition of the dark "miasma" of her own sins — her vision of her "heart of darkness" — and her critique of the racism implicit in the metaphor itself. Selina makes this critique in concluding that whites such as Mrs. Benton must confuse dark faces "with the heart of darkness within them and all its horror and fascination" (291). Lyle presents another, more sardonically and self-consciously colonized version of this idea. As he tells Harriet in his suave British way after relating how a white woman in Chicago screamed when he stepped into her elevator, such incidents "suggest a terribly dark and primitive side to your troubled countrymen" (422).

The interplay, in Lyle's and Selina's words, between a recognition of the universal truth of Conrad's metaphor and a recognition of its particular falsehood suggests the difficulties it presented for Paule Marshall as an author. Conrad's heart of darkness early offered her a compelling symbol for her interest in the importance of confronting the repressed,[27] and a compelling vehicle for expressing connections her work always insists on: the unity among races; the unity of the First and Third Worlds that makes people like Harriet accountable for the suffering of those like Merle. But the racism implicit in Conrad's use of Africans to represent the evil in Europeans denies these unities. Marshall's solution is to revise Conrad's symbol to reveal repression and oppression as two faces of the same phenomenon. In the confrontation between Merle and Harriet, she identifies Merle's hidden evil with a white imperialist's silencing intrusion on her inner life; in Harriet's midnight vigil she identifies Harriet's hidden evil with the self-destructive denial of her unities with the Third World.

Harriet's horrified vision of blackness superimposed on her own flesh — the recognition that she could not shut darkness out because it was part of her all the time — is her anagnorisis. It is more Conradian than Merle's recognition of the white "stillbirth" within herself except that once again the real evil, the man whose touch brings Harriet's stain to the surface, is not Black but white. At the same time, in its racist equation of black skin with evil, Harriet's revelation reenacts the very will to power she is finally acknowledging as the evil in herself. Her fearful recognition of herself as black is thus a flawed version of the "essential truth," revealed at dawn, that black and white are "one and the same" (459): "Dawn came. . . . moving slowly, with all the stateliness of a royal barge, into the heart of the darkness outside. They embraced — the darkness and the light, so that . . . she had the impression that the night, bedding down in the great folds of the hills, contained the dawn, and the dawn the darkness. It was as though they were really, after all, one and the same, two parts of a whole, and that together they stood to acquaint her with an essential truth" (459).

Following so closely on Harriet's vision of the "dark splotch" surfacing to "reveal her" (458), the image of night and dawn embracing completes Marshall's African-American recasting of Conrad's theme. Here the imperial barge moving into "the heart of the darkness" is not the voyage of imperialist explorers encountering in a peopleless landscape their own dark depths. It is the Bournehills dawn moving into the Bournehills darkness, an image of unity between races that are "really, after all . . . two parts of a whole" (459), like the dancers, "inseparable parts of a whole" at Sugar's (81). But Bournehills creates this unity all by itself. Night and dawn, end and beginning, bourne and born are superimposed in Bournehills, just as the double meanings of its name suggest.

With the picture of darkness and light superimposed, it is as if the camera moved back from Merle and Saul's bed to reveal their lovemaking as just one individual instance of an underlying "truth" of unity as fundamental as nature. In the same way, Merle, who "somehow is Bournehills" (118), contains its past and future in her own. Her journey to Africa is an individual journey of freedom, but behind it is the collective journey of exile it reverses.[28] The pain of Bourne Island's history is rooted in that journey in which all its losses began. The carnival pageant, by daring to reclaim this history and speak once again of these losses, celebrates the unity of "a People," which Merle affirms at a personal level by going to Africa to reunite her family. Merle's private losses of her daughter and of a voice in which to speak about her pain have been rooted in the losses of Bourne Island's history. Thus the places of silence associated with them, the flat in Leeds and her bedroom in Cassia House, have also been described in images of political and economic exploitation. By the same token her final journey to Africa expresses on a personal level the political themes of another journey of freedom: the pageant through which the dispossessed of the island, finding their voice in collective art, lay claim to the future by claiming their past.

This conflation of Merle's life with that of Bournehills, of her losses with Bournehills' losses and her journey with its journey, explains why the account of her departure at the end of the book issues in a prophecy of Cuffee's fire rekindled. As Saul leaves for home, where he now realizes he must, as Merle says, go back and "take a stand" (468), he passes Pyre Hill, an image of Bournehills' true capacity for change beyond anything his project envisioned: "it looked, as always, to be smoldering still, the fire that Cuffee had started, which legend would have it had burned for five years, refusing to die. It would flare again, full strength, one day" (472). On the way to the airport, the first rains of August slam up against the car, and Delbert jokes that the road will "take a walk any day now" (472).

Like so many images in the novel, this one double-exposes ends and beginnings, dispossession and power, changelessness and perpetually renewed life. The rains will wash out the road, as Delbert says, and the road crew will repair it again in the old ineffective way. But the same rains will bring the new shoots of cane to end what people in Bournehills call "the dead season," reviving a land that looked "too exhausted ever to bear again" (414). With the joke about Westminster Low Road, the place where Merle turned around to go back at the beginning of the book, the end of the book comes back around to its beginning. Bournehills will return for now to its old ways. But Merle is no longer at a standstill, and her journey into the future by way of the past is an indication that Bournehills, so steeped in history, may well be the scene of the fire next time.

After Ketu left their flat, Merle heard the final silence of nuclear annihilation. She responded with a silence of her own, unable to voice the "nameless and irrevocable loss" that her face revealed at the beginning of the book, and masking her pain with a compulsive talk that was part of her stasis: "Doing nothing. . . . And talking. Oh, God, going on like some mad woman all the time but doing nothing" (464). When the cathartic reclaiming of Caribbean history in the pageant brings her to speak of her marriage, setting its failure in the context of that same history, she is speaking into both silences, asserting their identity. This symbolic presentation of psychology and history as two faces of the same reality is connected, in all of Marshall's work, to her belief in women's power to name, to create, to give birth to a new order. At the end of *The Chosen Place*, Merle rides to the airport without speaking, having abandoned the "talk that was in itself a silence," her mind on the journey ahead. She has said that journey will end with a return home to take her stand as "a political party of one, strictly radical" (468). In keeping with this prediction, Marshall's last picture of Merle is of "a Third World revolutionary spirit" escaped from the novel, striding from Argentina to Canada, America to Africa, everywhere "speaking her mind," urging the oppressed "to resist, to organize, to rise up against the condition of their lives" (*Reena* 109). In this vision Marshall celebrates the power of women's voices not only to sustain their interior lives by recovering what they have lost as individuals, but also to recover history—to find again the collective memories that have been suppressed, and to ensure, both psychologically and politically, that the threat of annihilation will be met with "life persisting."

Chapter 3
Voice, Spirit, Materiality, and the Road to Freedom
Third World Feminism in *Praisesong for the Widow*

Thus saith the Lord God unto these bones, Behold, I will cause breath to enter into you, and ye shall live.

— Ezekiel 37: 5

Silence *is* like starvation. Don't be fooled.

— Cherríe Moraga

1

In *Praisesong for the Widow,* Marshall returns to her concern in *Brown Girl* with materialism, assimilationism, and their erosion of connections with community, the past, one's self. Here those themes are informed by the concern with spirituality to which the title calls attention, and which can lead readers to see this as Marshall's least political work. But such readings neglect the complicated role the material plays in this story of spiritual rebirth.[1] The major religious metaphors of the novel are all specifically concerned with the relationship between the material and the spiritual. Incarnation is the spiritual manifesting itself corporeally; transubstantiation is the material transmuted into the spiritual; resurrection is the body's awakening in a spiritual realm. Marshall uses these metaphors to present a web of complex relations between the body and the soul, the material and the spiritual, and most particularly between Euro-American material hegemony and an African-American spirituality that is itself expressed through a fusion of body and voice.

In *Praisesong* as in many narratives of spiritual awakening, what the old hymn writer disdained as "things of earth" are hindrances to spiritual progress. In Avey's story, however, the World and the Flesh are not mere allies of the Devil: things of earth do not stand in simple contradistinction to things less tangible and more true; nor is the body the simple antithesis of soul, as it often is in Western, but not African tradition.[2] Marshall's picture of the spiritual dangers of materialism is not a renunciation of the worldly as irrelevant to higher spiritual realities. On the contrary, it is of a piece with her relentless focus on the injustice underlying the material conditions of African-American life, especially in their connection to the conditions of African-American work. By the same token, the epiphany the novel depicts is what bell hooks terms "a politicized spiritual reawakening" (hooks and West 55). Silence and stasis in this novel are especially associated with questions of money and property, poverty and affluence, possession and dispossession. Most fundamentally they result from the power of the American economic system, from slavery to the present, to transmute the spiritual into the material, people into objects.

The materialism that imprisons Avey in silence and stasis by the time of her third Caribbean cruise on the *Bianca Pride* is not a sin but a form of violence a racist economy has inflicted on her, first through poverty and then through the fierce struggle against it that deadened her husband with self-alienating work.[3] The materialistic values into which this struggle plunged Avey have leached out her spiritual energy, but her worldliness is not therefore an ally of the body. Indeed, far from being coupled with the flesh in her psychomachia, this worldliness poses a mortal danger to the flesh, colonizing her body from within, restraining the erotic power that is allied to her spiritual energy. As Cherríe Moraga says,

> Women of color have always known, although we have not always wanted to look at it, that our sexuality is not merely a physical response or drive, but holds a crucial relationship to our entire spiritual capacity. . . . Simply put, if the spirit and sex have been linked in our oppression, then they must also be linked in the strategy toward our liberation. To date, no liberation movement has been willing to take on the task. To walk a freedom road that is both material and metaphysical. Sexual and spiritual. Third World feminism is about feeding people in all their hungers. (132)

The freedom road Avey eventually walks in *Praisesong* is both material and metaphysical, sexual and spiritual, and the novel's feminism is very much about "feeding people in all their hungers." One of the voices that speaks again in Avey's memory as she moves toward liberation is the collective voice of Martin Luther King's Poor People's March on Washington, which she remembers hearing as a threatening "hungry roar" in the background of her daughter's phone call home from the demonstration (140). Her desire to suppress this voice, in all its hungers, was bound up with the displacement of her own spiritual and sexual hungers by Jay's struggle for affluence. The economic violence responsible for that displacement is manifested in a particular aspect of materiality equated with masks, coverings, and camouflage: overlays of white luxury on white violence; superimpositions of white materialism on Avey's psyche. In this context Avey's recovery of voice and agency results from a visionary stripping away, the *seeing through* that the out-islanders of Carriacou know as *li gain connaissance* (218).

This seeing through strips away material reality to reveal a spiritual reality, but one that is not thereby divorced from the corporeal. Instead, it is experienced and celebrated bodily—in touch, massage, orgasm, dance. The skeleton, the core of the body, becomes the central figure for this spiritual reality in the novel, whose subtext is Ezekiel's vision of the dry bones: a vision of dismemberment and resurrection in which the reconstituting of the individual is at the same time the reconstituting of a people. By means of *li gain connaissance*, what was in Harriet's story a shattering confrontation with "an essential truth" (*The Chosen Place* 459) becomes in Avey's a healing discovery of the "pared-down, annealed, quintessential" (216), as a vision of the "bare bones" (249) of her heritage inspires her spiritual re-embodiment.

A conjunction of voice with journeys, and a concomitant link between silence and false, static journeys, recurs throughout the novel in many variations, all of them related to the interplay between the material and the spiritual. Each summer Avey made the journey to Tatem; twice each week throughout Avey's visit to Tatem she was taken on another journey, a "ritual" walk across the fields to Ibo Landing to hear Aunt Cuney's story (32), inherited verbatim from her grandmother, a former slave, commemorating yet another journey. "It was here that they brought 'em," the story began (37). Taken off the slave ship at the landing, the Ibos took one long penetrating look around and saw the whole history of African Americans from slavery to the present. Then they just walked back home across the water, singing, leaving the white folks "with they mouth hung open" (39). The whites' powerlessness in the face of the Africans' spiritual mastery of material circumstance is expressed in the comic silence of arrested action — the mouth frozen in an act that should be speech but is not. Seeing through to the heart of things, the Ibos refused to work for the white folks, whose character their *gain connaissance* unmasked. Instead they went home "stepping" and singing (38–39), leaving the enslavers static and speechless.

Marshall's description of Avey's adult life before the dream presents the obverse of this image. It pictures contemporary African Americans' ostensible mobility through labor in the American economic system as silencing African-American voices, masking African-American reality, and replacing meaningful journeys with empty, parodic journeys equivalent to stasis. Implicit in Marshall's description of this process is the analogy of an enslavement whereby people lose their homeland and their hereditary speech to become, in exile, objects of property.[4] The transformation is gradual. Avey brought to her marriage a legacy of ancestral speech, taking her new husband on the old pilgrimage to the landing and repeating the Ibos' story in the grandmother's words Aunt Cuney had passed down. Later, Aunt Cuney ceased to speak even in Avey's memory, as the journey of the Ibos was lost with the annual journey to Tatem that Jay's obsession with work made impossible. The pressure of two and three jobs at once, professional study, and career-advancing activities with the Elks and Masons ended his and Avey's annual trips to Tatem, their occasional nights out to dance, and their regular visits to old friends in Harlem (116). These journeys were later supplanted by others: a weekend tour to the Laurentians with fellow Masons, and the ride to the Statler for their annual luncheon. It is this latter trip for which Avey, mink stole over her arm, is poised in the dream when Aunt Cuney beckons her over the fields to the landing and then, in imagination, back to Africa with the Ibos.[5] Even as she appears, "Jerome Johnson" is waiting for Avey to join him in the car for the ride to the Statler, where he will sit this year on the dais as a Master Mason — the pinnacle of success in his grueling climb to affluence.

On the Masons' tour to the Laurentians — another image of the white heights Jay tried to scale — the endless snow-covered mountains depressed Avey with the thought of an old Eskimo woman abandoned to die "on some snowy waste" as the rest of her tribe "raced away toward warmer ground" (81). North White Plains is another name for a "snowy waste"; the tribe's journey south is the journey on which Aunt Cuney summoned Avey in her dream, a reversal of the journey toward affluence that began on the snowy night in their Halsey Street apartment when Jay made his despairing commitment to the American dream. In Marshall's description of that night and its aftermath, the issue of voice and the motif of journeys converge in a variety of ways that comment on African Americans' relation to American capitalism. What precipitated Jay's resolve, for example, was his recognition of another voice usurping Avey's during the argument brought about by his late nights at work, Avey's jealous fantasies, and the prospect of another child soon to be born into their poverty. The voice he heard in hers was that of a neighbor excoriating her drunken husband as she "herded" him home each Saturday morning, a voice that "spoke not only for herself but for the thousands like her for blocks around . . ." (108). Against this voice Jay and Avey had used their own talk — "Vaudeville-like jokes which they sprinkled like juju powders around the bed" — to ward off the grim possibilities it represented: " 'Oh-oh, here come your folks again, Jay.' '*My folks?* Who told you I was colored, woman? I'm just passing to see what it feels like' " (107).

The magic of these jokes was partly in their voicing of Jay and Avey's physical intimacy — talk, created in the marriage bed, that preserved it as a charmed space. That Avey should speak in this other woman's voice, the collective voice of the "thousands" of women whose marriages had been riven by poverty, showed that she and Jay, having lost the power of their unifying talk, had been divided and conquered like their neighbors. On the other hand, this voice that so horrified Jay was one he and Avey subsequently repressed at their peril. Hearing it speak through Avey that night, Jay thought of abandoning his family to poverty, then gathered his willpower to give up everything else, if need be, in order to work their way out of it instead. In that resolve, ironically, unremarked by him or Avey at the time, the real Jay "slipped quietly" out the door anyway (136), and "vanished . . . in the snowy wastes of Halsey Street" (138). Correspondingly, Avey began to experience a kind of banishment "not unlike the old Eskimo woman . . . who had been cast out to await her death alone in the snow" (141): the journey of exile that took her to North White Plains.

The image of the "snowy wastes of Halsey Street" is characteristic, both in its form and content, of the subtle double exposures that give this terse novel its special complexity. On the one hand, the image pictures a Jay who is vanishing already, at the first moment of his decision to embrace the American dream, into the upper-middle-class wasteland of North White Plains. At the same time it conflates the exile of the Eskimo woman (and implicitly of Avey, in North White Plains) with life in the wasteland of Halsey Street itself. In other words, the hard-won move to the suburbs, for which Jay and Avey sacrificed so much, in one important sense got them nowhere. In fact, the images of what would conventionally be represented as Jerome's climb up the ladder of success are ironically undercut by Avey's memory of this period of struggle as a "downward slide" (129).

Other images of climbing perform the same ironic undercutting: for example, Avey's nightmarish fantasy of herself, hugely pregnant in her fifth-story apartment on Halsey Street, having to be lowered down the stairs like some "stricken climber" being lowered "down a snow-covered mountain" in frozen clothes (101–2). This image resonates ironically with Jerome's attainment of white heights in the Laurentians, as does the image of her and Jay's angry voices "stranded on a peak" that Tuesday night after which Jay began his killingly strenuous ascent (105). The parallels suggest, once again, that Jay and Avey never actually got very far in their impoverishing climb to affluence; their journey and even their eventual destination merely duplicated the conditions of Halsey Street, but in a form they did not recognize. This sense that upward mobility for

African Americans is a form of stasis — one more means by which a white economic system keeps them in their place — is reiterated in other similarly double-exposed images throughout the novel. Together they provide part of the critique of American capitalism in which the novel's luminous spirituality is set.

Central to this critique is Marshall's meticulous tracking of Jay and Avey's loss of voice in their ironically static journey. After that snowy night, Avey, whose voice had so horrified Jay in its resemblance to the voice of their neighbor, "developed [her] special silence" (14), and Jay began delivering diatribes against "half these Negroes you see out here" (131), his words seeming to come from a "pallid" stranger "who had slipped in when he wasn't looking and taken up residency behind his dark skin" or "superimposed" its "pale outline" on his face "as in a double exposure" (131). As Jay was ventriloquized by this white intruder on his personality, so the African-American voices that sustained him and Avey in the early years on Halsey Street vanished from their lives: Mr. B., Lady Day, Lil Green, Ella, Ida Cox, Ma Rainey, Big Bill Broonzy, and Mamie Smith on the phonograph after work in the evening; the "black voices" that "rose" from the radio on Sunday mornings "like spirits ascending" (124); the voices of Paul Laurence Dunbar, Langston Hughes, and James Weldon Johnson speaking in Jay's ecstatic recitations of their poetry. With these ritual acts of speech vanished another: Jay's "scandalous talk" (127), a part of their lovemaking that Avey had "loved and needed" (129), and her talk when it was "her turn" to be "in command. . . . Until under her touch and the words she whispered to him . . . he was suddenly speaking again. But with his body this time. A more powerful voice. Another kind of poetry" (127). This bodily voice had brought about a private mental journey: "She slipped free of it all: the bed, the narrow hallway bedroom, the house, Halsey Street, her job, Jay, the children, and the child who might come of this embrace. She gave the slip to her ordinary, everyday self" (128).

In this novel the conditions of labor for African Americans are even more intricately related to silence and stasis than in *Brown Girl* or *The Chosen Place*. The description of Avey and Jay's talk in bed and of Jay's "more powerful voice" inciting Avey's mental journey of freedom point to the fact that in *Praisesong* more than the earlier novels voice is not only an expression of spirit but an attribute of body — even, more specifically, of sexuality. Here the loss of voice is itself paralysis. The body speaks; what silences the voice silences the body. In Jay's need to overwork to compensate for the crushing discrimination he faced, he and Avey lost his voice, Aunt Cuney's voice, Avey's voice, and a legacy of voices in poetry and music. Jay lost the "voice" of his sexuality; Avey lost the voice of her lovemaking and the journeys of self-transcendence that expressed her sexuality; both lost the will to dance in response to Black voices at home or at clubs in Harlem; both lost the ritual journey that had kept alive a slave ancestor's voice.

All these losses — interpenetrating forms of silence and stasis — are forms of repression, the opposite of what bell hooks calls "re-member-ing": the process whereby African-American women and men "know one another so well, our histories, that we can take the bits and pieces, the fragments of who we are, and put them back together, re-member them" (hooks and West 19).[6] Such re-membering is a recovery, in both senses: a recovery of self and a recovery from violence done the self. Jay experienced its opposite in his impulse to rail against "these Negroes" in alien white talk that disremembered his and Avey's earlier joyous sustenance in African-American music, dance, and poetry as well as his bitter experiences job-hunting in white America: "If it was left to me I'd close down every dancehall in Harlem and burn every drum! That's the only way these Negroes out here'll begin making any progress!" (131–32). This disremembering, which superimposed a white ideology on his own knowledge, was also a dismemberment, a cutting-off of his connections with his community and a mutilation of his personality: "Speaking of his own in the harsh voice that treated them as a race apart" (140).

Praisesong portrays these losses of memory, these silences and repressions, as a form of white violence, dismembering African-American selves by creating a need to lose the past.[7] Jay knows he was qualified for the jobs that racism kept him from getting, but he buries the knowledge, directing his anger into the self-violence of "hard, punishing little blows" to his hand as he says, "When you come this color, it's uphill all the way" (134), or into the self-violence of verbal attacks on other African Americans for "good-timing" (135). At Jerome's funeral Avey sees in his face the "pallid face" of the stranger who usurped his voice in these monologues (131). "Jerome Johnson was dead, but it was still alive; in the midst of his immutable silence, the sound of its mirthless, triumphant laughter could be heard ringing through the high nave of the church" (133). Whiteness, laughing in triumph over Jerome's "immutable silence," is superimposed on his very face; the image implies that he has finally been buried beneath it. "[S]tarting up out of his sleep the night of his final stroke," Jerome Johnson cried out, "*Do you know who you sound like?* . . . *Who you even look like?*" (132). Fleeing the collective Black woman's voice that overtook Avey's that night on Halsey Street, Jay opened the way for a collective white racist voice to overtake his, and the memory that haunts him on his deathbed, the memory of his words that Tuesday night, becomes an ironic commentary on his own situation. He sounds like a white person; at the end he even looks like a white person.

The connection Marshall draws between oppression and repression —

between white violence and the silencing of African-American memory —is even clearer in Avey's experience. After the 1963 bombing of the Birmingham church, she dreamed of finding, "amid the debris of small limbs strewn around the church basement," those of her daughters. "And it was the Sunday in the dream when Sis was to have recited 'The Creation' . . ." (31). Having memorized all twelve stanzas, even more than the fragmentary heritage Jay passed down in their Sunday rituals, Sis was to have kept alive a Black poet's voice by remembering. Instead that voice was silenced in her dismemberment, and as the white violence silenced her it also silenced Avey's inner voice, the voice of her dreams, by creating a need to forget. After the dream of Birmingham she either did not dream any more or forgot her dreams before waking (31). White violence produced in Avey a self-protective counterviolence directed, like Jay's, against herself. It produced a need to dismember herself by disremembering: a need to sever herself from her own knowledge.

Thus it is appropriate that Avey's re-membering begins with a dream she remembers: one, furthermore, that is a metaphor for another African-American woman's refusal to be repressed. When Aunt Cuney appears to Avey in her sleep, the time when Avey brought her words alive for Jay is long past, and the dream figure is silent. Like Alberta, however, who makes her relentless ascent out of Harriet's subconscious despite the iron will that has repressed her for so many years, or like Ettie, whose voice echoes through the very emptiness of its absence from Mrs. Benton's account of her, Aunt Cuney cannot be kept down. Avey sees her motioning first patiently, then urgently, in a "voiceless plea" (45), a silent exhortation that Avey join her in the old ritual journey (42). Although her voice, unlike her body, has not managed "to outfox the grave" (41), she expresses herself in no uncertain terms on the subject of Avey's clothes, tearing at them with startling violence.

As in the image of the colonial white incubus on Merle's mind, in *Praisesong* the superimposition of what is white on what is Black is a process simultaneously economic, psychological, and physical. Jerome's oppressive work imposes a white mask on him and subdues Avey's sexuality beneath mink stoles, silk blouses, and long-line girdles.[8] Even the colors she wears are "muted" (20, 48). Like the white face that gets confused with Jerome's, Avey's expensive clothes, signifiers of value in an economic system that defines their wearer as valueless, get confused in her mind with her sense of self worth.[9] Her colonized mind creates a colonized body—restrained, held in check, kept from "good-timing," its natural shape and expression elegantly concealed. As Susan Bordo points out,

The body—what we eat, how we dress, the daily rituals through which we attend to the body—is a medium of culture. The body, as anthropologist Mary Douglas has argued, is a powerful symbolic form, a surface on which the central rules, hierarchies, and even metaphysical commitments of a culture are inscribed and thus reinforced through the concrete language of the body. . . .

The body is not only a *text* of culture. It is also, as anthropologist Pier: e Bourdieu and philosopher Michel Foucault (among others) have argued, a *practical*, direct locus of social control. Banally, through table manners and toilet habits, through seemingly trivial routines, rules, and practices, culture is "*made* body," as Bourdieu puts it. . . .

Throughout his later "genealogical" works (*Discipline and Punish, History of Sexuality*), Foucault constantly reminds us of the primacy of practice over belief. Not chiefly through "ideology," but through the organization and regulation of the time, space, and movements of our daily lives, our bodies are trained, shaped, and impressed with the stamp of prevailing historical forms of selfhood, desire, masculinity, femininity. (13–14)[10]

Marshall's descriptions of the changes that come over Avey and Jay illustrate well this function of the body as a "locus of social control." Avey remembers the transformation in Jay: "He went about those years like a runner in the heat of a long and punishing marathon, his every muscle tensed and straining, his body being pushed to its limits; and on his face a clenched and dogged look that was to become almost his sole expression over the years" (115). Both of them are being shaped by the "movements of [their] daily lives," as the economics of being African American define those movements, into the "prevailing historical forms." For Avey this process is her social construction as a woman whose upward mobility requires assimilation to a middle-class white model of womanhood. The shaping influence of this construction exerts itself on her body not only, to use Bordo's terms, "Through the pursuit of an ever-changing, homogenizing, elusive ideal of femininity" whereby "female bodies become what Foucault calls 'docile bodies,' " (14)[11] but through the pressure to erase her individuality, subsuming it into her husband's just as she begins invariably attaching his name to hers in her inner colloquies.

One sign of the inscription of the gender roles of the dominant culture on Avey is that the transformations in her body begin to make her look like Jay.[12] She takes on not only her husband's ambitions but even his appearance, so that over the years as white culture reshapes Jay in its image and Avey in his, they come to look almost like "twins" (141). As Avey packs for her departure from the *Bianca Pride*, one sign of her impending freedom is her body's shift away from this "same facial expression almost, the rather formal way they held themselves" (141), as she finds unexpectedly the "warmth" of a smile "easing the strain from the held-in lip that had become a permanent part of her expression over the years" (27–28).[13] The frozen pose of Avey's snowy exile thaws as she begins to be liberated, body and soul, from the white culture superimposed on her. Avey's clothes are the visible sign of this superimposition, analogous to Merle's earring replicas of statues on Westminster Abbey, expensive tokens of economic subordination that she removes when her psychological subordination ends. Similarly, Avey's dream of her expensive clothes being stripped away is the prelude to a series of events in which she strips away the symbols of economic value that she has confused with herself.

The apparently bizarre violence of Aunt Cuney's attack on Avey's clothes is a response to the violence they manifest as enactments of the ideology that has cast her out to die in North White Plains. The power of vision the dream bestows on Avey leads, correspondingly, to a visionary stripping away of the trappings of luxury on the *Bianca Pride* that reveals them as masks for death, isolation, and a violence specifically directed at Avey as an African American. What the white luxuries and leisure conceal is evident, for example, at dinner in the Versailles Room the evening after her dream. In the Hall of Mirrors at Versailles, the West Indies, which the *Bianca Pride* now visits with its "imperial" presence, was robbed of itself — portioned out among the great imperial powers. *"Do you know how many treaties were signed there, in that infamous Hall of Mirrors, divvying up India, the West Indies, the world?"* Marion had asked (47). The gilt(guilt)-framed mirrors of the Versailles Room rob Avey of herself even more directly when she fails, for a moment, to recognize her reflection in one of them. This moment recalls her earlier experiences back home of failing to recognize herself in department store mirrors, the windows of the commuter train, the windows of stores and restaurants, "the simonized bodies of cars," and even the bathroom mirror of her house in North White Plains (48–49).

Patricia Williams writes that "the cultural domination of blacks by whites means that the black self is placed at a distance even from itself" (62). Taken together, Avey's experiences of self-distance reveal the same psychological dismemberment that has expressed itself physically in her loss of sexuality: a disconnection from her body so extreme that she cannot even recognize it as hers. At the same time they equate Avey's self-alienation with the experience of being made an object by a system that should, in mainstream American ideology, make her a subject. In this ideology the consummate subject is the consumer who is at home, whether in her house in White Plains or in a department store, among the icons of commodity capitalism. But instead of revealing her as this subject, the image of Avey's reflection in store and restaurant windows implicitly superimposes her on the commodities also seen in them, as if she were one more object to be bought like the "simonized bodies of cars" on which the image of her own body is also superimposed. Similarly, one source of her failure to recognize herself in the department store mirrors is the commodities most literally superimposed on *her*: her clothes. In its allusion to these other images of self-loss, Avey's reflection in the Versailles Room conflates her daily life, especially her life as worker and as consumer (represented even more literally in the mirrors of the dining room as she eats), with her historical status as a piece of territory to be "divv[ied] up" by white powers.

As Frantz Fanon's psychological analyses of colonialism make clear,[14] not only land but people were divided in Europe's plunder of Africa. In Avey, who chose a journey of White Pride instead of a journey to Africa, the imperialists' strategy of divide and conquer succeeded well, dividing her not only from her "tribe" but also from herself.[15] The result is that, to use Patricia Williams's pun, she has lost her "self-regard" — both in the sense of her and Jay having come to behave "as if there had been nothing about themselves worth honoring" (139), and in Williams's sense of losing the ability to view oneself from a vantage point outside the self.[16] Until Aunt Cuney's dream summons Avey to self-reflection from the perspective of her African-American heritage, the only such external vantage points Avey has make her look like a "stranger" to be appraised first by "not[ing]" her clothes in a quick list (48), just as the taxi driver on Grenada later takes a "quick inventory" of her (75). This view of herself — this form of self-regard that is the opposite of self-respect — is an intolerable contradiction that can be sustained only if, in these inventories of her appearance, she cannot recognize her hereditary status as an "object of property" among the objects in store windows.

It is not merely that Avey sees herself with the eyes of the (white) Other but that she has been refashioned, even her face with its now "permanent" strain, so that she *is* other. Then again, however, her recent experience of recognizing this otherness — seeing in the mirrors that she is now other than herself — is a hopeful sign. It signals her imminent self-recovery, especially the recovery of her body, which has been appropriated by a culture that devalues it. This appropriation of the body is also, of course, an appropriation of her "hungers," to use Moraga's term — the same intrusion on desire that severed her from Jay, erasing her sexual pleasure entirely ("her body left abandoned far short of the crested wave" [129]) and making his into a kind of property she had to "take" from him to free him of its burden ("Take it from me, Avey! Just take it from me!" [129]).

The appropriation of Avey's hungers is especially manifest in her efforts in the dining room to control her weight: "*Peach Parfait à la Versailles. . . .* She had eaten sparingly earlier in the meal in order to treat herself to at least part of the dessert tonight, a few sinful spoonfuls" (49). Eating the parfait is a "sin" in more ways than one. To begin with, it was a transgression for Avey and her friends to get to this dinner table. They chose the elite dining room out of determination not to let "these white folks keep the best to themselves" (46). Once there, they were assigned a table too near the service entrance and had to insist on being seated at a better one (22). The other diners, even when facing them, seem to have their backs turned (47). The difficulties associated with their eating here recall sit-ins — ironically so, since this is no Woolworth's lunch counter but the Versailles Room, symbol of the most august world powers, and since Avey's goal, once here, is to keep herself from actually eating very much. Her self-restraint collaborates to create a "docile body" fashioned in the image of a culture of long-line girdles and dieting. Even though she has rebelled against the power of those who do not want her to eat here, her abstemious, ladylike version of the sit-in — or of the Poor People's March on Washington — reinscribes on her body their power over her. Furthermore, the fact that eating at this table requires curbing her appetite rather than feeding it is a good indication that the culture to which she is trying to assimilate cannot provide what she needs to sustain her life.[17] Despite the richness of the food and its vast quantities, it does not feed Avey in any of her hungers; eventually, in fact, even the rigorously moderated amount she eats becomes sickening. The strange bloated feeling Avey first experiences in the Versailles Room is an unpleasant intimation, experienced all too viscerally, of the inordinate consumption of material wealth that is the essence of *White Pride*. It is also a symbol for the fact that Avey has, as it were, internalized the consumption itself, the devouring imperialism the Versailles Room represents.

Like the dead child Merle is portrayed as bearing within her, the "overly rich" mass of food Avey begins imagining inside her after the dream of Aunt Cuney represents an internalization of the oppressive culture imposed outwardly in Merle's earrings and Avey's elegant clothes. That the culture itself is a culture of consumption intensifies the metaphor, as does an image of the "small mob" of whites who seem to pursue Avey from one end of the ship to the other the next morning, "bringing with them their voices and the lingering smell of food" as they strive to engage her in their trivial chat about purchases and meals (54). "The voices . . . seemed determined to draw her down into the hollowness of their talk, to make her part of it . . ." (55). The white voices themselves are consuming; significantly, Avey's consumption of white material goods and pleasures has placed her in danger of having her own identity swallowed up *in other people's "talk."*

"Silence *is* like starvation. Don't be fooled" (Moraga 52). Not only is the white culture of consumption starving Avey with its empty excess; it is trying to fill its "hollowness" by consuming *her* through the process whereby she consumes *it.* The image of white culture seeking out Avey to devour her by implicating her in its consumption is a literalized image of the danger of assimilation, in which consuming and being consumed are identical. The paradox is the same as that implicit in Audre Lorde's question, "What are the words you do not yet have? What do you need to say? What are the tyrannies you swallow day by day and attempt to make your own, until you will sicken and die of them, still in silence?" ("Transformation" 41). For Marshall as for Lorde, being assimilated to white culture is an almost bodily assimilation of tyranny—a consumption of it—and the opposite of this swallowing is speech.

The links these images establish between whites' disproportionate consumption and imperialistic assaults on an African-American self are rendered even more complex in another of Avey's "surreal" visions (57), in which the games on the sports deck suddenly look to her like violence. She feels "as exposed and vulnerable" as the golf balls the players are "slashing into the sea"; the shuffleboard games seem "to turn for an instant into a spectacular brawl" with the cue sticks as weapons. When a grandmotherly woman fires a twelve-gauge, open-bore shotgun at the clay pigeon, Avey recoils "as violently as if the old woman with the gun had turned in the next instant and fired it at her" (56–57). As in the lawn tennis and plover shoots of the colonials in Merle's prints, white leisure in these images is a camouflage for violence. That it is racial violence is clear from a memory the sound of the hempen rings in the quoit games arouses, an incident of police brutality in Avey's neighborhood on Halsey Street. The resurgence of this memory of white violence—so strong she can still hear the thud of the billy club—is of a piece with her recovery of the ability, lost after the Sunday school bombing, to remember her dreams.

The visionary stripping away of elegant white leisure to reveal death, isolation, and violence reaches its climax in Avey's encounter with the bikini-clad old man who grabs her skirt as she goes by: "In a swift, subliminal flash, all the man's wrinkled sunbaked skin fell away, his thinned-out flesh disappeared, and the only thing to be seen on the deck chair was a skeleton in a pair of skimpy red-and-white striped trunks and a blue visored cap." Urging Avey to sit down with him and "Take the load off your feet" (59)—to stop moving, in other words—he is the opposite of the dead Aunt Cuney summoning her on a journey. A skeleton beckoning an aging woman toward stasis, he is an emblem of her impending death, appearing like the grim reaper to claim her. But the real threat he symbolizes is not physical death. It is the spiritual death that the illusory seductions of white culture represent for her. Once again Marshall presents economics and psychology as two faces of the same reality. The skeletal white rich man stands for a variety of desire that is death. He is also a figure for desire that is dead, as the desires indigenous to Avey's personality have been for the thirty years during which white culture has subsumed her. Seeing that culture stripped of its fleshly disguise, Avey flees in horror just as she flees the white "mob" (a term inevitably calling up its modifier "lynch"), looking repeatedly over her shoulder "as if she expected to see bursting through the door the noisy band who had hounded her from place to place all morning or the crowd from the sports deck with their cue sticks, golf clubs and guns" (60).

Like the earlier image, this one implies white violence directed toward Avey personally, despite the cordial camouflage of the chitchat that white people have tried to engage her in all morning. Indeed their talk itself is a kind of hounding, like the hallucinatory vision of pursuit by the whites on the sports deck. The violence is not only race hatred; more complicatedly, the implements of attack are the accoutrements of her persecutors' wealth. The cue sticks, golf clubs, and guns with which they pursue her connect the physical violence expressed in the incident of police brutality with, on the one hand, economic violence against those whose work produces the leisure of the sports deck (leisure they produce but cannot afford to buy) and, on the other, the psychological violence that the lure of assimilation to their culture has done to Avey.

The physical, economic, and psychological violence implied in Avey's near-hallucinatory perceptions, as if produced by a drug that "had dramatically expanded her vision" (59), takes on its broadest context in her parting glimpse of the *Bianca Pride*. The real motive of the "sleek, imperial" ship's "glacial presence in the warm waters of the Caribbean" is revealed for a moment when she turns for this last look back, "only to have her eyes assaulted by what looked like a huge flash fire of megaton intensity and heat, as the tropical sunlight striking the liner's bow and sweeping over the hull appeared to have set it ablaze" (16–17, 63). The ship returns to normal, "serene and intact," as her gaze shifts, but momentarily both images are coterminous, each "as real as the other" (63). Here in this double vision in a minimalist, stripped-down form is the apocalyptic imagery of *The Chosen Place*, which centered around the imperialist economy by which North does violence to South. Here is even the "imperial" barge itself, trespassing once again in a world its passengers see as exotically alien and which their civilization will consume in a last suicidal assault.

Throughout the novel this visionary stripping away of superimpositions of white culture, based on a double vision that sees through white masks to Black reality, occurs in counterpoint with another kind of double vision that sees African, African-American, and African-Caribbean realities as mutually superimposed. That these two kinds of double vision are really versions of the same process is clear in Avey's encounters on the wharf in Grenada. Here her visionary stripping of the disguises of white culture, the counterpart of Aunt Cuney's stripping of her in the dream, has another counterpart in the looks the out-islanders give her, looks of recognition that "[refuse] to see any differences" (235). It is as if, she thinks, "their eyes immediately stripped her of everything she had on and dressed her in one of the homemade cotton prints the women were wearing" (72). These looks both strip away the alien culture super-imposed on Avey and superimpose the islanders' seemingly alien identi-ties on her in the same instant.

A logical consequence of such paradoxical experiences is Jerome's spectral appearance on the hotel balcony, which is both a doubling and a separation, a superimposition and a stripping away. Because Jerome ap-pears as an externalization of Avey's self-doubts, he is in one sense a mirror image of her mind. But since these doubts are not originally hers but were imposed on her in the long process whereby she came to resemble him, for Avey to see them externalized in Jerome's specter is to recognize that they are, in fact, external to her. The process of doubling and splitting here is analogous to that whereby Avey's self-alienation from her mirror images was nonetheless a recognition that, in truth, the woman shopping in Avey's clothes, riding the train to Avey's job, and living in Avey's house was not herself. The specter speaks in the voice that Avey is beginning to hear as not hers, but it is also not his. Or rather, it is not "Jay's," because the specter is Jerome, a composite personality consisting of Jay and a superimposed whiteness, here represented in "the white lambskin apron and the white gloves he had been buried in as a Master Mason" (87).

The specter's anger that Avey has squandered money by deserting the cruise reveals one of the many ways in which her journey is being double-exposed on the Ibos'. The Ibos' goal in walking away from their ship, back across the water, was to wind up, as Avey will in many senses, back where they started, thus squandering the money paid for the voyage that was intended to turn them into objects. Jerome is fearful Avey will lose all that he gained for them and wind up back on Halsey Street. But such loss, another stripping away, is necessary for Avey to recover what was really lost in the years when Jay came to be "buried," even during his lifetime, "as a Master Mason." Those losses are encapsulated in the lost "small rituals" of Halsey Street: dancing to African-American music and making love with Jay "talking his talk" (144); on Sundays the "black voices" of the Fisk Jubilee Choir and Jay's recital of African-American poetry (124). "They had possessed qualities as transcendent as the voices on the radio each Sunday, and as joyous as their embrace could be at times in that narrow bedroom. And they had expressed them—these simple things—in the most fundamental way!" (137).[18] This passage locates all the small rites of Halsey Street along the continuum that links the "joyous . . . embrace" and "transcendent . . . voices" — the sexual and the spiritual. At both poles of this continuum Jay's voice, through ritual speech, expressed the power of the collective voice in which his and Avey's individual power was grounded. The magnitude of this power is hinted at in the image of Jay declaiming James Weldon Johnson, his voice recreating, albeit in an only partially remembered form, the voice of another African American recreating the Creation. Jay's voice talking his erotic talk is thus linked through a chain of associations back to the moment when God spoke the world into being — ultimate spiritual image of the power of speech.

"In order to perpetuate itself, every oppression must corrupt or distort those various sources of power within the culture of the oppressed that can provide energy for change" (Lorde, "Uses of the Erotic" 53). That is what happens when Jay rechannels his spiritual/erotic energy, replacing the rites of Halsey Street with the struggle for material prosperity. Thus it is logical that the end result of this struggle should be expressed as the distortion of yet another ritual, the Eucharist, through which the material becomes spiritual. The spectral Jerome on the balcony fears Avey will lose the "house . . . lot . . . insurance policies, annuities, trusts and bank accounts . . . government bonds and other securities" he bequeathed her — "The whole of his transubstantiated body and blood" (88). In life Jerome's sexuality became a kind of property; in death he bequeathed his wife his "body," having turned his very flesh and blood into capital. In this image of a man "transubstantiated" into property, late twentieth-century capitalism performs the function of slavery. The slaveholders got their wealth by making other people into objects of property; operating within the economic system they bequeathed, Jerome had to get his by making *himself* into property.[19] The image of his body transubstantiated into capital is another reminder that the spirituality of *Praisesong* is not antibody but antimaterialistic, with materialism seen, even more starkly than in *Brown Girl*, as the self-perpetuation of oppression through the distortion of desire in the oppressed. Hence materialism in this novel is portrayed as destroying the body as well as the soul: obscuring its meaning, draining it of life, especially of sexuality — rendering it, in short, merely material.

The point is important because of the warmth with which some white readers have greeted a novel that may appear quite safely focused on a criticism of African Americans for aspiring to too much material prosperity and thereby tragically losing touch with their roots in a distant and much poorer continent. It is crucial to remember that it is not only Avey's connection with Africa with which she has lost touch; it is her "rage" at white injustice and violence. Furthermore, her *material* resources, as well as her spiritual resources, are essential to carrying out the final project she envisions of caring, *spiritually,* for Marion's "sweetest lepers" by providing them with a sense of their deep cultural connections with Africa. Their physical journeys to Tatem will have to be paid for if these children are to make the spiritual/mental journeys she envisions. And finally, the root of Avey's materialism is a white materialism that is bound up with the legacy of slavery. At Jay's funeral, seeing the pale stranger's face superimposed on his, hearing its laugh triumph over his "immutable silence," Avey clenched her gloved hand into a fist ready to strike at the face, as "the first note of a colossal cry could be heard forming in her throat" (133). On the hotel balcony that indecorous cry, restrained so long ago by the funeral director, erupts: "'*Too much!*' Loud, wrenching, issuing from her very center, it was a cry to make up for the silence of years" (138). The two words into which Avey's self-liberation is condensed derive their force precisely from the way they explode the distinctions between her buying into capitalist ideology and being sold.

2

In *Talking Back,* bell hooks describes her desire, when she wrote her first book, to know whether the oppressed can recover "a wholeness of being" that existed before oppression. Evoking a "way of knowing . . . learned from unschooled southern black folks," she unlearned the white understanding of "self" as unitary and isolated, recognizing the term instead "not as signifier of one 'I' but the coming together of many 'I's', the self as embodying collective reality past and present, family and community. Social construction of the self in relation would mean, then, that we would know the voices that speak in and to us from the past, that we would be in touch with . . . our history. Yet it is precisely these voices that are silenced, suppressed, when we are dominated. It is this collective voice we struggle to recover" (31).

The form of speech Avey recovers in her outburst, described as a "litany," heralds her move closer to one of the most powerful springs of collective speech in her heritage, the world of the African-American church. So powerful a source of voice is this world, in fact, that in Avey's dream it gives Aunt Cuney a voice even though she does not speak. Aunt Cuney is silent, but Avey, because of their shared reservoir of language, knows the very words in which she is pleading: "*Come/Won't you come . . . ?* . . . *Come/Will you come . . . ?*" (143). Having answered this silent plea, Avey—alone on an island where she does not know a soul, a solitary widow on the balcony of her single hotel room—ends her "sleeper's wake" by moving back into a network of kinship and community associated with the stripped-down, ritualistic speech she is recovering: "prostrate before the darkness, a backslider on the threshing floor, at the mourner's bench" (143). Remembering her life, recovering the sense of connection with a collective soul she and Jay had lost, Avey begins to reunify her fragmented self on the threshing floor, that solitary place of self-encounter that is nevertheless the heart of a communal space.

When the image of the threshing floor returns on the journey to Carriacou, this solitary communal space is seen, in particular, as the focus of church "Mothers' " voices (194). The Mothers on the boat ride are the old women among whom Avey is seated and whom she recognizes as figures from her past: "the presiding mothers of Mount Olivet Baptist" whose voices "propelled the sermon forward each Sunday" and who, when sinners were on the threshing floor, helped with their "exhortations . . . to bring them through" (194). In these women's "soothing, lilting words full of maternal solicitude," the individualistic but collective "mother's voice" of *Brown Girl* has been stripped down to something more basic: a ritual voice that itself divests Avey of "troubling thoughts, quietly and deftly stripping her of them as if they were so many layers of winter clothing she had mistakenly put on for the excursion" (197). The image recalls Aunt Cuney, whose religious exhortation ("*Come/Won't you come*") makes her in a sense the first of these religious Mothers. Aunt Cuney, however, was temporarily banned from her own church for mingling the sacred and the erotic. By crossing her feet during the Ring Shout, she was seen as defining her step as dance rather than worship. After that, it was said, Aunt Cuney made the trips to the landing her religion. Thus in summoning Avey to the landing, Aunt Cuney summons her to her own heresy of encompassing the spiritual and the corporeal in the same circle of self-expression.

Avey's sudden abandonment of concern with refashioning her body is part of a move into this circle and out of cultural values that require self-subordination. One of Patricia Williams's discussions of self-division is especially relevant here:

> Into [the] breach of the division-within-ourselves falls the helplessness of our fragile humanity. Unfortunately, the degree to which it is easier in the short run to climb out of the pit by denying the mountain labeled "colored" than it is to tackle the sheer cliff that is our scorned mortality is the degree to which blacks internalize the mountain labeled colored. It is the degree to which blacks remain divided along all sorts of categories of blackness, including class, and turn the speech of helplessness upon ourselves like a firehose. We should do something with ourselves, say the mothers to the daughters and the sons to the fathers, we should do something. So we rub ointments on our skin and pull at our hair and wrap our bodies in silk and gold. We remake and redo and we sing and pray that the ugliness will be hidden and our beauty will shine through and be accepted. And we work and we work and we work at ourselves. Against ourselves, in spite of ourselves, and in subordination of ourselves.
>
> We resent those of us who do not do the same. We resent those who are not well-groomed and well-masked and have not reined in the grubbiness of their anger, who have not sought the shelter of the most decorous assimilation possible. (120)[20]

Having finally let go of the reins on her anger the night before, in a wild lashing out that spilled the contents of her pocketbook on the floor, Avey very specifically leaves the shelter of decorous assimilation in her trip down the beach, by leaving the white hotel behind and going off on a walk without even the shelter of a hat (153). The walk will lead her to the quite different shelter of Lebert Joseph's rumshop. The fact that she has left her pocketbook, empty, tossed with its still spilled-out contents on the bed in an unlocked room has the same meaning as her going out in disarray without making the proper toilette to maximize the value of her clothes. As Williams says, to a remarkable extent in our culture that regards possessions as "the description of who we are and the reflection of our worth," property "is nothing more than the mind's enhancement of the body's limitation" (124).

Almost literally an extension of the body, a pocketbook represents property both in its role as commodity and as a container of money. Letting go of the impulse to "work at" ("Against . . . in spite of . . . in subordination of") herself to overcome her body's supposed limitation, Avey need no longer clutch to herself the property that was "the mind's enhancement" of her body. Not only does the pocketbook, as ornament, enhance a woman's body; in obscene slang (as well as in some literature), it is traditionally a symbol for her body, or rather for her sex. In Avey's case the symbol of the pocketbook suggests the displacement of her sexuality by property, her filling up with material excess that must be emptied out (a foreshadowing of the subsequent emptying of the "overly rich" food she has consumed [207]). By extension, as in other images implying slavery, the pocketbook thus suggests the making of Avey herself into property. A simultaneous symbol for Avey's affluence and for her sex as it has been constructed by the struggle for affluence, the image of the pocketbook is a striking contrast to the symbol for Avey's sex in the imagery of the Halsey Street rituals:

He would lie within her like a man who has suddenly found himself inside a temple of some kind, and hangs back, overcome by the magnificence of the place, and sensing around him the invisible forms of the deities who reside there: Erzulie with her jewels and gossamer veils, Yemoja to whom the rivers and seas are sacred; Oya, first wife of the thunder god and herself in charge of winds and rains . . . Jay might have felt himself surrounded by a pantheon of the most ancient deities who had made their temple the tunneled darkness of his wife's flesh. (127)

In this image of the flesh as temple of the spirit the material is spiritual; it is to this fusion that Avey must return. For Avey as for the aunt who mingled the sacred and the erotic so heretically in the Ring Shout, the kingdom of heaven — or the abode of the goddesses — must be entered corporeally. The imagery of infancy that describes Avey's awakening in the hotel room after her vision is thus not only a metaphor for rebirth on some disembodied spiritual plane. Her sweating, her struggle to dress herself, and, later, her vomiting and defecating on the trip to Carriacou are explicitly associated with children's physicality, and a crucial dimension of her spiritual rebirth must be the return to her sense of herself as a body. Avey walks out into the morning in a disheveled state that looks like disregard of her body but is actually a new regard for it, as she wanders away from the steadily receding column of hotels until these monuments to Western materialism turn "insubstantial as mirages" and then disappear (154). The logic of this image is the same whereby the flesh of the wealthy white man is seen to dissolve away from his skeleton. Restored to itself, African-American sight sees the very body of Western materialism as immaterial. By leaving the mirage of this materialism behind, Avey can arrive at the opposite pole of African and African-American spirituality: Joseph's circular mud hut, "seedy, run-down, stripped almost bare," with "the hushed tone of a temple or church" (159). Here once again the stripped-down is the sacramental, and the sacramental, associated in turn with a visionary power to see through meaningless superimpositions to the heart of things, expresses the more meaningful superimpositions of a collective self. Freedom of voice and the impulse to journey are natural concomitants of this power. Indeed, Avey finds herself talking so "freely" here that she wonders whether the speaker is herself, and in response to her host's invitation to the Big Drum dance of Carriacou she hears "herself (or whoever it was speaking in her voice)" asking how long the trip takes (183).

Through her "angry litany" on the balcony, through Lebert Joseph's "litany" of invitations ("You must come"), through what is obviously a confession before the bowed priest in "the almost sacred light" (168), Avey is drawn into the world of ritual speech to which the title of the novel alludes. With the loss of the Halsey Street "rituals" she lost "the praisesongs of a Sunday" (137) — ritual, collective acts of speech that tie the single, isolated individual, represented here by a widow, to the community. "In time . . . we must move past always focusing on the 'personal self' because there's a larger self. There's a 'self' of black people," says Sonja Sanchez (Tate 134). Through a coming to voice that involves ritualized speech,[21] the widow is connected once again to this "larger self" — in Eugenia Collier's words, "the essential collective Black self" (295).[22]

Lebert Joseph asks what Avey *is*, equating her personal identity with the larger self of her nation: "'And what you is?' . . . 'What's your nation?'" (166–67). His performance of the Bongo and the Juba draw her into the collective memories of this self she has lost. The metamorphoses the dances produce in him — making him seem taller, correcting the defect in his leg, making him seem younger, even transforming his movements into those of a woman (179) — are indications of the immersion in a wider community that makes him not one person but many. His identity, who he "is," is the unified multiplicity of the many nations who dance the dance of the Big Drum. Furthermore, as Collier points out, Joseph is an incarnation of "Legba — trickster, guardian of the crossroads where all ways meet" (312).[23] A magical, protean figure, he stands at the crossroads on Carriacou as he waits to escort Avey up the hill to the ceremony (230, 232–33);[24] both literally and figuratively he occupies a position at the crossroads of Africa and America. In this role, as Collier says, he "contains many linkages: Africa and the Diaspora; the carnate and the spirit worlds; the present generation, the ancestors, and the yet unborn" (312).[25]

Henry Louis Gates Jr. describes this linking function of Esu Elegbara figures, of whom Legba is a version in Benin and Haiti (*Signifying Monkey* 5): "Each version of Esu is the sole messenger of the gods. . . . master of that elusive, mystical barrier that separates the divine world from the profane. . . . In Yoruba mythology . . . his legs are of different lengths because he keeps one anchored in the realm of the gods while the other rests in this, our human world . . ." (6). Like Joseph, Esu can appear in both male and female guises, and like him Esu is multiple but also a unifier: "If plurality comprises one form of Esu's power, a second form is his power to connect the parts" (37).

The two forms are intimately related in Marshall's portrait of Lebert Joseph. As he looks at Avey with his jeweler's loupe, *li gain connaissance* is a technique of recognition, a rescue of memory. Paradoxically, the figure who most embodies this technique of stripping away to a core of "simplicity" also embodies multiple, superimposed realities: a good emblem of the way the spare, "annealed" simplicity of this terse novel is at the same time a multiplicity of double perspectives. At one moment Joseph looks tall, at another short; he is old and feeble but walks "with a forced vigor that denied both his age and infirmity" (161); he lies shamelessly and speaks the deepest truth. But these superimpositions reveal his essentiality. In his duplicities and multiplicities he is "the core, the hub" of the ritual song and dance, because he is the very embodiment of unity. He is related to people all over the world: "sons and daughters, grands and great-grands in Trinidad, Toronto, New York, London" (236). He sings the "Beg Pardon" *"not just for me one"* but *"for tout moun'"* (236). His wrinkles establish his kinship with all of Africa: "lines etched over his face like the scarification marks of a thousand tribes" (161). Avey perceives him as "one of those old people . . . who have the essentials to go on forever" (161).

In addition to the linking function Collier cites, Marshall's emphasis on speech and silence makes Legba's association with language crucial to her use of the figure. Gates describes Esu Elegbara as the very symbol of the power of language. In particular he is master of *ase*, which Gates translates as "logos," "more weighty, forceful, and action-packed than the ordinary word" (Gates, *Signifying Monkey* 7). Like the lost African-American "Creation," then, Joseph is a figure for the aboriginal African power of language, with which Avey has lost her proper connection. By interpreting the text of divine will, Esu is one " 'who loosens knowledge' " (9) — a good description of Joseph's function in Avey's rescue of memory. Esu is thus a figure for unity and knowledge; he is also a figure for the power of the Word in a sense comprising action as well as language. As such he represents the end of stasis in a form involving both language and unity: " 'He *alone* can set an action in motion and interconnect the parts' " (Gates 37). Often portrayed as "an inveterate copulator possessed by his enormous penis" (Joseph jokes about the Excursion as a time for sex and appears at the crossroads with a large staff in hand), Esu is, Gates says, "linguistically . . . the ultimate copula, connecting truth with understanding, the sacred with the profane" (7). Significantly in this context, Avey's "putting . . . back together again" climaxes in the achievement of doubleness: the "distance" she attains through orgasm, which stands as a metaphor for the "distance" or doubleness she comes to see, paradoxically, as a sign of being whole.

This paradox is illuminated by Gates's interpretation of the divine trickster topos, which "functions as a sign of the disrupted wholeness of an African system of meaning and belief that black slaves recreated from memory, preserved by oral narration, improvised upon in ritual . . . and willed to their own subsequent generations, as hermetically sealed and encoded charts of cultural descent" (*Signifying Monkey* 5). Marshall's use of this figure, who becomes in her text a symbol for the transmission of an African legacy to subsequent generations, is thus itself part of her own transmission of the same legacy. Of special importance is Joseph's doubleness and the doubleness he engenders in Avey, who, approaching the crossroads where he stands waiting to take her up the hill to the ceremony, feels herself "to be dwelling in any number of places at once and in a score of different time frames" (232). The description resonates with those of Joseph as "everywhere at once" during the ceremony and as belonging to past ages as well as the present (242, 233). Avey's assimilation to this figure is revealed in her feelings of ubiquity and time travel, her final confirmation as an Avatar(a), and her bemusement at "their strangeness, her own of the past few days and the man's" as she climbs the hill (233). The dual-gendered, old and young, multivoiced Joseph is a figure for the doubleness Avey must achieve in order to hold past and present together in her life, as he does.

Avey's initial sense that Joseph's speech, full of puzzling words such as "nation" (175), is merely strange (175) is a symptom of what would be in Fanon's terminology her own "cultural estrangement": "Every effort is made to bring the colonized person to admit the inferiority of his culture

which has been transformed into instinctive patterns of behavior, to recognize the unreality of his 'nation,' and in the last extreme, the confused and imperfect character of his own biological structure" (*Wretched
of the Earth* 236).[26] In this description a denigration of one's own body is
part of the loss of spiritual sustenance in the past and of political connection with one's nation. The journey on which Joseph guides Avey is a
process of decolonization that restores her body, her past, and her nation
through the mediation of the embodied and embodying spirituality of
African and African-American religious ritual. Thus the first experience
into which Joseph tricks Avey is the sickness brought about by the rough
water en route to Carriacou, which evokes African rituals of purging.[27]
That it occurs during her childhood memory of getting sick during an
Easter sermon ties it as well to African-American religion, which from
slave times has provided a means both of protesting and transcending
material circumstance, locating "richness, protection and power" in
gifts of the spirit while at the same time deploring the unjust material
conditions of African-American lives. It is this unity of material and spiritual concerns, so integral to African-American Christianity, that Marshall explores with the superimpositions of body and soul, materiality
and spirituality, in her account of Avey's passage toward the Big Drum
ceremony. The complexities of these superimpositions are well illus-
trated in the dream of the Easter sermon, with its call to resurrection
"When you find yourself buried" — as, for example, under "the shameful
stone of false values, of gimme gimme gimme and more more more"
(201). Urging that this stone be rolled away from the soul's door, the
preacher's voice, which becomes "God's voice" (203), brings out of Avey
the mass of "overly rich" food (207), symbol of her worldliness, that she
has felt in her stomach since the evening after her dream of Aunt Cuney.

This casting out, a response to the heightened speech of the preacher
with his electrifying "strangled scream" (199), is itself a kind of speech,
the opposite, as in Lorde's image, of swallowing tyranny. It is also a bodily
counterpart of Avey's spiritual coming to voice in the rumshop. There
Avey, rigorously self-contained for so many years, participated in a confession, a ritual making-public of what is most private. When she vomits,
supported between the church "Mothers" whose voices (*"Bon, li bon"*)
bring her through like a sinner on the threshing floor, what is inside her
becomes public in a visceral self-revelation that is the physical counterpart of her confession to Lebert Joseph. After the last of the food is
"expelled" as excrement (207), Avey is laid in the "hot, airless dark"
in the deckhouse: "A multitude it felt like lay packed around her in the
filth and stench of themselves, just as she was. Their moans, rising and
falling with each rise and plunge of the schooner, enlarged upon the one
filling her head. Their suffering — the depth of it, the weight of it in

the cramped space—made hers of no consequence" (209). Avey's sense of a collective suffering that makes hers "of no consequence" gets her beyond the isolationism that Jerome, whose American dream kept him and Avey apart from the Civil Rights movement, evinced when Marion called home from the Poor People's March in Washington: "What's she doing down there anyway? . . . When did she ever have to go without three square meals a day?" (141). Having escaped the hollow, monolithic, all-consuming white voice linked to the "smell of food" on the *Bianca Pride*, then finally having emptied herself of all she has consumed under its influence,[28] Avey is free to recover her collective Black voice.

To recover this voice is simultaneously to hear it in memory and to speak with it across time, as part of a "multitude" whose moans she can now recognize as an extension of hers, "enlarg[ing]" on the one that fills her head. This is a new image of self-dissociation to replace the old image of Avey staring baffled at herself in the mirror. Since she is alone, the moans she hears outside her are actually hers, but she does not, as in the case of the reflections earlier, feel totally dissociated from this external self-manifestation. Instead, the moans outside her are an extension of an *unvoiced* moan inside her head. That she hears her voice as coming from outside herself is an apt reflection of the fact that her authentic voice belongs to the "larger . . . 'self' of black people." In this image the "multitude"—unlike "the thousands" at the march or "the thousands" speaking in the voice of the angry woman on Halsey Street—are not just something external that she wants to block out; they speak for her when she cannot speak. In a similar way, Aunt Cuney in the dream is silent herself but communicates the words she and Avey share as a legacy of other African-American voices, and this interior silent-but-speaking dream voice gives voice, in a form Avey perceives as external to herself, to the silent discontent that has filled her head for thirty years.

Avey's purging recovers the memory of Black voices: "the inflammatory voice from the pulpit" (197), and then the voice of the slaves. The bodily speech of her purging is also a journey: a kind of reverse Middle Passage back to the legacy of Africa,[29] but in the hold of a slave ship. Avey's violent retching and the inarticulate moans she speaks/hears on this journey recover a voice prior even to speech. In her coming to voice, language itself must be stripped away to reveal meanings it cannot articulate. Snatching her dress from the skeleton man's hand and striking out at the "derisive" white face projected on the "dark and empty air" of the hotel balcony, she made a "murderous, growl-like sound" (142); mourning Jerome's death in life brought out of her "A hint of the angry, deep-throated cry" of "some Dahomey woman warrior of old" (130).

Not surprisingly, to go back further beyond even this nonverbal language is to move away from language toward music, a modulation with a pivot point in the preacher's voice, speaking words but in the "strangled scream" of a blues singer (199). Moving through this sacramental voice that seeks "higher ground" (199), and then through the moans of the slaves in the depths of the slaver, Avey awakes in Carriacou: the domain of Rosalie Parvay's "plainsong or . . . chant. . . . curious, scarcely audible" (220), and of the Big Drum's plangent note expressing "feelings . . . beyond words" (244–45). Here she can recover the voice of her and Jay's private rituals, then the voice of Africa.

3

Implicit in Avey's recovery of these lost voices through the rituals of baptism, healing, and incarnation is the complex relation between the material and the spiritual in her pilgrimage. When Rosalie Parvay, singing her chant, bathes and massages her, Avey's body is finally restored by that supreme physical act of spirit, the "laying on of hands" (217), as she re-members herself by remembering Aunt Cuney bathing her as a child in Tatem. Like voice, memory—which in Marshall's work is always the root of voice—is an attribute of body in this novel. In order fully to remember her heritage, Avey must experience the memory *physically*.[30] She moves back through the physical sensations of childhood and the hold of the slaver; to recover her body is to recover the history of its subjection and degradation crossing the ocean in a slave ship as well as the happiness of a child riding the ocean waves with her father. Then she moves beyond the slaver toward the bodily memory of something she never knew about consciously at all, the "nation" that Joseph recognizes in her style of dancing. This process of bodily recovery is paradoxically at the same time a process of material loss, as the "glitter and the excess" (139) of her material life are gradually stripped away to reveal the true nature of her own materiality. Her disheveled, ungirdled journey down the beach toward Lebert Joseph's hut is thus part of the process whereby the glitzy white heights of the ski-slope shaped hotel, evoking the journey to the Laurentians, fade into mirage. So is her further physical and figurative disrobing by the "Mothers" who perceive that she has worn too many clothes for what is emphatically not a journey of wintry exile. Earlier she tried to protect her fancy clothes from Aunt Cuney, used her six suitcases of clothes as "a barricade" against the out-islanders (73), and drew on her gloves to differentiate herself from these people who seemed to see no differences. For her ritual bath, in contrast, Avey is naked. Packing for her escape from the cruise ship, she moved from closet to suitcase "noiseless as a sneak thief" (10) — as if, in other words, the possessions she gathered did not belong to her. In a sense they did not. The vast load of clothes had nothing to do with the Avey hidden under the mink stoles and silk blouses. This real Avey comes to life beneath Rosalie's resolute "kneading and pummeling" of her "inert" thighs, which restores a memory of Jay "talking his talk" as they made love, then brings her to that "long pleasurable distance" she has not experienced in years (223–24).

On Halsey Street, Avey escaped the material circumstances of her life through physical self-expression—by means of the body. On Carriacou she escapes materialism (this time another version of the entrapping material circumstances of her life) through a repossession of her body. This repossession is an escape from materiality in two directions. On the one hand it is a return, in Rosalie's "sparsely furnished" room (215), to the materially impoverished but spiritually rich world of her childhood. In another direction, her physical/spiritual restoration is a slipping-free of it all as when lovemaking released her from the material conditions of her life in Brooklyn. Such escape into "pure self" (128) would not be possible, however, without an immersion in physicality.

This paradox underlies the connection between the physical and the spiritual in general in Avey's pilgrimage. For while her restoration is an escape from materiality, it can happen only through a re-membering of the material, a putting-back-together of the body. "Your daughter has been putting me back together again" (229), she tells Joseph later. This physical remembering is identical with the act of memory that brings "inert" flesh back to life by reincarnating the past in the present and, specifically, resurrecting a lost voice. Jay's voice was lost with the loss of his and Avey's small rituals as stasis overtook him in a parody of another ritual, that of transubstantiation. Rosalie's baptismal laying on of hands restores his voice not only by recalling his love-talk to Avey's mind but by reenacting the powerful "voice" of his sexuality in Avey's body. Rosalie's ritual—the reverse of Jerome's ritual "transubstantia[tion]" of self into inert property—resurrects Avey's "inert" body, moving her from stasis to the journey of self-transcendence she used to make on Halsey Street.

Underlying the fact that Avey's spiritual rebirth restores her body to her, freeing it for this transcendent journey, is the first cause of an African-American woman's loss of freedom: the system of slavery that, as Collins says, "commodified Black women's bodies as units of capital" (51).[31] For an African-American woman to possess her own body, in Marshall's account, is not only to resist the "cultural estrangement" that convinced her of its "confused and imperfect character" but, even more basically, to resist "being the object of property," a unit of capital. The emphasis on corporeality in Avey's story is thus ultimately about her self-redemption from slavery—her rejection of her objectification, her self-reclamation as a subject. Once she has taken this step she can, like the Ibos, walk home across the water, as she does figuratively in the Big Drum dance: "She moved cautiously at first, each foot edging forward as if the ground under her was really water — muddy river water — and she was testing it to see if it would hold her weight" (248).

"Only as subjects can we speak. As objects we remain voiceless — our beings defined and interpreted by others" (hooks, *Talking Back* 12). In *Praisesong for the Widow* the end of silence is the end of stasis because the recovery of voice and the recovery of the body-as-subject are the same. Avey's bold move out onto the muddy river water is an escape into the voice of Africa and away from the white voice that ventriloquized Jay, making him merely the object through which it spoke, an object it "defined and interpreted." "Speaking of his own as a race apart," Jay was made an object by this voice both because it ventriloquized him and because the words the voice made him say objectified him by assigning him, as himself one of "these Negroes," a white racist definition. Jerome's self-objectifying voice is the essence of self-definition by exclusion of an other — ironically, since *he* is the other that is excluded. It is revolt against this white voice, in fact, that finally ends Avey's status as observer outside the circle of the dance. "*If it was left to me I'd close down every dancehall in Harlem and burn every drum!*" Avey hears these words "in her ear" at a crucial moment in the ceremony (247). To escape the internal/external voice that speaks them she makes the most definitive act of rebellion possible — moving closer to the drums, then taking her "single declarative step forward" into the dance (247). Recovering "something of the stylishness and sass she had once been known for" as a dancer then restores in her memory Jay's proper voice, the unmistakably African-American voice of their private evening rituals: "*Girl, you can out-jangle Bojangles*" (249).

This voice, emerging in Avey's consciousness as she moves in the circle of old people enacting an ancient ritual, fuses the erotic and the spiritual, old age and youth, to establish one of the central paradoxes of the novel. Having seen through the white materialism of the *Bianca Pride* to the skeletal memento mori underneath, Avey goes on to find in the "bare bones" and "burnt-out ends" of the ancient ceremony on Carriacou the source of what Marshall described in Merle's eyes as "life persisting." In *Praisesong* this theme is bound up, as it was not in *The Chosen Place*, with the problem of old age and death. Avey's dance with the old people on Carriacou, for example, is a redeemed version of her combats with old people earlier. She responded to Aunt Cuney's dream-summons with a bitter, resistant fight. Her tormented introspection at the hotel in Grenada ended with another fight, as she struck blow after blow at the image she wanted to strike earlier — the pale, triumphant face of the stranger that imposed its face on Jay's and usurped his voice. After her argument with Lebert Joseph about the trip to Carriacou, "She felt as exhausted as if she and the old man had been fighting — actually, physically fighting . . ." (184). Avey's wild fights with her dead Aunt Cuney, the dead Jerome Johnson, and the ancient Lebert Joseph are, at one level, pictures of a woman in her sixties wrestling with old age and the prospect of death. As she comes to see, however, the real death that threatens her is the "megaton intensity" of the fire concealed beneath the "glacial" *Bianca Pride*; the exile of the Eskimo woman in the white north plains as her "tribe" journeys south without her; the death emblematized in the white man's skeletal summons; the burial under a pallid, alien anti-self that killed Jay years before Jerome Johnson died.

Avey's first reaction to the dream figure of Aunt Cuney was the realization that she should be a skeleton: "Standing there unmarked by the grave . . . with a hand that should have been fleshless bone by now: clappers to be played at a Juba" (40). Lebert Joseph should be a feeble old man, but he has "the essentials to go on forever." He and Aunt Cuney summon her not to death but to the collective life eternal of the thousand tribes Lebert Joseph represents—the collective journey of the "tribe" instead of solitary exile, old age, and dissolution in North White Plains. Aunt Cuney and Lebert Joseph will go on forever because, bound as they are to the life of a community past and present, their lives do not end with their individual deaths. That is why, as Rosalie says of her father in a description that applies also to her and all the old people of Carriacou, "He's a man gets on like he and death had a wager and he won" (227). The voices of these old people are united in songs passed down for generations; their dance, "the restrained glide-and-stamp, the rhythmic trudge, the Carriacou Tramp," is "designed to stay the course of history" (250). To "stay the course" is to persist; to "stay" something (as in "stay her hand") is also to stop it. To stay the course of history is both to last through the course of history and to stop the flow of time, to preserve the past from the changes of the present. It is also, perhaps, to dam up the "course" of history in order to redirect it, for the feelings of connectedness Avey has through the dance—"the threads streaming out from the old people around her"—enter her with a "brightness" that speaks "of possibilities and becoming even in the face of the bare bones and the burnt-out ends" (249).

In *Praisesong* even more than in *The Chosen Place*, life persisting—the "essentials to go on forever"—has to do with achieving an understanding of the self as something simple, absolute, authentic, as "essential" as the bare bones at the core of the body. At the same time this self is not unitary but multiple, a multiplicity of superimposed lives. In this novel, life persisting has to do with the persistence, through the individual, of a collective life whose sustenance is memory. In the America of which Avey is inevitably a part, the sustenance of memory, in turn, depends on a deliberate move away from the conditions that enforce forgetting. Avey's jour-

ney home — back to the South in her dream, back to the real Caribbean
the cruise ship will not visit, back to her African roots through the dance
— is a recovery of the Ibos' power to make this journey of freedom, which
was, for the grandmother who told the story, not literal but imaginative:
"They sounded like they was having such a good time my gran' declared
she just picked herself up and took off after 'em. In her mind. Her body
she always usta say might be in Tatem but her mind, her mind was long
gone with the Ibos . . ." (39). The Ibos' journey, one of the many avatars of
the myths of escape back to Africa, had its origin, too, in imagination: in
that "necessary distance of the mind" from one's material circumstances,
the seeing through to a deeper reality, that Avey comes to embrace.

Avey's restored sexuality brings back her fullest power of achieving
such physical / spiritual transcendence. In one of Marshall's most complicated double exposures, this power links the physicality of Avey's dancing
and lovemaking with the spirituality implied in the image of distance
from the material world — the slave's ability to separate her body from
her mind.

Too much! Couldn't they have done differently? Hadn't there perhaps been another way? . . . Would it have been possible . . . to have wrested, as they had done
over all those years, the means needed to rescue them from Halsey Street and to
see the children through, while preserving, safeguarding, treasuring those things
that had come down to them over the generations, which had defined them in a
particular way. . . . What would it have taken? . . . Awareness. It would have called
for an awareness of the worth of what they possessed. Vigilance. . . . And strength.
. . . and the will and even cunning necessary to withstand the glitter and the
excess. And distance. Above all, a certain distance of the mind and heart had
been absolutely essential. ". . . *Her body she always usta say might be in Tatem, but her
mind, her mind was long gone with the Ibos. . . .*" (139)

Joyce Pettis has pointed out that although many African-American
women writers have addressed the "schism that occurs when blacks —
particularly women — ignore the politics (and lessons) of race, class, and
gender and blindly subscribe to the American dream," Paule Marshall
is the only one who has addressed implicitly the question of "how African Americans can remain culturally moored and psychologically whole
while participating in economic enterprises that almost guarantee fragmentation" (*Toward Wholeness* 115). It is this question that the image of
"distance of the mind" answers, by establishing a perspective from which
the spiritual and the material are held together in the same twofold
vision. The techniques of superimposition Marshall uses throughout the
novel to fuse the past with the present, the metaphysical with the physical,
the individual with the collective, the New World with Africa, literal journeys with metaphorical journeys,[32] are *formal enactments, in the narrative,*
of the wholeness paradoxically created through this distance of the mind.

Not only does this distance prevent the "fragmentation" almost guaranteed by the struggle to acquire material comfort; it is the perspective necessary for assuring that people can be fed "in all their hungers."

One expects in a novel of old age some treatment of the issue of the decay and dissolution of the flesh.[33] Marshall's novel both meets and deflects this expectation, describing her aging protagonists' spiritual rebirth in old age as a rebirth of the body and its hungers, a restoration of lost sexuality. The deflection reinforces the political and economic themes of the novel. For in *Praisesong* the dissolution of the body is not a consequence of old age but a violent dis(re)memberment, expressed physically in Avey's loss of sexuality—a disconnection from the body so extreme that she cannot recognize her own reflection. The dissolution of self brought about first by entrapment in the material circumstances of poverty and then by entrapment in white materialism is a degeneration into the stasis of object. Flesh is transubstantiated into stocks, bonds, property, commodities, units of capital; the body, disremembered so that what is African in it is lost, is dismembered into its component parts, the individual scattered among the dry bones of the other dismembered selves with which it should be in connection.

"Only as subjects can we speak. . . ." The opposite of the objectification that is dis(re)memberment in *Praisesong*, most painfully experienced in the hold of the slaver, is the resurrection implied in the name of the ship in which Avey has that experience, the *Emmanuel C.* The double visions achieved through this name exemplify the kind of superimpositions Marshall achieves through allegory. Slavery, like crucifixion, attempts to reduce the spirit to flesh; incarnation (Emmanuel, "God with us") is the spirit made flesh; resurrection is the triumph of spirit in the flesh. Metaphorically the *Emmanuel C* crosses the ocean in two directions at the same time, bearing Avey into physical bondage in the New World by transporting her as a slave in the airless hold and at the same time bearing her back home to her spiritual roots in Africa. This double journey is simultaneously crucifixion and resurrection, because what unifies the two journeys of the boat is their troping of memory, the opposite of the objectification that is dis(re)memberment.

The final memory that surfaces for Avey is a memory of her true name, another version of "Emmanuel." It stands for the link between individual and community that is necessary to sustain a collective life by remembering it, incarnating the past continually in the present. Avey's calling of her true name—Avatara—confirms the knowledge the old people express in their unexpected genuflections: a seeing through to the self in Avey that is an avatar of something larger, communal.[34] Just as Jay "emerged from the music every evening" as "the self that would never be seen down at the store," Avey's self—an Avatara incarnating other selves—emerges from the music of the Big Drum ceremony. This self made whole by incarnating others is a redeemed version of Jerome Johnson's self that, incarnating profoundly other selves by speaking for white pride, lost wholeness by making *itself* other. *Praisesong for the Widow* means both a praisesong for the widow to sing — a fellowship of voice in which to merge her isolated self — and also a song of praise *for herself*.[35] Having sunk to reverent awe before the computer console that controls the movements of the *Bianca Pride*, Avey ends by reverencing African-American heritage, honoring herself and being honored as one of its avatars.

An avatar is an incarnation; incarnation is an embodying of the spiritual. Once again this superimposition of the metaphysical and the material as Marshall represents it has to do with voice. To incarnate Aunt Cuney's grandmother, the ancestor for whom she was named, Avey must speak the words the grandmother spoke. As Angelita Reyes says, the grandmother "never lost sight of the Word, or Nommo, as empowerment. In this instance, Nommo is female energy. . . . The tale is the empowerment of the Nommo" (188). The initial setting for this empowerment will be North White Plains and the "glacier buildings" of Manhattan (255); its audience will be "those young, bright, fiercely articulate token few for whom her generation had worked the two and three jobs," whom Avey will accost like the Ancient Mariner: "As they rushed blindly in and out of the glacier buildings, unaware, unprotected, lacking memory and a necessary distance of the mind (no mojo working for them!), she would stop them and before they could pull out of her grasp, tell them about the floor in Halsey Street and quote them the line from her namesake . . ." (255).

In this image the audience for Avey's transmission of the Nommo is defined specifically as those who think they speak well: "those . . . fiercely articulate token few." The word "articulate," however, is a marker of and from the vocabulary of a (white) voice external to them, belonging as it does to the repertoire of mildly surprised, racist praise bestowed on "a token few" as seals of approval for successfully assimilating to white speech patterns. The word "fiercely," on the other hand, suggests the iron determination with which these young people have struggled for this articulateness, which must be in certain senses a loss of voice. And it bespeaks their tacit sense that, for all their assimilation to the "glacier" world in which they make their living, they are as vulnerable here as all the other images make them out to be — blind, unaware, unprotected. There is "no mojo working for them," the mojo having been precisely Jay and Avey's intimate talk, with its satirical reversals that rejected cultural "passing." Their desperate motion is the circular motion of Avey's wintry exile as that mojo failed. Their rushing "in and out of the glacier buildings" recalls all of her sojourns in frozen white wastelands (North White Plains, the "glacier" cruise ship, the ski-slope-shaped white hotel) where the stasis of her circular motion presented an unapprehended mortal danger.

The journey to Carriacou requires a different language for the island-ers—their original patois, which they insist on speaking exclusively as soon as they get to the wharf (76). Avey's journey with them issues likewise in a new language for her—or rather, a return from her "special intim-idating silence" (21) to the language of her origins. Aunt Cuney's sum-mons of Avey back to Africa by way of Tatem and the landing is identical with the summons for Avey to take up a legacy of women's voices be-queathed by the grandmother who continued to speak through Aunt Cuney, whose voice, now silenced, Avey is called to reincarnate in her own.[36] " 'It was here that they brought them,' she would begin—as had been ordained" (256). This "coming to voice" to which Aunt Cuney calls Avey is different from that Merle achieves—less individualistic, more ritualized. It is to be part of a collective remembering, a speaking of words that have been, as in all inherited rituals, "ordained." And this remember-ing is the essence of bell hooks's "re-membering": a reunifying of frag-ments into a whole self, and of reunified selves into a whole community.

4

"Afrocentric communication maintains the integrity of the individual and his or her personal voice, but does so in the context of group activity" (Collins 99). The African-American feminist vision of this novel centers around its working out of the way a woman can maintain her integrity as an individual and the integrity of her individual voice in the context, on the one hand, of a sexism that Marshall portrays as always interwoven with racism and, on the other, of the need for African-American women to speak together, collectively, in the voice of a "larger . . . 'self' of black people" that includes both women and men. One aspect of Avey's self-loss in the thirty years of her exile is her co-transformation with her husband into something alien to herself. A comparison with two white feminist novels is illuminating. Like Avey's awakening, Edna Pontellier's is associated with the casting off of a non-self represented in clothing imagery: "It sometimes entered Mr. Pontellier's mind to wonder if his wife were not growing a little unbalanced mentally. He could see plainly that she was not herself. That is, he could not see that she was becoming herself and daily casting aside that fictitious self which we assume like a garment with which to appear before the world" (Chopin 1047). Sim-ilarly, in Doris Lessing's *The Summer before the Dark*, Kate also sheds a false self and the habit of trying on opinions as one would try on dresses from a rack. But in neither case is the protagonist's husband also associated with the same compulsion to "wear the mask," as is the case with Avey and

Jay. By portraying the tyrannies of race, gender, and class as aspects of each other, Marshall presents the issue of Avey's false self in a more complex way. On the one hand, Avey's false self is a mirror image of her husband's personality (the tyranny of gender); on the other, this personality she mirrors is also false, a construction of the tyranny of race as it in turn is shaped by (and shapes) an African-American family's experience of class in the 1950s and 1960s. Avey's transformation into Jerome's "twin" is the result of all these tyrannies in interaction.

The deft subtlety with which Marshall captures that interaction culminates in the sequence of events leading up to Avey's claiming of her name at the Big Drum ceremony. On the white balcony Avey has a horrified vision of her own face at her funeral, overlaid with the same white stranger's face that triumphed over Jay. Perhaps, she fears, her children will hear the same laugh that exulted over Jay's "immutable silence." But this fear is projected into the future; no white face is described as actually having overtaken Avey. Instead it is implicitly *Jay's* face that has superimposed itself on her to make her his twin as his struggle for self-reliance in a racist economy takes its toll on both their bodies. An out-islander sees in Avey another face — sees her, in fact, as the "twin" of a Carriacouan she has never met. After mistakenly calling her Ida, the man reassures her, "Don' ever let anybody tell you, my lady, that you ain' got a twin in this world!" (72). Avey is swept by a rush of indignation — "Twins!" Such comparisons always suggest that after all one has less individual integrity, is less special and unique, than one had imagined. But Avey's woman-twin is the reflection of her own African past — that is, of a *genuine* self — whereas her man-twin looked like her because, as his wife, she had been made into his image by the double pressure of the racism that transformed him into Jerome Johnson in the same ways it transformed her, and the sexism that drew her inexorably into being "Avey Johnson" — a woman who could not call her own name, even in her mind, without attaching her husband's name to it. The encounter with the man who calls her Ida is a redeemed version of the scenes in which she sees herself in the mirror as someone she doesn't know. Here, she is herself the mirror image of someone she doesn't know, as a stranger who doesn't know her "recognizes" her anyway.

In the early days Avey's unity with Jay — the unity of voice that made up their "mojo," for example — was something good: a solidarity. Paradoxically, their twinship actually represented a separation from each other in which their bodies, identically tensed by their ordeal, could no longer communicate in the language they used to speak. That language, again paradoxically, drew them together because it allowed so fully for the expression of their individual selves. When at the height of the Big Drum ceremony Avey reasserts her individuality by moving away from Jerome's white voice, it thus follows naturally that she should recover his African-American voice speaking the language of the private rituals that united them most closely as a couple. At the moment she frees herself to act on her own accord, she recovers her intimacy with Jay, even as the individuality of her dancing, full of her own special "stylishness and sass," mirrors the Ring Shout she used to imitate as a child in Tatem.

These acts uniting individuation with connection culminate when Avey voices her name not as "Avey Johnson" (showing that, no longer Jerome Johnson's twin, she is defining herself on her own terms, separate from her husband), or even as Avey Williams (she establishes an identity by separating herself also from her father's name), or even as plain Avey (and here we see that merely stripping down to an individual self is not enough), but as both "Avey" and what that name is "short for": *Avatara*, the singular name that nonetheless establishes her as not singular at all but the slave grandmother's double. "Rather than defining self in opposition to others, the connectedness among individuals provides Black women deeper . . . self-definitions" (Collins 106).

The Chosen Place and *Brown Girl* end with women as makers of journeys. *Praisesong* ends with a woman as the leader of journeys, a speaker, even an oracle—a ceremonial speaker who affirms her heritage by passing her voice down to the next generation, making them heirs, as she was heir, to a woman's voice. On her way to the airport at the end of *The Chosen Place* Merle is engaged in a mental journey, already gone like the grandmother with the Ibos, having achieved what Avey would term "a necessary distance of the mind" (255). As Collier points out, the grandmother Avatara "expresses a vital dynamic of displaced Africans—the body here, the mind there. She, however, is aware of the split, and for her it is an extension, another dimension of the self" (311). In other words, doubleness is part of Avatara's victimization as a slave, but she turns it to her use as a power, much as the people of Bournehills transform their dispossession into determined self-possession, their enforced stasis into a refusal to be moved, their enforced silence into resistance. Avatara thus stands for the distance of mind Avey sees at the end of the novel as "necessary," so that when Avey comes to incarnate her, that is what she is incarnating—the "vital dynamic" Collier describes.

In all of Paule Marshall's books, a woman's recovery of voice is a recovery of kinship with other women. *Brown Girl* ends with the recovery of a mother, as Selina leaves for the Caribbean to root herself in her mother's past. *The Chosen Place* ends with Merle's journey to recover a lost daughter. *Praisesong* ends with Avey's recovery of a daughter whom she had tried to abort, and whom, in her self-alienation, she succeeded temporarily in losing: Marion, who even in infancy promised to have more to say than her older sisters.[37] Just as Avey's journey to Grenada and Carriacou reminded her of Tatem and her own childhood, it also reminded her often of this daughter, who is never present directly in the action but whose voice keeps rising in Avey's mind. Marion has already identified with a collective suffering that goes beyond her individual life — the "hungry roar" in the background of her phone call — and has made the journey to Africa. Born after the Halsey Street rituals had faded, Marion had to seek out her heritage for herself, angry at what she saw as her mother's "infuriating silence" (14), so alienated from her father that by the time of the Poor People's March they "hardly spoke to each other" (141).

"I was not willing to be orphaned by silence," Jewelle Gomez says (205). "Cast out" and "banished" like the Eskimo woman, Avey begins her journey of freedom when a woman's voice, breaking the silence in her memory, draws her back into a network of kin. By claiming a voice, Avey claims her past through relationships to her great-aunt, her great-aunt's grandmother, and the Ibos who rejected slavery. She also claims the future by reclaiming Marion, orphaned by the silence in her parents' memory. As a journeyer home and rescuer of memory, Avey recovers her motherhood by recovering this lost daughter, who begged her to travel to Africa, scorning the *Bianca Pride*—insisted, that is, that she remember who she was. By so doing, Avey also reaches out like a mother to all the dispossessed children who have had no voice to reclaim for them their lost past — the Ibos' exile and their journey home.

Merle, too, ends as a rescuer of memory, a traveler, and a speaker. Her journey begins at the end of *The Chosen Place* with an affirmation of her motherhood, the trip to Africa to reclaim her child. Whatever the result, the voice with which she speaks thereafter, like Avey's at the end of *Praisesong*, is a mother's voice. This is the voice Paule Marshall celebrates in all her work — a voice strongly individualistic but also strongly collective: the voice of her own mother, which she heard in the kitchen as a child and with which she merged hers as a writer; the voice to which she paid tribute in her portrait of Silla. The mother's voice at the end of *Praisesong* will speak up against the materialistic values, rooted in an ideology of white supremacy, that warped Silla's power to their own ends. Even so, Marshall's final conception of Avey is not far from her first portrayal of a mother who, "in this white-man world," could "take [her] mouth and make a gun" (*Brown Girl* 70). Silla is betrayed into using her voice in collaboration with forces inimical to it and to her. But even as she arrives with the white policeman to destroy Deighton's haven of Peace, her indomitable personality stands apart from the alien power into whose service she has put it temporarily, just as, in the deafening roar of the machines at the war factory, the whine of her individual lathe rises for a moment above the sound of the others (*Brown Girl* 99–100). Despite the use to which she is allowing it to be put, Silla's strong voice, propelled by an "indestructible will" (*Praisesong* 161) like that of the old people on Carriacou, bespeaks her power, and the power of all the other women whose voices speak in hers, "to stay the course of history" (*Praisesong* 250).

This is the same power Avey evinces at the end of *Praisesong for the Widow*, having joined the timeless dance of people who live as if, like Aunt Cuney, they had "outfox[ed] the grave" (41). In Avey this power is more genial, more generous than Silla's, much more the function of a power struggle resolved than one in which, as in Silla's case, she is still embroiled. Merle also achieves a sense of power like that Avey achieves, but after an almost lifelong struggle for it. Avey's comes to her like grace: a gift of the spirit at the end of her turmoil on the threshing floor. Avey's escape from silence and stasis through ceremonial speech, song, and dance implies the connection that ritual establishes between temporal life in a world of material realities and a spiritual source of empowerment beyond the "things of earth."

The figures who lead her to the rituals she needs belong to this transcendent, atemporal source of power. There is an otherworldly quality to Aunt Cuney's dream-summons and Lebert Joseph's sudden appearance just at the right time. One is a figure from beyond the grave; the other is the archetypal guide-across-the-threshold of the hero journey as well as the ancient protean trickster of African folklore (Collier 312).[38] Bercita Edwards, who brings Avey finally to speak her true name, has a face like that of a skeleton — "a ravaged landscape of dark hollows and caves where her wrinkled flesh had collapsed in on the bone" (251), as if she also had escaped the grave. In addition, the "wispy white hairs" on her chin make her "An old woman who was at once an old man. Tiresias of the dried dugs" (251). With his simultaneous male and female life history Tiresias is, like Lebert Joseph, another figure for the uncanny knowledge that comes from double perspectives. In their conflation of life and death, their magical status as beings of the real world and some Other world, and their various kinds of doubleness, all of these guide-figures embody a "distance of the mind" (255) from temporal reality. They lead Avey to a recognition of her kinship with them, as an avatar of the collective memories they also represent.

In contrast, to the extent that Merle has an external impetus, something she has been hoping will "happen . . . apart from me . . . to bring me back to myself" as she says (230), it is the combination of the carnival and Saul. Saul is deeply flawed, full of self-doubts, by no means a guide — the polar opposite of Lebert Joseph with his infallible immemorial wisdom, Aunt Cuney with her absolute certainty of the path Avey should take, Bercita Edwards with her *gain connaissance* like that of Tiresias. Avey's and Merle's journeys of freedom differ correspondingly. Carriacou, as Avey sees it from the plane, seems "more a mirage rather than an actual place.

Something conjured up perhaps to satisfy a longing and a need" (254). The trip to Carriacou is the last, crucial part of the journey presented to Avey as by magic — as if, like the words in Aunt Cuney's story, it "had been ordained." Merle sells almost everything she has to get back to Africa, an unburdening of material possessions somewhat like Avey's casting off of the psychological burden of her material inheritance, and producing a similar relief, but again the result of a longer struggle. Merle lives in a desperate search for wholeness for eight years or more, her bedroom a symbol of her "conflicting parts" (401). Avey lives for some eighteen years in her elegant, well-ordered world without acknowledging her lack of self-reconciliation.[39] Once she sees it, however, a ritual for becoming whole is magically available to her and, having found herself "buried," as the preacher would say, she is resurrected in the space of three days.[40]

All these differences contribute to the difference in tone between the endings of Marshall's most overtly political novel and what is, on the surface, her least political novel. Two striking images bring *The Chosen Place* to a close. One is the fiery legacy of an old revolution that will be rekindled in the future; the other is the destructive, regenerative rain. Both are part of the subject announced in the title of book 1, "Heirs and Descendants." *Praisesong* ends with images of generations and their continuities, the theme of "Heirs and Descendants" from *The Chosen Place* but without the bitter overtones the words take from that novel's concern with old wrongs that never die. There is no revolutionary fire on the final page of Avey's story; the image would not fit the tone of the ending, which has a serenity and sense of completeness, of having arrived at a goal long sought, that recalls other novels of old age and acceptance. But the peace and self-reconciliation are infused with a promise "of possibilities and becoming" (249) that one would ordinarily associate with the ending of a novel of adolescence: a sense of vocation achieved, the proper quest finally embarked upon. *Praisesong for the Widow* ends with a sense of arrival, after so many years, not at a resting place but at the right point of departure.

Nor is the youthful quality of missionary zeal in Avey's resolve to tell strangers her tale and lay claim to her grandsons every summer, as Aunt Cuney laid claim to her, grounded solely in the joy of a homecoming to African-American culture. Like the Ibos' journey of freedom, Avey's is a response to what her expanded vision showed her when she took a long, hard look at the life white people intended her to have. Merle must incorporate the memories of slavery, colonialism, her father's racist exploitation of her mother, and First World violence against Bournehills — memories of being overpowered — into whatever self-empowerment she can achieve. In the same way, Avey's liberation of her powers requires that she remember the search for her daughters in the rubble of the Birmingham church, hear again the thud of the billy club and the white stranger's laugh above her husband's silence, relive her original passage to America in the hold of a slave ship. These almost intolerable memories inform her joyous reconnection with African-American heritage just as, even at the most ecstatic center of the ceremony on Carriacou, the drummer pauses occasionally to play a "single, dark, plangent note" distilling "a thousand sorrow songs" (244).

As in prophetic African-American Christianity, Avey's recovered religion of the landing is no mere turning of vision upward to pie in the sky. The distance of mind and heart that Avey achieves is the double vision of the novel itself. This vision is rooted in anger at white violence, insisting that anger be recovered where it has been repressed, but it is also full of spiritual calm. It is infused with rage at material dispossession and with joy in the possession, at the same time, of a spiritual plenitude that scorns material excess. For all its sacramental overtones, Avey's vocation as a speaker and journeyer is as deeply rooted in political vision as Merle's. The "miracle" she will commemorate is a slave revolt; the story "ordained" for her to tell is a story of spiritual, intellectual, and physical resistance to oppression.[41] By the same token, "the struggle . . . against forgetting" is as political in this novel as in *The Chosen Place*, because to rescue African-American memory in a context in which the cause of forgetting is white violence is a revolutionary act. In Avey's and Jay's lives the primary, most pervasive expression of white violence was through an economic system that fostered African-American poverty. To escape that poverty, they bought — or were sold — into "the glitter and the excess" of this system whose basis in white supremacy defined them as having "nothing about themselves worth honoring" (139). The cold "snowy wastes" into which Jay vanished and Avey was exiled in the wake of that violence recall images from other feminist novels about aging: Margaret Drabble's *The Ice Age* and Lessing's *The Summer Before the Dark*, for example. But in *Praisesong* the snow represents more than the coldness of death; it represents, specifically, the threat that assimilation to white culture poses to a Black soul. The real battle Avey must wage is not against old age and death but against this death-in-life — emblematized in the rich white man who should be alive but is already a skeleton. At the same time, it is a battle on behalf of the life emblematized in the "bare bones" of the Carriacou ceremony, in the skeletal but vigorous Bercita Edwards, and in Aunt Cuney, who should be a skeleton but is not: a life that outfoxes even the grave.

The trickster-magician-guide who conjures up the "mirage" of Carriacou "to satisfy a longing and a need" is not Esu or Bercita or Aunt Cuney, of course, but Avey, whose power of expanded vision turns a literal journey to Carriacou into the spiritual journey she needs, making a real journey imaginary just as the mythmaking powers of a slave made the Ibos' imaginary journey real. The Avey who "emerge[s] from the music" of the Big Drum is Marshall's portrait of the artist as an old woman — one who, like Lebert Joseph, uses her dearly bought *gain connaissance* to win the "wager with death." Like Joseph, Bercita, and Aunt Cuney, she triumphs over the grave by affirming her individuality through identification with the "larger self . . . of black people." As Mary Helen Washington says, "Black women who struggle to 'forge an identity larger than the one society would force upon them . . . are aware and conscious, and that very consciousness is potent.' "[42] The power of Avey's magical guide-figures is not external to her; it is the potency of her consciousness in the act of re-membering and resurrecting itself.

Knee bone connected to the leg bone
Leg bone connected to the ankle bone . . .
Them bones, them bones, them a-dry bones . . .
Oh, hear the word of the L-O-R-D!

Jay sang Ezekiel's story on Sundays with the Five Blind Boys: "like spirits ascending, black voices rose" (124). Aunt Cuney can rise from the grave, after all, because Avey has the power, despite the violence done her, to re-member herself and the "larger self" she incarnates. It takes "cunning," she has realized, to achieve the "distance of the mind and heart" that sustains the journey of freedom. By the end of the novel the great-aunt's cunning in outfoxing the grave is Avey's, and the voice that rises with Aunt Cuney's resurrection is Avey's own.

Chapter 4
Daughters
Conflations of Discourse

The two basic challenges presently confronting Afro-Americans are self-image and self-determination. The former is the perennial human attempt to define who and what one is, the issue of self-identity. The latter is the political struggle to gain significant control over the major institutions that regulate people's lives. These challenges are abstractly distinguishable, yet concretely inseparable.

— Cornel West, *Prophesy Deliverance*

"You begin everything with 'My father says this or that' or 'My father's gonna give me this or that' — but what do *you* say, what do *you* want?"

"I don't understand," Beryl began and turned to the others, then swung back to Selina. "I say the same thing he says."

— *Brown Girl, Brownstones*

1

Toward the end of *Daughters* the protagonist has a dream similar to Avey's at the beginning of *Praisesong for the Widow.* Her former lover tugs urgently at her arm as she resists — so forcefully that they are soon fighting each other in "an all-out brawl," to the glee of the white observers on Columbus Avenue: "Go to it! Go to it! A battle royal. A nigger show" (383). Ursa's old thesis advisor from college, the one who rejected her proposal to study egalitarian relations among women and men in slave communities, is there among the yuppies, "jubilantly waving" the proposal he suppressed. The similarities with Avey's dream are obvious: the urgent, desperate force of the African-American figure who draws the heroine physically, even violently, back into a dyad she has tried to leave behind; the nightmarish sense that the dreamer's private, inner conflicts must be fought out in a public arena where their meanings are up for grabs by unsympathetic spectators; the dangerous, disorienting effect of class conflict on the heroine caught in its vortex; the presence of a history teacher (Crowder, Aunt Cuney) involved in the rescue — or suppression — of memory.

The differences between the dreams are equally striking. The most obvious is the change in the sex of the heroine's antagonist, which raises a host of issues about what Ursa's thesis proposal referred to as "gender roles and relationships" (11). The same issues are raised by Marshall's signifying on yet another novel,[1] evoked in the reference to a battle royal and three earlier references to Ursa's tendency to "disappear down some manhole" (7, 84, 329). The presence of *Invisible Man* as a subtext in *Daughters* is a tribute to the fiction of an author whose essays Marshall has often identified as a major influence on her work. Within that context, however, *Daughters* elaborates many shades of difference between Ralph Ellison's account of an African-American man and Marshall's feminist vision of African-American women, men, and their relations some forty years later. In *Daughters*, the images of an invisible man — and an invisible woman and even an invisible couple — comment not only on race and class relations but also on gender relations, and on the mutually shaping interactions among them.

Central to this commentary is Marshall's consideration of voice and silence, which has broadened here to include a consideration of many kinds of discourse as they are shaped by gender, race, class, family structures, and the relations between the First and Third Worlds. One part of this concern is with the relation between public and private forms of discourse, an illusory dichotomy that the novel collapses through a system of superimpositions. Depicting these two forms of discourse as interdependent, even identical, the novel offers another dichotomy in their place: on the one hand, kinds of discourse that sustain oppressive hierarchies by producing silence, division, and invisibility; on the other, decolonizing acts of speech that make connections, establish equality, and subvert or destabilize hierarchies by violating the rules of discourse that help maintain them. These issues emerge in their complexity in a set of episodes that double-expose the public and the private: political speeches and a bedroom conversation, academic prose and lovers' talk, spoken words and the interior conversations of the psyche. One of these episodes is Ursa's dream of the public battle royal, together with the intimate, private scenes to which it alludes. Another is the private argument between Estelle and Primus about whether to attend the Planning and Development Board reception, together with Estelle's subsequent public performance of "Statues," replete with private but simultaneously political meanings directed at Primus. The last is Ursa's heroine-journey, with her private, preparatory reenactment of a public ritual on the beach at Government Lands and the subsequent fulfillment of her two tasks:

to disrupt Primus's final campaign speech and to initiate a conversation with his keep-miss, which becomes a private counterpart of his public silencing.

Related to the conflation of the public and private in these episodes is the fact that throughout them the interactions among gender, voice, class, race, discourse, and power are played out in the double realm of the psychological and the political, which are superimposed in ways that build on the techniques of the earlier novels. The core of this superimposition is the heroine's relationship with her father, whom even she calls by his political nickname, "the PM."[2] Her psychological struggle for autonomy from him, which parallels and in the end actually becomes part of his and Triunion's political struggle for independence from the United States, points to what Cornel West describes as the inseparability of "the issue of self-identity" and "the political struggle to gain significant control over the major institutions that regulate people's lives" (22). The question of "gender roles and relationships" comes to center on precisely this intersection, where the women characters' triple struggle for personal independence, political independence, and mutually sustaining relationships is most fraught with potential contradiction, and where the interrelations among the mother's voice, the father's voice, and children's voices become the crux of political and psychological conflict.

In keeping with the many double visions of the novel is its focus on couples, including two pairs of sister/friends, one African-Caribbean and one African-American, as well as the long-term lesbian couple on whose support Ursa's friend Viney calls in an emergency. This couple, mentioned only briefly, is perhaps at the end of the "lesbian continuum" on which the other two women couples could be somewhere located.[3] Astral, who touches her friend Malvern "for the first time ever" when she is dying, interprets Viney and Ursa as "bare bare wickers" (312); Malvern responds that maybe lesbians "have the right idea" (312). The couple on whom Viney calls for help have been in a stable relationship since college, as have Viney and Ursa in their friendship, which is sustained by talk.

The dialogue of women, their "intimate, loving palaver" (87), is perhaps the single kind of discourse most valorized in the book, whose climax centers upon women bridging gaps between themselves through conversation. Emerging for a moment from her stampeding monologue that circles angrily around Primus, Astral's eyes finally "clear long enough for her to actually see" the dying Malvern (311); Ursa opens up in a conversation with her mother while Primus sleeps; Astral and Ursa talk in an explosion of honesty that defies Primus's method of keeping them apart. These conversations take place outside the circle of the father's voice and destabilize the hierarchies in which, true to his name, he holds the prime position. There are of course many other hierarchies in which his position is subordinate instead, and the intersection of his silencing in those hierarchies with his silencing of women in the heterosexual couples of which he forms a part is one of the subjects of the novel. The same kind of intersection is a major problem in Ursa's relationship with her lover Lowell. Both of these pairings, and the complicated interplay of gender, race, class, silence, and voice they involve, are at issue in Ursa's dream of the battle royal.

2

In the background of the battle royal dream is the problem to which its literary signifying alludes: that of the invisible man. On one level, this is the same problem that reverberates through Ellison's novel, in which the dispossessed hero's invisibility is bound up with the dispossession of his voice. On another and interestingly related level, Marshall's version of the invisible man is summed up in the dilemma Viney describes in part as "The black men-black women ratio thing" (71). Her search for a man who will be "useful" (102), unlike her fickle lover Willis, has its political parallel in Mae Ryland's search for a candidate: "The right one's got to be out there somewheres . . ." (299).

Such passages point to a major preoccupation of the novel: what women like Viney, Mae, and Ursa see as African-American men's disappearance from African-American women's world — politically, psychologically, economically, emotionally, sexually, and just plain demographically.[4] This problem of the invisible man takes its most striking form in Viney's image of herself at the police station after her son's arrest, with "this hole the size of me next to me . . . the wind pouring through it. . . . the outline, the space where some decent, halfway-together black man should have been. . . . it's not that I can't manage on my own. Hey, I'm doing it every day! It's about dealing with what's still out there . . ." (330–31).

The image of Viney standing next to a blank, man-shaped space in her personal/political battle for her son against "what's still out there" belongs at one pole of a series of images of Black heterosexual couples confronting the institutions that regulate their lives. At the other pole is the statue of Will Cudjoe and Congo Jane: "Coleaders, coconspirators, consorts, lovers, friends. You couldn't call her name without calling his, and vice-versa, they had been that close" (14). Somewhere in the middle of the series are Mae Ryland and Sandy Lawson raising their clasped hands at the end of Sandy's campaign speeches. Somewhere in the middle, too, are Ursa's parents "like bas-relief heads on a medallion or a specially minted commemorative coin" (356), with Estelle's "profile . . . superimposed on the PM's" (355). The "coin" commemorates, presumably, their early political campaigns, but also the struggles of people like Jane and Will who preceded them. Also in the middle, but closest to the pole represented by Jane and Will, is the picture of Justin Beaufils and his wife, crusading for Triunion's freedom from colonial dependency, writing their position papers and making their speeches together, sharing the podium equally (304).

All of these images of women and men united as couples — at times, in fact, fused or "superimposed" — have to do with speech. This is true even of Viney's picture of the man-shaped absence, which is, among other things, an image of a man-shaped silence. As this image suggests, *Daughters* is about the gendering of African-American invisibility and about the role played in that gendering by the suppression of voice. But it is also about the potential for a revolution in gender roles implied in an equalizing of voice: a revolution that Marshall portrays as necessarily going hand in hand with the struggle for racial equality if the latter is to succeed. In this novel, revolutions fought by heterosexual couples in which the woman has an unequal voice eventually fall prey to betrayal, as the man's silencing of the woman translates into a silencing of his constituents and even of himself. Mae, for example, shares equally in the work of Sandy's mayoral campaign, but her role in the public discourse of the campaign is as a warm-up speaker who then takes her place, whether on or offstage, in the audience. Afterward, she strides with "a few brisk Congo Jane steps" to clasp raised hands with him (280). The image for that one moment is of equals. But Mae's inequality of voice in this partnership is a forecast of what comes later, when Sandy's highway project ends her brief role as South Ward liaison. Mae's warm-up speeches pictured Sandy making people of color visible at City Hall, a visibility she equated with opportunity to speak at the center of power: " ' . . . Useta be the only black face you ever saw in there was the janitor's. . . . there's gonna be a lot more black, beige and brown to be seen up in all white that's been there since forever, a lot more of us having a say . . ." (274–75). Thus it is particularly ironic that, far from giving African Americans more visibility at City Hall, Sandy collaborates to protect white commuters and visitors from the sight of the ghetto. Not surprisingly, his sellout heralds Mae's departure from a center of government dominated by whites who, she says, "couldn't stand the sight of me down there" (296).

The issues of silence and invisibility here raise one of the novel's major questions, the question of the different roles that Black male and female representative voices play in regard to the hegemonic discourses of white political and economic power. Mae's role as liaison, listening to the people's voice and speaking their concerns to their male representative, is as a subordinate, mediating voice between two voices in a chain of communication — a typical woman's role in many contexts. Ominously, the man on the top of such a chain does not listen directly to the voice at the bottom. The woman's voice operates as a signifier of that other voice, but because of its subordination as a mediating link, what it most obviously signifies is the silence of those at the bottom of the chain as well as its own, intermediate silence. Thus it is hardly surprising that after a brief time Sandy treats Mae's voice in exactly this way — as an absence. Far from transmitting the people's voice any further, he no longer even hears it through the intermediary. And the silencing of his constituents is equated with their invisibility, even to him. "[To] run a road through us," Mae exclaims, "like we ain't even here" (294).

The silencing of the ward's female representative is not merely representative of the ward's silencing; what Marshall represents through Mae's story is far more subtle. In the sequence of events that leads to Mae's demotion, an African-American woman's gender subordination in the discourse of a political campaign, reinscribed as the subordination of her voice in the political discourse of City Hall, *is the same as* the race and class subordination not only of herself and other African-American women but of African-American men as well, including Sandy. For Mae's disappearance from City Hall in response to Sandy's sellout signals his absence from the center of power too, despite his ostensible presence. Thus the image of him and Mae on the stage after his stirring speech, clasping hands high like Jane and Will, is replaced by another: Sandy descending a flight of steps flanked by two white men, who talk to him simultaneously as he looks back and forth like a spectator at a tennis match (285). Sandy has become a gap, a silence — a "windy hole" (380), as Viney would say — between the whites who control the discourse into which he has succeeded only too well in insinuating himself.

The gap that is Sandy in this image is precisely the hollow core on which the stability of the hegemonic discourse of Midland City Hall depends. He personifies the invisible space, the silence, walled up at the core of that discourse. And the personification is a reminder that it is, after all, not just voices but *persons* whom this kind of discourse is designed to contain. The men between whom Sandy is wedged look like plainclothesmen, Ursa recognizes later, and the ride he takes with them looks like an arrest. The other arrest in the book is of Robeson, for talking back to a white police officer. Both incidents are about arresting speech — about consolidating an oppressive hierarchy by silencing African-American males. That fact renders even more ironic the police officer's emphasis on "*Ms.*" Daniel's lack of a man to join her in speaking on her son's behalf.

Marshall presents a similar but even more nuanced picture of the connections among gender, silence, and Black invisibility in the portrait of Estelle. Like Mae, Estelle is allotted a subordinate place in the discourse of a man's political campaign, this time as speaker of "a few words" after the main speech (131, 230). And like Mae, although more unofficially, she comes to take on the role of liaison with the impoverished district the candidate represents. As Primus becomes more and more a puppet of white interests, he increasingly delegates to Estelle this job of listening to his constituents while he betrays her with his mistress Astral and betrays his constituents with what comes more and more to be his master, the Planning and Development Board. The argument over whether Estelle will attend the Board's reception for what she scorns as "visiting firemen" (226) from the United States illuminates the dynamics of voice, power, gender, and discourse that Marshall explores through their relationship. When Estelle complains, in this dispute, that Primus is no longer around to hear what his constituents are saying, she is raising, in *her* representative voice, the issue of Primus's increasingly unrepresentative voice. As they argue in their bedroom, Primus's domestic conversation with Estelle, who is speaking both as his wife and as the liaison for Morlands, shifts toward public oration: " 'Wha' the rass, Estelle, do you think that any of us . . . like having to run behind these white people with our hand long out? Do you? . . .' His voice rose. He stepped to the edge of the platform out at the monument" (234).

The conflation of public and private discourse at this moment underlines the equivalence between Estelle's gender inequality in her relationship with Primus on the one hand and, on the other, the inequality between Primus's constituents and the white powers with whom he is slipping into alliance. What he actually says to Estelle in his self-defense, however, adds complications beyond those explored in the story of Sandy and Mae. Primus's bitter reference to himself as "a so-called representative of the people" shows that he understands painfully the issue Estelle is raising (232). With nothing hopeful to say to his constituents, he absents himself from their gathering in the hope of speaking on their behalf at the gathering of United States businessmen. Ironically, this choice shows to what extent Primus's ability to speak to his constituents, be there to hear their voices, and voice their concerns to "the great people — Them!" are all dependent on his ability to intervene successfully in a discourse that, as Estelle sees much more clearly than he, excludes his voice by definition. To Primus's statement that he will propose a cannery for Morlands, with a housing scheme for the workers, she responds immediately, "No, you won't! You'll talk about what they want to talk about. . . . Infrastructure. We never have enough infrastructure for them. How I hate that word. I've seen it happen every time, and I've had it!' " (234).

In her essay "Sex and Death in the Rational World of Defense Intellectuals," Carol Cohn has shown that in the language of defense analysts with its vocabulary of "clean bombs," "collateral damage," and "Christmas tree farms" and its lack of a word for peace, a perspective that takes into account the value of human life is not simply absent; it *cannot be voiced*. The discourse does not admit of it. "This language," she says, "does not allow certain questions to be asked or certain values to be expressed" (128). It is, for example, impossible in the vocabulary of nuclear defense-speak "to talk about humans" (131). Not only is the language narrow; more dangerously, "it is seen by its speakers as complete or whole unto itself—as representing a body of truths that exist independently of any other truth or knowledge" (132). Marshall offers a similar perception here of the exigencies of "talking business" (234) in a neocolonial setting such as Triunion's P and D Board receptions. The people's interests Primus wants to represent simply cannot be spoken for in a discourse designed to represent United States business interests. To these interests the privileged word "infrastructure" represents a body of truths independent of the images of human need with which Primus, in his bedroom oration, moved Estelle to change her mind about attending the reception. In the business talk he must speak with the "firemen" there is, in contrast, no way to voice this need. The discourse does not admit of it. Thus Primus's efforts to speak about a cannery to the "firemen" succeed only in bringing him to a position similar to Sandy's position as a silent space enclosed by the discourse of white power. He ends by laughing and clinking glasses with the white men who refuse even to hear his idea as Estelle, who left the group in outrage, watches from the sidelines (239–40).

Despite the fact that the reader also watches through Estelle's and Mae's eyes, Marshall's portrait of Sandy and Primus is by no means unsympathetic. Especially in Primus's case she represents with painful clarity the kind of pressures that finally mire him in collusion with interests inimical to those of the people who elected him. In a different class context, the image of Primus genially clinking glasses is the image of Ferguson, choked with the unvoiced speech he had prepared, saying only "Fine, sir, thank you, sir." The difference in class, however, raises the question of whether Primus has more possibilities for power than Ferguson—a question Marshall presents, interestingly, through the lens not of class but of gender. Next to Primus, a man for whom this silence must be nearly intolerable, she positions a woman, Estelle, for whom it actually is intolerable, just as City Hall was intolerable for Mae after Sandy failed to give people of color more "say" (275).

This positioning raises the complex question of how unequal distributions of power among politically progressive women and men in their fight for justice are interwoven with the inequities they fight. Mae and Estelle's inequality of voice in their political partnerships with Sandy and Primus, signifier of their gender inequality more broadly, is of a piece with the class and racial inequality between these men's constituents and the white men to whom they sell out. This does not mean that Primus would have been more successful with the cannery if Estelle had had a bigger voice in his campaign, or that Sandy could have kept the highway out of the ward if Mae had shared the podium equally. It does mean that the unequal position the woman is assigned in each case is a measure of the man's potential for selling out. Quite literally the measure, because after the election, these women come to constitute the relationship between the voice of the people and the man's voice, so that the allotment of unequal voice to the woman predicts the man's eventual unequal allotment of voice to the people he supposedly represents. The woman's inequality in the political partnership turns out to be *the same thing* as the man's potential for being co-opted into perpetuating the class and racial inequalities that, together with gender inequality, sustain the political and economic system. In the struggles against oppression this novel depicts, failing to unite the struggles for race, class, and gender equality is a fatal flaw.

At least since the time of Sojourner Truth, feminist theorists have warned against this flaw, arguing the futility of fighting class, race, and gender oppression as if they existed in isolation from each other.[5] In Rose M. Brewer's words, "Social constructions of black womanhood and manhood are inextricably linked to racial hierarchy, meaning systems and institutionalization. Indeed, gender takes on meaning and is embedded institutionally in the context of the racial and class order: productive and social reproductive relations of the economy" (17). As the women of the Combahee River Collective put it, "We . . . often find it difficult to separate race from class from sex oppression because in our lives they are most often experienced simultaneously. We know that there is such a thing as racial-sexual oppression which is neither solely racial nor solely sexual, e.g., the history of rape of Black women by white men as a weapon of political repression" (275).

The relationship to which such analyses call attention—what is often called the "intersection" of gender, race, and class—has in recent years become the multiple focus of much feminist theory.[6] Actually describing this "intersection," however, is much more difficult than calling attention to it. Deborah King provides a useful model for exploring the "interactive oppressions" of racism, sexism, and classism operating as three "interdependent control systems" in "multiplicative relationships" (265, 270). In her model, the relative importance of any single factor—race, sex, or class—varies depending on "the socio-historic context and the social phenomenon under consideration" (272). Akin to King's method in its success at avoiding a hierarchizing of oppressions is Gerda Lerner's proposal for a model that sees race, class, ethnicity, and gender as "mutually constitutive" aspects of each other (see "Reconceptualizing Differences"). Even more successful, in a different vein, are some works on the experimental margin of feminist theorizing that escape completely the necessity for describing "interactive oppressions" in the linear, sequential exposition traditionally required of theoretical writing. Most notable here are such works as Patricia Williams's superimpositions of fiction, autobiography, allegory, parable, history, and legal theory, or Mab Segrest's simultaneously confessional and theoretical accounts of the processes whereby her racial, class, sexual, and religious identities were socially constructed.

Daughters is Paule Marshall's most ambitious use of superimpositions in this same project of rendering the ways in which the "interlocking" of oppressions actually operates. The differences between Avey's dream of Aunt Cuney and Ursa's dream of the battle royal reveal the increasing challenges she has set herself in fashioning a way to represent the "multiplicative effects" of various forms of dispossession. This is one of the most remarkable achievements of *Daughters*: its success in representing gender, class, and racial oppressions as forces that, in Elizabeth Minnich's words, "intersect, interact, coalesce, *and* differ" (68), all at the same time — forces working themselves out in the murky complications of people's daily lives.

Consider, for example, the way Avey's and Ursa's dreams portray silence as constructed by race, class, and gender. In *Praisesong* the summoner is silent, pleading for Avey to travel the ritual path that would lead her memory back down the ladder of upward mobility, away from the "special intimidating silence" born of the tension between her white-identified class standing and her African-American heritage. This path leads back to the old Avatara's voice at the landing and forward to the new Avatara's voice at the same site. It leads back, that is, to a silenced history of slave resistance and forward to the moment when, by voicing that history, the heroine can reenact the resistance, freeing herself and those to whom she speaks. At issue in this dream is the way racism works to suppress and repress the voice of a community, particularly a collective women's voice. Aunt Cuney is silent because she needs Avey's voice in order to transmit hers. Avey is silent because of the way her new class standing — which is bound up both with the racism she has experienced and with her absorption, as a wife, of the particular effect racism had on her husband — cuts her off from the heritage of speech Aunt Cuney represents.

The silencings portrayed in Ursa's dream derive in a related but more complicated way from the same interlocking oppressions. The dream scene in *Daughters* centers on two contexts, Ursa's conflict with Crowder and her stroll down Columbus Avenue with Lowell. The first of these, like

the dream in *Praisesong*, equates a silencing of the heroine with the silencing of the history of slave resistance. In this case, however, the heroine is
silenced despite the fact that she has privately lost neither that history nor
the woman's voice that transmitted it to her. Having carefully preserved
the memory of Will Cudjoe and Congo Jane as a legacy from her mother,
Ursa is nonetheless prevented from voicing it in her senior thesis at
"Mt. H." The reasons are implied in her advisor's name, which suggests
that he has managed to force Ursa out of a predominantly white public
discourse — to crowd her out — and also that he is not just a single individual performing an isolated act of racism. Superimposing the world of the
ivory tower on the streets of Manhattan — revealing, that is, the ways in
which they are really the same place — Crowder's individual presence at
the battle royal associates the whole crowd on Columbus Avenue with one
of the "major institutions that regulate people's lives"; the crowd's behavior in turn identifies as a form of racial harassment the exclusionary
discourse he represents. Ironically, Ursa's proposal itself, which is quoted
in an earlier scene, called attention to the kind of institutionally enforced
silence that Crowder's possession of her words represents: "*A neglected
area in the study of the social life of New World slave communities has been the
general nature of gender roles and relationships. This paper examines the relatively
egalitarian, mutually supportive relations that existed between the bondmen and
women and their significance for and contribution to the various forms of resistance to enslavement found in the United States and the Caribbean*" (11).

These words Crowder brandishes — words that are physically present
but invisible and therefore effectively absent — are one form of silence
represented in *Daughters*, a form that might be called inaudible speech.
In this form of silence, a woman directs words in her mind (or here, on
paper) to an external audience to whom in actuality she either cannot or
does not choose to transmit them. One example is the parallel inner
dialogue with a man that often takes place in a woman's mind as she
engages in an actual dialogue with him. "What're you talking about?
Where're you getting all this nonsense from?" Ursa demands of Lowell,
thinking, "Please. You're not telling me anything I don't know" (266). In
a similarly heated argument, Primus says that Estelle loved their honey-
moon/political campaign, and Estelle assents mentally, "*Not only loved it!
I used to feel we could move Gran' Morne just the two of us!*" But instead
of voicing this memory, she shoots back, "Don't be so sure about how
much I loved it!" (230). In both cases, something about the way "gender
roles and relationships" operate in the lovers' private discourse imposes
silence — a silence signified by words that appear, at least on the surface,
to speak the opposite of the truth. There is a helplessness about these
words that suggests the conversation has taken on an impetus of its own,
one that forces the woman to be untrue to her memory. It suggests too

that the rules of the discourse serve neither speaker, but some other purpose beyond them. In both cases the memory thus being silenced is that of an earlier, much more mutually sustaining relationship. Somehow in these gender conflicts the history of a couple's relationship gets silenced and betrayed, and that silencing further inflames the conflict.

Ursa's visible-but-invisible words in the dream are a version of this same phenomenon, but one that superimposes a broader cultural and political history on the picture of a private conflict between a woman and a man. The superimposition clarifies the public, other purpose beyond them being served by the rules of these lovers' private arguments. The unspeakable words at Lowell and Ursa's battle royal are not about their personal heterosexual relations, as in the private argument of which the dream is a visual translation. They are instead about the history of heterosexual relations in slave communities, and the reason they are unspeakable is the role played by the white historian Crowder as gatekeeper of one kind of public discourse. In the discourse that Crowder controls, as in the lovers' private discourse, the history of their relationship gets silenced and betrayed. And the double exposures of the dream say that these two betrayals are the same. A related passage makes the same point:

> Jane *and* Will Cudjoe . . . You can't call her name or his without calling or at least thinking of the other, they were so close.
>
> "I like that," Lowell Carruthers had declared back in the days of the free zone. "We need to get back to thinking like that, being like that again if we're ever going to make it."
>
> It was unacceptable, the man had said, handing the proposal back to her the moment she stepped in his office. (377)

For a moment in the final paragraph of this passage, the pronoun "It" seems to refer to the whole preceding idea — the concept of Black women and men "being like that again." Then the actual referent comes into focus: the proposal. At the microlevel this is another of Marshall's superimpositions. What Crowder objects to is actually both antecedents: the proposal's description of history *and* the possible future it might predict. That neither will "do," in his view, is the double vision of the "squinting pronoun."

A crucial aspect of the battle royal in *Invisible Man* is that the blindfolded contestants are invisible to one another. The fact that Crowder's suppression of African-American men and women's history works toward exactly this end establishes the logic of a white historian's presence in the dream version of Ursa's fight with a lover. It is in his interest, and the interest of the crowd he is part of, that Lowell and Ursa should not see each other clearly — that they should be holes at each other's sides. It is as if the "brawl" were his personal triumph, achieved by interfering with

African-American women's and men's ability to re-member their shattered earlier relations with each other.

A portrait of this kind of re-membering earlier in the novel identifies the recreation of an egalitarian history with its mutual voicing by a woman and man, and with a fusion so complete that the question of their visibility to each other is simply irrelevant. It was in the "free zone" — the space in their bed where, with "their bodies interchanged and their voices melded" (99), they could discuss "every and anything" (94) — that Ursa told Lowell about Will and Jane, and Lowell responded, "We need to get back to thinking like that" (94, 377). The end of the "free zone" is an important gloss on Ursa's dream, because it shows how the silencing of Lowell and the silencing of their "melded" voice as a couple are as much factors in the battle royal as is Ursa's silencing at Mt. H.

These other silencings are the second context for the dream scene in *Daughters*. Like the first context, this one represents a particular kind of silence as the work of racism, and as in the case of Mae and Sandy, it asserts a connection between silencing and invisibility. Ursa dates her and Lowell's talks in the "free zone" back to "The time before Davison" (96), Lowell's racist boss whose appropriation of Lowell's voice recalls the silencing of Jay Johnson. Racism in the economic system silenced Jay by making him a speaker of white people's monologues. The racism at Lowell's workplace, which he dares not leave for fear of being unemployed, makes him an obsessive talker and makes Ursa, consequently, an invisible woman: "Has he heard her? Does Lowell Carruthers even see her? She doubts it, although he's looking directly at her across the table. Davison. Davison's face is in the way" (37). In the after dinner stroll that provides most directly the material of Ursa's nightmare, Ursa says silently, "I know, Viney, I should turn and take a cool walk in the opposite direction and let Mr. Carruthers go on up Columbus Avenue raving to himself like one of the crazies out here. It would be blocks before he even noticed the hole at his side" (54). Racism, by suppressing her lover's authentic voice — whose timbre she once heard in her own (93) — has rendered her a female counterpart of Viney's invisible man. Ellison portrayed racism as subverting, redirecting, or usurping an African-American man's voice: most insidiously, perhaps, his voice as a public orator. He also portrayed racism as capable of rendering African-American men invisible to each other as well as to whites. In *Daughters*, Marshall portrays racism as capable of rendering African-American men *and women* invisible to one another, most insidiously by its silencing role in their private conversations, which are never completely separate from various kinds of public discourse — Primus's public orations, Ursa's writing of history.

The association of Lowell's ravings with the voices of the homeless signifies the economic foundation of this invisibility and this silencing. As with the white usurpation of Jay's voice, the fact that Halcon Inc. "takes over [Lowell's] voice" (56) is a function of his precarious class standing. Davison's racism casts Lowell, "the Davison jones on him" (383), metaphorically in the role of one of the "crazies" the state hospital "demobilized" during the era of the "cowboy in the White House" (57, 45). But it could just as easily "demobilize" him for real, by making him unemployed, possibly even homeless. The image functions in much the same way as those that suggest equivalences between Jay and Avey's experiences in poverty and in affluence. Like other images of Ursa and Lowell — as looters struggling over a handbag in a riot (269), or as targets for spectators' pennies — it pictures upward mobility for African Americans as an easily reversible illusion in which, in terms of the race-class system, nothing substantial is changed.

The potential effect on Ursa and Lowell's relationship of the class instability associated with their experience of racism is expressed in another image of invisibility linked specifically to gender relations. Pausing before a store window in their walk up Columbus Avenue, they watch a display of bicycles mounted as if racing to a neon finish line at the top of a hill. As the lights flash off occasionally, the faces of the white couple next to them "linger ghostlike in the plate glass," while Ursa and Lowell's reflections disappear "each time the window goes black" (55). The image reflects again how precarious is their very presence on Columbus Avenue, but this time the reflection raises the question of what their precarious class standing has to do with their tenuous status as a couple.

The tyranny of gender is crucially interwoven with this tyranny of race and class in the constructing of African-American invisibility as *Daughters* portrays it. Sexism works in complicity with racism, which also works sometimes to activate sexism. Viney's "ratio" speech hints at the structural reasons no anonymous "Someone useful" (331) is around to take Willis's place. In the representation of Lowell's weekend absences from Ursa, Marshall highlights one of these reasons in particular, the Vietnam War, which means that Lowell must fill in for another absent father, which means that he cannot be with Ursa. There is, in other words, a chain of absences into which men such as Lowell get linked inevitably. Even so, in the image of Lowell walking along talking to what he does not realize is a hole at his side, the absence is one for which he, not a larger system, bears most immediate responsibility. Lowell has cast Ursa as invisible woman by using her in traditional sexist ways: making her a sounding board for his voice without listening to hers, an audience whose face he no longer even sees, an unreciprocated source of emotional support. In this sense his sexism works in complicity with the racism that is always conspiring to make Ursa an Invisible Woman anyway. On the other hand, Davison's racism not only operates in collusion with Lowell's sexism but works as the initiating cause of the particular enactment of sexism in this scene. Davison mistreats Lowell, which results in his obsessive monologues, which render Ursa invisible *to him in particular.*

Jay's ventriloquizing was represented in an image of a white face superimposed on his, obscuring *his* personality. Davison's possession of Lowell's voice is represented in an image of a white face obscuring *Ursa's.* The variation highlights the way in which *Daughters* pictures racism and sexism reinforcing each other as silencers. By the same token, Lowell's resistance to the racism that has usurped his voice functions in effect as resistance against the sexism, too, by reestablishing a connection in which Ursa is not merely the blank space that the voice of Halcon Incorporated, speaking through him, has made her. "Steeling himself to be silent," he holds on to Ursa's arm as if it could "save him from both his outrage and his runaway tongue" (57). Lowell reaches for Ursa's help in silencing this crazed, possessed voice that erases his authentic voice at the same time it erases her: this "runaway voice" (53) that makes him absent to her just as it makes her absent for him. The move for her help in resisting Davison's ability to make Lowell an invisible man establishes Ursa's visibility too.

But Marshall presents the gender relations in this scene, and in the dream, as more complex than even these involuted interplays between racism and sexism suggest. Part of this complexity involves Ursa's choice, at the time of the dream, actually to act out the fantasy of walking off and leaving Lowell with an absence at his side. In yet another image related to those of invisible men, at the time of Ursa's dream Lowell is figured as a "hollowness" inside Ursa the size of the Grand Canyon (334), not because he has left her but because she has walked out on *him*—or perhaps more accurately, in terms of the other controlling metaphor of the novel, because she has in a sense aborted him just as she aborted the product of their sexual union. Ursa's internal "canyon" is clearly a parallel to the man-shaped hole next to Viney, but in this case the woman, rather than the man, is responsible for it. Lowell's absence here is Ursa's absence, which is her empty womb: a symbol for their failure to create a relationship that Ursa felt could sustain life. At the same time the empty womb stands for the painful breaking of ties with other people that Marshall portrays, especially in the later imagery of Ursa's split from her father, as sometimes necessary for autonomy.[7]

This father is another invisible man, but with an ironic twist. For the most part he is not physically present in Ursa's life, but his psychological presence often keeps her from what popular psychology would call "being there for" Lowell. Ursa does genuinely need autonomy within the relationship with Lowell. In a sense, that is the definition of "relatively egalitarian, mutually supportive relations" between men and women

(11) — mutual autonomy within a context of mutual support. But she also absents herself emotionally from Lowell because of her *lack* of autonomy from this other important man in her life, her father. In the conversation that causes their final rift, Lowell complains that, like Triunion, she is "Independent in name only" (268), all the time operated "by remote control" (269). "Oh, sure, your body's around," he says. "Habeas corpus. We have the body, but that place and De Lawd — especially De Lawd — have your head. He alone comes in for at least ninety-five percent of your thoughts" (265).

The argument about Ursa's colonial dependency on her father establishes the identity of the psychological and the political in her superimposed struggles for self-identity and self-determination. It is in this double psychological and political context that Ursa and Lowell's ability to re-member their history of egalitarian relationships becomes critical. The question of how to rescue the memory, and the practice, of the egalitarian relations between women and men in slave communities is at the center of Marshall's consideration of gender in *Daughters*. Ursa's proposal focused on egalitarian relations *"and their significance for and contribution to the various forms of resistance to enslavement found in the United States and the Caribbean"* (11). Egalitarian relations in slave communities thus imply the three contexts in which gender is especially at issue in this novel: African-American women's struggle for autonomy; their struggle, at the same time, for personal connectedness with Black men and other Black women; and their struggle for a corresponding political connectedness — for racial solidarity in a common struggle for freedom.[8] The title of the novel, glossed by the epigraph to book 1, refers to all three of these struggles: *"Little girl of all the daughters, / You ain' no more slave, / You's a woman now."*

Autonomy and connectedness are salient terms in Carol Gilligan's consideration of women's "different voice," and her perception of the ways their interrelations are troubling for women is relevant here.[9] More relevant, however, are the more complex ways in which many African-American feminist theorists have avoided the simple dichotomy of autonomy and connectedness by including a third term linked to both of the others: the mutual struggle of African-American women and men for what might be called collective autonomy. These theorists have shown that for African-American women, what Cornel West identifies as the inseparability of the struggle for individual autonomy and the struggle for control of the institutions that regulate African-American lives has involved special problems, precisely because of this triple context of Black feminist struggle. Such feminists as Barbara Smith, bell hooks, and Audre Lorde pointed out from the beginning that African-American women's fight for control of these institutions implies solidarity with men ipso facto—hence their vigorous rejection of white feminist separatism even as they insist on resisting sexist oppression. As the Combahee River Collective wrote, "Our situation as Black people necessitates that we have solidarity around the fact of race, which white women of course do not need to have with white men, unless it is their negative solidarity as racial oppressors. We struggle together with Black men against racism, while we also struggle with Black men about sexism" (275).[10]

The "Angela Davis article" that Ursa cites in her thesis, presumably "The Black Woman's Role in the Community of Slaves," sheds light on one of the many ways in which Marshall conceptualizes these issues in *Daughters*. Davis portrays the loss of the tradition of egalitarian relationships as concomitant with their displacement by white gender ideologies originally alien to slave communities. Embedded in her argument, then, is the implication that the feminist struggle in which she was involved at the time was not a betrayal of solidarity with African-American men but a recovery of an equality that white supremacy had succeeded in great measure in suppressing.[11] Eleanor Holmes Norton used a similar argument in the early essay she contributed to *Sisterhood Is Powerful*: "We are perhaps the only group that has come to these shores who has ever acquired the chance to consciously avoid total Americanization with its inherent, its rank, faults. On the road to equality there is no better place for blacks to detour around American values than in foregoing its example in the treatment of its women and the organization of its family life" (401).[12] Marshall's representation of Crowder and Davison as silencers and, thus, provokers of the battle royal between Lowell and Ursa makes a point similar to those of Davis and Norton: turning African-American women's and men's relations with each other into a battle of the sexes is part of the work of white institutions.

In her use of images of absence and invisibility Marshall derives strength from her literary solidarity with Ellison while struggling at the same time against his novel's relative blindness to gender issues. Taking an image that is about the tyranny of race in Ellison's novel—the central image of invisibility—she makes it function, with all those thematic overtones it has already, as a locus for considering the racialized tyranny of gender in African-American women's lives as they struggle for individual autonomy, for connections with men and other women, and for collective racial autonomy from the white institutions that regulate their lives.

The changes she makes in the contestants in the battle royal as Avey's dream becomes Ursa's dream raise exactly these three contexts. Most obviously, the fact that Avey struggles with a woman and Ursa struggles with a man shifts dramatically the relation between the dreamer's needs and those of the figure who tugs so desperately at her arm. In *Praisesong* the appearance of the dream messenger signals a need in the dreamer. This woman ancestor stands for the return of the repressed, presence after absence, voice after silence. The need she communicates so urgently is hers insofar as it is a need for her voice to be resurrected. But her need is identical with Avey's need to resurrect Aunt Cuney's voice in herself; it is also, more generally, identified with the needs of a whole community whose voice and memory are imperiled. In *Daughters* the other person in the dream is no ancient, timeless female ancestor but a man Ursa's own age, clutching at her arm as to a "stick being held out to someone drowning" (383) even after Ursa has tried to end their romantic involvement by taking "a cool walk in the opposite direction" (54). The question of "gender roles and relationships" makes the relation between Lowell's needs and Ursa's needs much more complex than that between Avey's needs and those of her aunt. Lowell needs rescue; indeed, he is one of the "fiercely articulate token few" whose static circular passage in and out of Manhattan's "glacier buildings" Avey planned to disrupt with her narrative. But what does it mean in terms of gender roles for a woman to have a man pulling on her arm as if it were a lifeline? How can Ursa achieve autonomy, or indeed how can she achieve a mutually sustaining connectedness, in such a situation?

The tug-of-war raises, very literally, the issues of being attached, being separate, being free, being connected. It takes up again the question raised in *Praisesong* as to how an African-American woman is to be free and achieve her own voice while at the same time establishing through that voice a connectedness that affirms rather than erases her self. Aunt Cuney is a female redeemer-guide figure, and Avey's liberation is expressed in her capacity, and resolve, to become such a rescuer herself. But the semimythical stature of Aunt Cuney and of Avey after she reclaims her status as Avatara means that in Avey's story the ways in which this role can be problematic for women do not arise. Half of Ursa Beatrice's name reminds us of the extent to which women in Western history have been mythologized as spiritual guides, the meaning of their lives on their own terms negated and redefined in terms of the lives of men they inspired.[13] But the other half of her name alludes to a woman rescuer from quite a different tradition than Dante's Beatrice, one who achieved her own freedom as well as that of others. The constellation Ursa Major contains the "drinking gourd" that slaves looked for in their journeys to freedom. The slave escape mentioned specifically in *Daughters* is that of Harriet Tubman, whose story is told by Robeson's friend Dee Dee and was told to Ursa in her childhood by Estelle (66–67).

The allusion to Harriet Tubman in Ursa's name implies all three contexts of Paule Marshall's consideration of gender. It refers to the struggle for autonomy, in that Tubman won her freedom by fleeing to the North, as Ursa's mother prepared her to do from childhood by launching her on "the lone voyage" in a rowboat (390). But Tubman returned South nineteen times to rescue over three hundred other slaves (Flexner 96), replicating in their lives her individual journey of freedom. Each mission risked that freedom on behalf of others; on the other hand, her individual autonomy was enacted in the acts of rescue themselves, and could ultimately be guaranteed only by success of the collective struggle for which she risked it. Significantly, the single return South to which Paule Marshall calls attention in Tubman's story is her mission to rescue her father (67).

It is on the eve of her own return south to rescue her father, in fact, that Ursa's dream of the battle royal occurs, and the most immediate inspiration for the dream is not her breakup with Lowell but the impending break with her father, which her mission paradoxically implies. This almost patricidal gesture of ruining her father's career is nothing short of revolution, as "the PM's" nickname, which identifies him symbolically as the neocolonial patriarchy, suggests.[14] The name equates Ursa's psychological and political struggles for independence, superimposing her struggle against her neocolonial status as a still-dependent adult child with her sense of responsibility to the still-dependent neocolonial state of Triunion, from which she fled north for freedom but to which she must return. But the PM's nickname, as Marshall has pointed out, is ironic: "an empty symbol of power and authority in a country that still takes its orders from America and the West" (Dance 4). So Ursa's political struggle for independence, which is equated with her struggle for independence from him as his daughter, is also *his* struggle for political independence from the First World domination that makes his power illusory. For him to win that struggle, epitomized in the struggle for possession of his voice, she must win her own struggle for autonomy from him.

All these double exposures in the picture of Ursa's relation to the PM are a brilliant representation of the way African-American women's struggle against sexist oppression by African-American men is tied to and complicated by their common struggle, *with* those men, against a white supremacy that in part imposes its sexist oppression of African-American women *through* those men.[15] The reason that Ursa's rebellion against the PM is also a rescue of him is the interlocking nature of their oppressions — of her gender oppression by him and of the racial and class oppression of both of them by the colonial powers with which Primus has come, against his own better interests, to be in league. Primus wants Ursa as a star in his "constellation" (54); the "constellation" created by the *Woodrow Wilson's* presence in Triunion's harbor (181) stands for the fact that the United States wants Triunion — and Primus — in *its* constellation. In these connections Marshall not only portrays with elaborate subtlety the mutual dependence of liberation focused on gender, class, and racial issues; once again her superimposition of the political and the psychological insists on the interlocking nature of the outer and inner dramas of imperialism.

As is the case with Lowell in the dream, Ursa's role as a man's rescuer in the struggle against and on behalf of her father has to do, paradoxically, with her ability to silence his voice — or rather, the voice that has run away with his. The progress of Primus's recolonization manifests itself in his increasingly obsessive talk about the Planning and Development Board's resort scheme, which is the subject, his mistress complains, of "Every word out his mouth . . . !" (308). Ursa dreams of Lowell begging her for rescue in a context that alludes to his need for her help in silencing his "runaway voice" (53) that makes her invisible. But at the time of the dream she is about to return south to rescue her father from all that is represented by *his* runaway voice. She can succeed only by providing his opponents with the facts they need to silence him at his final campaign speech. Ursa's rescue of her father, however, has the added twist that, even as she works toward a collective freedom for Triunion in which both he and she will participate, and for which he fought in his earlier days, the freedom she achieves in this journey south will include freedom from the PM's patriarchal domination of *her*. Behind the dream of Lowell's need for rescue, that is, is another context in which a woman's personal and political connectedness with a man, and even her ability to rescue him, are actually dependent on her ability to cut him off from — or out of — herself.

The breakup with Lowell was figuratively an abortion, leaving Ursa with a hole inside her. More complicatedly, Ursa's simultaneous rescue of and break from the PM is figured in an episode whose dominant imagery combines abortion, miscarriage, birth, a children's ritual, and revolution. Alone on the beach at Morlands, she scales Little Gran' Morne, which children scale each Sunday in a reenactment of the slave revolt. At the top "the canyon inside her begins to shrink" — an image that evokes the beginning of labor — as she "puts aside Lowell Carruthers" (384). The birth or abortion that will distance her from her father, in other words, is related to her ability to distance herself from Lowell. On the way down, "the grass made slick by the rain last night simply slides out from under her. . . . Her right hip strikes the edge of a rock, pain knifes through her, and then she is free-falling the last foot or two to the ground" (389). With this slide — Triunion's term for a miscarriage — the metaphor of Ursa giving birth shifts to a metaphor of her own free-fall out of the womb: the miscarriage of Primus's treason against the people. Because her separation of herself from his domination will bring about this miscarriage, it is simultaneously her birth as a mature woman, "no more slave."

Ursa's actual act of revolution, "the main task of the day" (390), which she undertakes after the pain of the fall eases enough for her to move, occurs in the narrative hiatus between the description of her pain on the beach and her pain in bed that night. The excised narrative, appearing as a blank on the page, is thus itself a figure for the act the hiatus represents: a silencing, a cutting-out like the abortion Ursa had at the beginning of the book but imagined, then, as incomplete. Ursa's abortion is "meant to suggest her attempt to cut away the subtle seduction and domination that has long characterized her relationship with her father," Paule Marshall has said. "It's only at the end of the novel, when she brings about the PM's political defeat, that she's finally free of this incubus" (Dance 10).

What Ursa's heroine journey has to do with Lowell is more ambiguous. As he recedes in her mind at the apex of her revolutionary climb the "canyon" shrinks: clearly a suggestion that expelling him is part of her struggle for autonomy. But the ways in which the image simultaneously refers to her relationship with Primus superimposes on this set of meanings another possible meaning of the act for her and Lowell. It is possible that the impending birth and abortion her heroine journey signals will in fact make room for Lowell in her life. The fact that "everything" will no longer be about the PM, as Lowell complained it was earlier (266), may allow her, as a reborn autonomous woman, to have a more "egalitarian relationship."

Even so, the analogies between the rescue for which Lowell implores Ursa in the dream and the rescue she imposes on her father without his consent raise a number of questions. Are her only choices to become Lowell's lifeline or to degrade them both in a "nigger show" (383)? Must she rescue Lowell, that is, out of allegiance to the race despite the ways in which her own needs may conflict with that rescue? Or is Lowell's rescue tied so intimately to Ursa's—just as her father's is tied to hers and just as the rescues for which Harriet Tubman jeopardized her autonomy were implicit in that autonomy—that she cannot save herself without rescuing him?

By raising these questions, the symbolic context of Ursa's dream presents an intricate picture of the way gender complicates the relations between her struggle for self-identity and for autonomy from oppressive institutions. But there is a further complication. Even as Marshall portrays Ursa's struggle with Lowell as fraught with general implications that transcend their lovers' quarrel, the novel is infused, as her novels always are, with a realist's fidelity to particulars. Whatever the larger issues, in the "real life" represented in this insistently realistic novel, Ursa might understandably decide that Lowell, with his neurotic fastidious rituals and his symbolically protective watchdog Mitchell, is not the man she wants to be connected with most intimately. Indeed it is Ursa's right to a consideration of the particulars of the case that is at issue in the dream.

For exacerbating all the complexities of her struggle with Lowell is the fact that, in the eyes of the white audience for their relationship — pinned by the white gaze intent only on seeing "which of them will go down first" (383) — there is no room for complexity. What that gaze does, in fact, is to create the situation in which Ursa's resistance to the role of lifeline — perhaps justified in terms of gender relations — is stripped of its complexities so that it can be interpreted as a battle royal — that is, a betrayal of racial solidarity.

Thus part of what is at issue here is the way the problem of gender roles gets racialized in a society in which the relations between African-American women and men are politicized by the generalizing gaze of a racist white audience whose interpretations leave no room for particulars. In the background of the Angela Davis article that Crowder found unacceptable as a source for Ursa's thesis, for example, was a much more widely disseminated piece of hegemonic political discourse, the Moynihan report of 1965, with its interpretation of African-American men as emasculated by matriarchal African-American women. A host of writers have exposed the sexist and racist inaccuracy of this report,[16] whose ruling metaphor of matriarchy has nonetheless come to be part of the hegemonic discourse whereby the gender roles and relations of African Americans are presented as a battle royal in the media, and which continues to have serious implications in policy making.[17] Marshall's picture of whites enjoying a fight between Ursa and Lowell is, among other things, a good image of this whole process: the blind, destructive white gaze actively intruding on private relations through the power of hegemonic discourse to assert publicly its own interpretations ("A battle royal") and suppress others ("the history of egalitarian relations.") The crowd's limited and therefore limiting gaze sees a battle royal where Paule Marshall, on the other hand, makes the reader see the intricate difficulties of male-female relations as exactly this context of racialized gender roles and gendered race relations complicates them.

Another reworking in *Daughters* of a scene from *Praisesong* adds yet another dimension to these issues raised by the struggle for autonomy in Ursa's dream. Once again the reworking involves a change in the sex of a character with whom the heroine comes into an intimate, problematic connection:

A thin, ragtag man her age wearing a faded Hawaiian shirt whose missing buttons exposed his bony chest. Did she remember him, he wanted to know. . . . "I was one the little children your mother uses to let come and play with you in the yard when you all came to spend time in the district. . . . You must remember me . . ." / She didn't remember him. / "I saw in the paper the other day that you was back in the island. . . ." He drew closer, his voice dropped, and as if they were Siamese twins sharing the same heart, Ursa felt the heart in the man's bony chest speed up. He had heard, he whispered, his carious breath in her face, that they were hiring at a stone quarry outside town, but he needed bus fare to get there." (107–8)

Avey hears of an unsuspected "twin"; Ursa hears the twin's voice — and recognizes the twinship by feeling the man's heart speeding up, as if it were in her own body, as he nears the most daring part of his speech. Avey is merely addressed as if she were her twin; Ursa actually feels the twinship — unexpectedly, shockingly, physically. The shock is underscored by the image of this as a Siamese twin, a man with whom she shares the same body.

In *Praisesong*, in which voice is an attribute of body, coming to voice is associated with a ritual that fuses communal speech and dance. In *Daughters*, in which coming to voice is associated with conversation, language is a bodily connection. Nowhere is this more clear than in the early relationship between Estelle and Primus, when they make love on Gran' Morne: " 'Mwen renmen ou,' she said, as he had taught her. It sounds better in Creole, he had said. 'Mwen renmen ou!' He brought his face back up to hers briefly. She tasted herself on his lips. 'Creole with an American accent. I love it,' he said, using her favorite expression" (137). The image of Estelle tasting herself on Primus's lips, echoed by Primus's speaking of her words and her speaking of his, identifies as a single connection their fusions of voice and body. Such fusions explain in yet another way what invisibility has to do with voice in *Daughters*. If speech is a form of bodily connection, then silence, especially through the substitution of one voice for what should be two, becomes a form of physical absence. Lowell talks without seeing the almost silent Ursa, who might as well be a hole at his side; Viney talks to the police chief alone, with a man-shaped absence beside her; Astral rants on about her problems with Primus, "blind" to her dying friend Malvern (311). The opposite of such images of couples in which one partner is an invisible man or woman is the image of the couple in the "free zone," with "their bodies interchanged and their voices melded" (99).

The images of talk as bodily connection in the free zone and on King William Street pose some interesting questions in the context of Marshall's consideration of women and voice. Avey comes to voice by discovering that she is not one but many, a revelation for which the discovery of an unknown woman twin is a symbol. But this discovery coincides with her ability to stop being the "twin" of someone else, her husband, whose authentic voice, along with hers, she can recover only by differentiating herself from him. The paradoxes here reject traditional white Western notions of individuation and autonomy. For Avey, self-identity both equals and does not at all equal individuation in the sense of

Freudian-based psychology. The Siamese twin image in *Daughters* poses the issue in even more sharply paradoxical terms. How can a woman individuate herself in a world where at any moment a man may accost her on the street and establish a natural and legitimate claim to her very body as his own?

Like Lowell, this man demands a kind of rescue, and like Lowell he is connected to Ursa by their mutual past. Like Lowell, he has the capacity for speaking in such a way that his voice seems to come from Ursa's own body. As with Lowell in the free zone, Ursa's unity with this man appears simultaneously as voice and physical connection. Furthermore, as in Lowell's case, Ursa's inability to individuate herself from her father threatens her unity with this other man. The PM used to chase him away from Ursa when they were children in order to enforce the class distinction between them, and the man's desperate speech to Ursa is one of many things that make her suspect her father's part in exacerbating poverty on the island (108). Ursa's feeling of unity with this man, in other words, is part of the painful process of separation from the PM that culminates in her decision to make contact with Justin Beaufils, another of "the gang of little fowl-yard children" whom Primus tried to shut out of his daughter's life (304).

The superimposition of these two unions of voice and body — Ursa's unity with Lowell and her unity with the man on the street — expresses with extraordinary, almost visceral force Paule Marshall's insight into the interpenetration of the personal and the political. That Ursa's psychological separation from her father should be a prerequisite of the ability to form a mature adult heterosexual attachment is, by itself, a routine insight of Western psychology after Freud. That Ursa needs autonomy as well as connectedness is in some ways a routine insight of Western feminism both African- and Euro-American. That this differentiation of herself from her father in the move for psychological autonomy should be identical to the claiming of a political solidarity that abrogates the class differences sustained and exacerbated by patriarchy is something else again.

The equations implicit in this insight — the equation of autonomy and connectedness, of separation with unity with revolutionary solidarity with independence individually and collectively — help to explain why the heroine's coming to voice, so important in the earlier novels, takes place offstage in *Daughters*. In a sense it is so unspeakable an act of rebellion that it is best represented by a blank space on the page, a narrative silence. But in another sense, the fact that the narrative procedure silences the heroine's individual coming to voice magnifies that process by conflating it with the coming to voice of a people. At the crucial moment,

Ursa simply listens silently, her head bowed, with the rest of Primus's "constellation" in the darkness behind him, as his audience shouts the questions her sabotage enabled them to ask.

Ursa's coming-of-age is an achievement of individual autonomy through a private, psychological break from her father. But this achievement of autonomy issues in someone else's speech. In an important sense this is true for Avey too. Her journey of freedom will lead her back to the landing to speak someone else's words. But she is the orator at the end, unlike Ursa, who remains on the margins of the audience, as she always has, listening to the voices she has helped to liberate. It is noteworthy, too, that although Justin's supporters lure Primus's audience away to hear him and his wife speak (395), the narrative gives us the people's words but not theirs, just as whatever Ursa said in the course of her subversion of her father is not represented in the narrative.[18] In the text, that is, these *individual* words appear as silence. Primus is not simply replaced, as speaker in the spotlight, by another man; he is replaced by a couple who, however, choose not to step into his spotlight but to inspire his audience to speak up for themselves.

The choice to remain silent and invisible instead of usurping the oratorical spotlight raises again one of the novel's most central concerns about discourse, the issue of the representative voice. In a system in which the economic structure of a "democracy" like Triunion is dominated by multinational corporations, representational politics is itself mere representation: "a 'puppy show' (meaning puppet)" as Roy called the first elections to which the United States, by government invitation, sent a delegation of guns (222). To shatter this illusory representation of democratic representation, something other than a representative voice is required. Thus Ursa at the climax of her revolutionary act is not portrayed as speaking; she does not take on a representative voice. Neither, significantly, does Justin or his wife. We know that Justin makes speeches, but we do not hear them directly. We know that his wife speaks, but we do not hear her either. We know that Ursa spoke to one or both of them, but we do not hear that conversation. They are all behind the scenes, silent, when the people themselves speak up from the audience. Later we learn that Justin invited Primus to join forces: a Père Bossou, perhaps, to stand with Will Cudjoe and Congo Jane.

The figure of Congo Jane here, Justin's wife, does not allow her voice to be represented by Justin; she speaks for herself, equally. Congo Jane with her musket was the equal of Will with his. But in the battle that Justin and his wife fight on behalf of the people, things are different. She will not be elected; he will be elected. She will not speak in Parliament; he will speak. Her very representation in the narrative illustrates the difficulties they face. Because she is represented primarily through a narrator who sees women as rightly subservient to men, we do not even know her name; to Celestine she is only "the wife . . . he went and find in Spanish Bay" (304). Even Estelle, who says that Justin and "his wife" are just as she and Primus were (360), does not tell Ursa the wife's name, and Ursa does not ask. Whatever equality "Justin's wife" and her husband seek to establish, the way the discourse of present-day Triunion is gendered means that they cannot be spoken of equally in the same way that Congo Jane and Will Cudjoe were spoken of long ago. You couldn't call Will's name without calling Jane's, "they were so close" (377). But the name of Justin's wife need not, it seems, be called at all. If the existence of such gender inequality in and of itself predicts a sellout on the man's part, then Justin is in danger. If what counts is the man's refusal to reproduce that inequality in his personal and political relationships, then Justin represents something new.

It is in this distinction between Justin's campaign and those of Primus and Sandy that we might look for an answer to Peter Erickson's question, "How do we know that Justin Beaufils won't reproduce the trajectory of Primus' political career?" (270). The many parallels between them certainly raise the possibility of such a reproduction. Justin has laid the groundwork, however, for a different kind of intervention in the discourse of power than Primus was able to achieve. He lays that groundwork in his sharing of voice with his wife during the campaign, in his invitations to Primus to join him, and most importantly in his choice not to usurp the spotlight from Primus at the windup speech but to be absent, letting the people speak instead of him. Justin chooses, that is, to be an invisible man for the sake of his constituents, unlike Primus and Sandy, whose invisibility betrays their constituents. Like Estelle and Ursa, he chooses a place of invisibility and silence from which to destabilize the discourse of power. He does speak later; perhaps he too stands on a platform in a spotlight. The fact that we do not know for sure, on the other hand, is significant. By placing this speech offstage like all his others, the narrative spotlights not him as a speaker, but the people whose speech he inspires.

Justin's name is interesting in this regard. It implies a resurgence — and insurgence — of justice, but through a network of relationships. Like Merle's last name, his implies kinship. He is Beaufils, a stepson — the spiritual son of Primus, in one sense, because he follows in his footsteps in so many ways. This kinship with Primus implies, as well, a kinship with Primus's daughter. Ursa and the man on King William Street are metaphorically Siamese twins; Justin, another of the impoverished children from whom he tried to separate her, is metaphorically her stepbrother. Their resurgence in Ursa's life plays the role here of Alberta Lee Grant's return or Aunt Cuney's return. But in *Daughters* this return of the repressed is quite literally the resurgence of the oppressed. Ursa had forgotten these dispossessed people, as Primus intended; at the end their just brotherhood with her is reestablished despite him.

3

In *Brown Girl*, "the mother's voice" is at the crux of Selina's psychological, artistic, and political growth. It is the force against which she must define herself as she shapes an independent voice capable of talking back even to Silla, and as she eventually develops an alternative means of self-expression through dance. It is also the force against which she strikes out in her efforts to define some alternative conception of power. Selina's "oppositional world view" (to borrow bell hooks' term) is never articulated directly in the book; all she manages in response to Silla's pronouncement is a consciousness of "her own small truth that dimly envisioned a different world and a different way" — a still "undefined" truth that she would like to "shout" to all the Bajan mothers to "give the lie" to Silla's argument (225). Yet even as "the mother's voice" deploys the world-view against which Selina rebels, it sustains Selina's growth as an independent woman, providing the nourishing ground for the very success of the rebellion against it. The father's voice is more elusive and problematic. Deighton's talk of "land home" is uplifting (12), a source of images to counteract Silla's of "buying house." But his voice is ultimately a self-betrayer, as he resigns himself so completely to another personality that his cry of surrender lacks even a personal pronoun: "Need you, Father, need you" (169).

In *Daughters*, the father's voice would at first glance seem to be the all-important one. Certainly it plays the role most analogous to that of the mother in *Brown Girl*. "[T]hat voice of his!" (233) is dazzling, powerful, seductive, the expression of an impassioned, magnetic personality like "that voice" against which Selina feels herself helpless (*Brown Girl* 180). Ursa keeps the PM's letters in her headboard to have "the sound of his voice on paper within easy reach" (44). Estelle warns herself in an argument, "Don't listen to that voice of his!" (233). Yet, as was the case with Deighton, this father's voice is subject to appropriation. In particular he falls prey to the danger inherent in the role of representative voice, which is that the position of representing one group to another also opens the intermediary to influence from the other direction. Under this influence the attempt to speak truth to power, on behalf of what Merle would call "the Little Fella," shades into the discourse of "the great people — them!" explaining to the Little Fellas why, after all, their voice cannot be heeded. Such explanations inevitably entail double-talk; as Primus tells

Celestine when the incriminating xeroxes are delivered, "I'm gon have to talk muh talk tonight to explain this one, bo" (395). But, as Celestine says later, the people "din want to hear any ol' talk about he's still trying his best for them" (395).

The ol' talk Primus had planned to lay on the people, a public political discourse he finally does not get to engage in, is paralleled by the "ol' talk" he keeps promising Ursa (385), a promise on which he never delivers. This other "ol' talk" is to be private, cozy, intimate, father-to-daughter, the epitome of sincerity. But that the word he uses for it is identical to the word Celestine uses for the rhetorical counterpart of pulling the wool over his constituents' eyes hints at the reason he cannot engage anymore in this kind of discourse either. Primus tries to keep separate the public and the private spheres, in duplicities increasingly symbolic of his self-division. But there is no such separateness. The public silence that his political duplicity necessitates reinscribes itself as a private silence. For his daughter and wife are also his constituents, and at the point at which he keeps promising Ursa an ol' talk, domestic peace dictates that he cannot in fact afford to answer the most candid questions of the daughter whose voice he has so signally failed to represent.

The position of power in a hierarchy silences subordinates and is therefore a position of being deceived, and self-deceived. Up on the platform at the monument Primus stands "under the rigged spotlight" (407), his family seated just beyond its reach in the darkness to one side of him (376). The deceptions implied in "the PM's" position of being looked up to as speaker include the irony of his nickname, to which Marshall called attention in her interview with Dance (4). The power the PM's windup speech represents is representation only: a show "rigged" by someone higher up in the hierarchy than he. What happens to Primus at the monument, in the peripeteia, is that this speech is overthrown by another kind of discourse, as his individual voice is replaced by multiple voices attempting, as Ursa would have done in their "ol' talk," to initiate a dialogue. As a counterpart, what happens behind his back is that the women his voice had silenced and divided have a conversation.

The parallels between these public and private climaxes of the novel call attention to something the novel examines at many levels: the interdependence — even sometimes the identity — of private discourse and public, especially political discourse. In the case of the conversation between Astral and Ursa, this interdependence has to do with the interdependent role that the divisions and duplicities caused by class hierarchy play in Primus's psyche, family life, and political life. A silence associated with class division is at issue in the case both of Primus's domestic betrayal and of his political betrayal, which mirror each other. And in both cases

Primus's psychological self-division is an internal counterpart of a class division that he in turn, through the private and political acts resulting from his self-division, helps to sustain.

Primus's need for lovers from both classes, whom he works hard to keep apart, is an aspect of his self-division, the same division of class allegiances that eventually translates into his political betrayal of his home district. Primus comes from the poorest part of the island, but from a family that could afford to send him to a fancy private school where, on the other hand, he was poor in comparison to his schoolmates. He espouses what sound like socialist principles but expresses a credulous awe for the United States as a place where, as in a Horatio Alger story, "the impossible is possible" (47), giving Ursa "the silent treatment" when she refuses to realize his American dream for her to have "CEO big on the door" of her office in a Fortune 500 corporation (47).[19] These internal psychic divisions translate themselves into acts that reinforce the class divisions they reflect. Primus keeps Ursa apart from her "twin" and from Justin; he stands in the way of dialogue between Estelle and Astral; he finally invests in a financial deal that will help to shore up the class distinction between Morlands and the First World "Fortune 500 and friends," as Estelle calls them, who will take for their "playground" the land Primus once wanted to use for hospitals, farming cooperatives, model villages, canneries, housing schemes (357).

To heal the divisions the PM's internal divisions create, it is necessary to initiate speech in place of the silences for which he is responsible. Thus Ursa's Siamese twin speaks to her on King William Street; Ursa communicates with Justin; Justin reveals Primus's duplicity to the people for whose interests he is no longer speaking; they respond by shouting questions instead of listening silently to his speech; and, for one shocking moment, Astral speaks her mind to someone who is regarded as her superior in terms of class.

In this, Astral is a revealing counterpart to Ettie, Alberta, and Carrington. None of those subordinate characters speak in the novels in which they appear; the "life persisting" for which they stand persists in indomitable silence. The figure of Astral breaks this silence, shedding an interesting light on the progression of Paule Marshall's meditation throughout her career on the question of voice. For the climax of this book is not the liberation, as one might have expected, of the heroine's voice, which speaks its most revolutionary words offstage. It is the twin liberation of the people's voice at a public meeting and then, in a private meeting, of Astral's voice, in response to the heroine's mediating voice as her mother's emissary.

In this liberation of Astral's voice from the silence that the hierarchy of class would impose on it, both kinds of discourse that the novel valorizes come into play: conversation (especially between women) and speaking truth to power. The dialogue between Ursa and Astral becomes both of these when Astral unexpectedly voices her resentment at Ursa's class privilege over her, epitomized in Primus's command to Astral at the swimming pool: "Astral, bring a towel and something cool for Ursa to drink when she's done. Some soursop juice, if you have it" (211). The casual command, taking its power for granted, established a discourse whose rules deprived both women of a voice in which to protest. Astral could not speak up because of the economic power behind the command. Servants do not talk back without jeopardizing their jobs. The daughter, furthermore, must not talk back to the father — certainly not to protest his treatment of his mistress. And the mistress cannot, in public, speak up without humiliation to claim that her status as kept woman should entitle her to more respect than she would get as a maid. What Astral does in her conversation with Ursa the adult is to voice — and initially it is not a voice she even recognizes — the anger she was forced to repress during these visits of Ursa the child:

"I used to hate that you had to stand there on a Sunday holding that towel and tray. Even before I was old enough to understand, I didn't feel it was right . . ."
"Always getting on like he thought you was some child I had for him!"
Who said that? Astral Forde looks wildly around her as though the outburst had come from someone other than herself. Some Judas with both longing and rage in his voice had spoken, betraying feelings she kept secret even from herself. (405)

Ursa and Astral's openness in this conversation — their risk-taking, however inadvertent it may be — has the effect of breaking one of the threads that entangles gender subordination with class subordination. In the scene at the pool the combination of class privilege and male privilege gave Primus control of the discourse, silencing both women. Further, Ursa's class privilege was conflated with his privilege as a master/keeper/employer of a mistress/employee, because as his daughter she could not speak up to dissociate herself from that male privilege being exercised on her behalf. Primus arrogated to himself, in other words, the right to represent Ursa's needs. But what he actually ended by representing — as in his other role as a representative voice — was the class hierarchy inevitably voiced through the kind of discourse in which he spoke for her. As a grown woman, the daughter who is "no more slave," Ursa evades this discourse by speaking up for herself without an intermediary. And Astral, breaking the rule of self-censorship that helps to position her in the hierarchy, replies. By abrogating the effect of Primus's commanding speech at the side of the swimming pool, breaking the rules of the discourse he chose as the one that would define the relationships among the three of them, the women's dialogue eliminates his male privilege as one of the sources of their (nonetheless still numerous) differences. The canceling of male privilege as a factor in their relationship thus both derives from and enables the liberation of women's speech — specifically, women's speech in conversation.

Even more specifically, coming to voice in this novel requires not just speaking but, at a more nuts-and-bolts level, breaking the rules of discourse that apply in patriarchy. Interestingly, the first consequence of this revolutionary act, in the case of Astral and Ursa, is a realignment of their relationship into that of mother and "loving daughter" (405). With Primus removed from the space between them, Astral need no longer perform services for the child Primus imagined she had had "for him"; instead she can experience the relationship as something for her own benefit, receiving Ursa's service — the offer of her dinner on a tray covered with a towel — as a daughter's office of love. The role reversal is not romanticized; it cannot cancel Ursa's class privilege. It does, however, subvert the class hierarchy, by insinuating into it the complexities of the mother-daughter hierarchy, the only relationship Ursa and Astral could establish in which Ursa would be cast as the subordinate. Nor does Marshall romanticize the encounter more generally. After the outburst and Ursa's reply, Astral retreats, "fiercely holding onto the silence." But the subtle shift in relations here is all the more dramatic for the realist's fidelity to Astral, to which she quietly calls attention in Ursa's reminder to herself: "Let it be. Don't push her. She's said far more than just three or four words this time. Besides, you wouldn't want her to behave completely out of character" (405).

Astral's outburst is the private counterpart of the liberation of the people's voice at the monument; they are even in a sense the same. In both cases there is a voicing of resentment at a power structure that has imposed silence; a breaking of the rules of a discourse that enforces gender, race, and class hierarchy. The public liberation of the people's voice is thus paralleled by the liberation of women's voice through conversation. Both liberations occur because Estelle, from the place of silence, uses Ursa's mediating voice to disrupt the silences created by the discourse that defines Primus's place in the private and public hierarchies of family and state.

It is thus the mother's voice in *Daughters* that undoes the wrongs associated with the father's voice. But Estelle's is not a voice like Silla's, which is an orator's voice despite the private contexts of her pronouncements. Rather, the voices that actually sound most like Silla's in this novel are those of Celestine and Astral, whose interior monologues are silent declamations. Estelle's voice, in contrast, works through conversation, and not even necessarily through conversation in which she is a direct participant. It is Estelle who has the ol' talk with Ursa that Primus did not have, and it is his self-exclusion — his silence, that is — that makes their talk into an implicit conspiracy. Estelle initiates it, indeed, with an announcement that she is breaking a rule — "breaking my vow of silence on certain subjects" (358). This is a reminder that the rules of a discourse are demarcations of what is off limits — signs of silence. Ursa and Lowell's relationship after the end of the free zone had to be held together by just such a rule, which Lowell expressed as "Something about keeping our two cents worth of advice to ourselves" (264). The breakdown of this rule initiates a terrible argument and, they assume, the breakdown of the relationship. But Viney suggests that they might instead have cleared the air for a new and freer, more intimate dialogue.

Viney's optimism points to an important premise of the treatment of voice and silence in *Daughters.* Just as conversation is valorized in the novel, those rules of discourse that create silences in conversation — which amount to doublenesses — are exactly those that must be violated in order to reestablish what Ursa calls "wholeness and unity" (40). From another angle, it is Lowell's and Ursa's doubleness that necessitates the code of silence in the first place. Ursa realizes later that, in breaking that code, Lowell said things she needed to hear "from someone other than myself" (382); similarly, Lowell did not want to hear that he should quit his job, something he himself suspected. The rules of discourse in this case — the demarcation of what cannot be said — were intended to silence internal voices that the other person's external voice might otherwise too clearly echo.

Indeed, just as divisions between people are expressed as silences in this novel, so are internal self-divisions, which suggest a failure of internal conversation: the fact that one aspect of the self is not in dialogue with another. The doubleness in Primus that necessitates Estelle's rule that no one, on Ursa's first day home, talk about anything political is the sign of such a self-division. The logical consequence of that division is a runaway voice like Lowell's — an opaque, self-obsessed voice impermeable to anyone else's and thus capable only of a monologue in which talking is a form of *not* talking: "*Selling Mile Trees!* He arrived in Morlands late last night to announce that this was what he intended doing. . . . They would discuss it in the morning, he said, but he was too tired, too blasted tired, to talk about it tonight. . . . Talking faster . . . than they had ever heard him, his voice hoarse from exhaustion, his face haggard" (385–86).

4

The picture of Primus being progressively overtaken by — "runaway" with — a voice that is clearly not his raises the question as to how the dispossessed can disrupt the dominant discourses that silence them. In the imagery of *Daughters*, it seems impossible to do so from the center where Sandy and Primus stand: "almost shoulder[ed] . . . between" the two white men talking simultaneously to Sandy on the steps of City Hall (285), or hemmed in by the coercive business talk at the firemen's reception. The most effective acts of resistance Marshall portrays are from the margins, the background, the blank places of invisibility to which Black women, in particular, are consigned.

Estelle's power to rescue Primus from the self-loss manifest in his self-absorbed monologues, for example, comes from her ability to initiate, from the margins, conversations that disrupt hegemonic discourse by abrogating the silences its rules dictate. In the case of her sending Ursa to talk to Justin and Astral, the very conversations she is initiating are themselves against the rules. Her other most significant intrusion into hegemonic discourse, however, is by means not of voice but of a resisting silence, in the game of statues that moves her from the margins to the center of attention at the "firemen's" reception — a counterpart to Ursa's revolutionary children's game of "Monument" on the beach. Interrupting the American businessman to whom she is talking, she asks if he ever played "Statues" as a child. She then illustrates by whirling around and assuming a frozen pose, "standing rigid in the silvery gray dress with the draped top" that Primus had made her wear, with her rum held high in her right hand and her left arm bent, "holding her evening bag as if it were a tablet." She continues frozen even after the man guesses the riddle correctly; he responds with a stupefaction that spreads throughout the room as everyone else falls silent too, "all of them turning into statues of themselves" (241).

Estelle enacts this drama in a room the entrance to which is adorned with "two caryatidlike statues" (238), as if the sign of this gathering were the freezing of woman's motion into ornament, decoration, mute static support. Estelle is present at the reception as just such a decorative support, by virtue of her gender. Less obviously, Primus is here for essentially the same purpose, by virtue of his race and his neocolonial status. In the Windsor Room, memorial of British imperialism, Estelle's voice is called on to enact what hooks calls "a talk that [is] in itself a silence," the "right speech of womanhood" (*Talking Back* 6–7) — but also, in this context, the right speech of a Third World man. Estelle is an expert at this kind of talk, a womanly form of control that Marshall, like many feminists before her, portrays as merely a form of powerlessness in the larger scheme of things.

To counteract this powerlessness, Estelle takes control of the silence the dominant discourse imposes on her and Primus, using it dramatically to protest that discourse — in fact to silence it, if only momentarily. Against the lie on which all the conversation is based — the lie that the First and

Third Worlds are actually engaged here in dialogue rather than an act of ventriloquism in which both parties speak the same monologue — Estelle poses a silent representation of the truth. The substitution she engineers, silence for talk, merely reveals what her and Primus's talk has been all along. Estelle's game of statues turns the decorative stasis she has been assigned into an act (in both senses) of Liberty, thus exposing the game being played at the reception for the charade that it is. By representing her dispossession, the silent tableau bespeaks her resistance to it.

In this charade representing a charade, Estelle's enactment of Liberty bears an interesting relation to a scene in one of Jessie Fauset's novels, *There Is Confusion*. The heroine, a dancer, has been cast as "America" in a theatrical pageant but must wear a white mask because it is deemed not seemly, or perhaps simply not realistic, for an African-American woman to represent America. At the climax of the dance she appears in this mask as "a regal, symbolic figure" (232). Fauset uses this "figure" to raise questions about partials and universals; about political representation, artistic representation, and their intersection. From the beginning of the production of African-American art, many white critics have taken it for granted that Black characters represent only a part of experience and therefore cannot, like white characters, embody the universal. As Fauset's heroine finds out in her attempt to get jobs as a dancer, whites can dance any part, but she can get only those roles designated specifically for a woman of color. Whites can represent her, but she cannot represent them. The fallacy translates her political dispossession as an African American directly into her dispossession as an artist.

Elizabeth Minnich's discussion of universality in *Transforming Knowledge* raises the issues that are at stake in Fauset's novel. Minnich describes the fallacy of "taking the few to be proper grounds for generalization to all so that one group becomes representative of all (as others do not become representative for it)" (75). As she says, "One way to see this error, generalizing — even universalizing — from too few instances, in *any* discourse is . . . to notice who is marked, who carries a prefix. Those who have no particularizing prefix are those who have been taken to be 'the thing-itself,' the few who stand in for the universal or general" (77–78).

The real mask at issue in the universalizing of a particular African-American woman by means of a white mask is the masquerade of whiteness as a universal. The reason whites think they can dance any part is that they see their particular experience, at its deepest level, as everyone's: they represent everything; people of color can only represent themselves. In this view, whether African Americans are a part of America is irrelevant; only a white can stand for the whole, for what is "typically" (232) American. At the end of the performance, having experienced for once the liberty of universality that whiteness confers, the dancer is a star. She is encored again and again and someone shouts, "Pull off your mask, America!" (232). The cry reverberates with irony. It raises the question as to who, after all, might be said to "wear the mask" of universality. And it asserts that the whiteness of "America" in the pageant is indeed a mask, because America in this particular case — as in many others — is Black.

Fauset's heroine wears a mask to conceal her racial difference from the whites who make up most of the audience. In the world portrayed by *Daughters*, silence works, among other things, to obscure and elide difference and therefore contain it. Such masking of difference is the role scripted for Estelle's voice at the reception, and it is exactly this role that her performance of the regal, symbolic figure of Liberty subverts. Estelle's specific job is to "know how to talk to them" in order to make the Americans feel at home in a Third World country (236), a role Primus urges on her because he thinks it makes them more receptive to his plans for Morlands. Estelle knows that it will simply enable them all the better to impose on Triunion their discourse of infrastructure, tourism, and tax breaks without hearing the different language of development that Primus wants to speak. In the discourse the firemen control, Primus's plan for a cannery is unspeakable precisely because it would voice an explosive difference between his perspective and theirs. Estelle's disruption of "the usual small talk" (168) that is designed to mask such unpleasant differences spotlights them dramatically, for what she does in her pantomime is to use silence to unmask the differences the smalltalk is intended to contain. Thus the first effect of her pantomime is to force the fireman she has been chatting with so amiably to experience, for a moment, what her American accent is supposed to obscure: that he does not understand her. "Now you speak the kind of English I don't have any trouble understanding," he says (238). With appropriate irony, this countrywoman to whom he is so sure he can relate more easily than he can to the people of Triunion presents to him, as a riddle, the very icon of his nation's relation to other peoples: the Statue of Liberty. Assigned to elide difference by representing "home," Estelle chooses instead to *represent* difference — by representing "home" with a vengeance. Even when the fireman guesses the riddle, he continues to stare in bemused silence, drawn irresistibly for a moment into her form of discourse just as she was forced into his. In this marginalized silence, which Estelle causes to usurp the role of the central discourse at the reception, he and the other visitors re-present what they really are: United States businessmen stupefied at the spectacle of Liberty wearing an African-American face.

Like all Paule Marshall's multidimensional symbolic tableaux, this one pictures much else as well. First, in this neocolonial setting Estelle's mime provides an ironic commentary on the American version of liberty that the firemen are proferring the poor, the sick, the huddled masses of

Morlands, whose needs cannot even for a moment be voiced at the reception. As Viney's grandfather would say, "The woods are on fire out here . . . and we need everybody that can tote a bucket of water to come running" (102). Clearly, these fire-men's relation to the blaze is not that they have come to put it out. Second, Estelle in the silvery tunic dress Primus coerced her into wearing, with her glass held high as a torch of liberty and her evening bag before her like a slate, is appropriating the costume of the decorative woman at a political reception for another, oppositional set of meanings, refashioning it into an image of woman as guide to freedom. Her representation of that image functions differently for her two audiences, the firemen and Primus. The Statue of Liberty summons the poor of other countries on a journey—to the United States, haven for those who yearn to breathe free. The Carnegie Foundation summoned Primus on a journey to the United States, where, as Roy says, "he butt up on a federation of Sirens singing sweet in his ears" (204). Estelle reverses the invitation of the Statue of Liberty, summoning the wandering Odysseus home.

By using, as a form of speech, the silence to which she has been relegated at the reception, Estelle silences the dominant discourse, turns attention to the margins, and succeeds, at least, in communicating exactly what she means to this most important member of her audience. Enacting her silent commentary on the way this discourse has silenced him, she silences his meaningless chitchat along with all the rest. On the other hand, her game is a desperate act of self-defense, like Merle's catatonia or Viney's occasional long, numbed silences. "She was stone that couldn't see, couldn't hear, couldn't feel. So that she didn't, couldn't, see the growing stupefaction on the man's face. . . . spread to . . . every face in the room. . . . Nor did she hear when the conversations . . . faltered and died . . ." (241).

Estelle's act, which gives her a momentary control over the silence and stasis imposed on her and Primus, passes back and forth from a sign of agency to a sign of oppression. Her confrontation, her sudden insistent visibility, turns into a retreat in which the blindness of stone protects her from confronting what she cannot bear, but also keeps her from seeing the success of her act. Although she could not make Primus's silenced speech on behalf of Morlands be heard, she has forced the silence itself —the silence at the core of the business talk, *her* silence—to be heard by those whose discourse is designed to contain it. What Estelle's act does for one moment is to make that unacknowledged silence, that invisible space at the core of hegemonic discourse, loud and visible.

More unambiguously successful is Estelle's other intervention from a place of silence into a silencing discourse. Again she engineers this intervention from the margins, and again it has the silencing of Primus's ventriloquized voice as one of its goals. This intervention, however, goes further by liberating a voice — the lost voice of Primus of which Estelle has been the custodian — as well as silencing one. It is without ever overtly saying exactly what she wants done, but only by wondering aloud to Ursa "what Mr. Beaufils would have to say about" the prospectus (359), that Estelle instigates the process whereby Primus's voice, appropriated by the P and D Board, gives way to that of Justin. By inciting Ursa to enable Mr. Beaufils to "say" something about the prospectus, Estelle calls forth a counterdiscourse to challenge the slick advertising hype that Primus has allowed to supplant his talk of cooperatives and model villages. But Justin, after all, as Estelle reported to Ursa, says the same things Primus used to say in his early days. What Estelle instigates, that is, is the return of Primus's own repressed voice.

5

Estelle from the beginning of *Daughters* is the mother Avey becomes at the end of *Praisesong*: the mother who does not forget. She is repository and transmitter of voices, custodian of history. In Ursa's childhood she strides beside her bed declaiming the words of Sojourner Truth. In her very first conversation with Primus on his Carnegie tour, she woos him with the history of his island, a forecast of the role she will continue to play as re-memberer. In the game of statues, which in essence voices his silence, and in the silencing of his appropriated voice before he can consummate his self-betrayal at the monument, she summons back to voice the silenced half of his divided self by freeing his constituents' voices, initiating dialogue. In the same way, she disrupts the silence that, according to the rules, should have been maintained between her and Astral as wife and mistress of the same man, and between her daughter and Astral.

The mother's voice in these contexts is an empowering, freeing voice, but one that operates behind the scenes — or even, paradoxically, through silence. This is not to say that Marshall's portrait of Estelle repeats the old idea that women exert their power most effectively from their appropriate place behind the scenes, without asserting themselves as individuals. On the contrary, once again the dichotomy implicit in this stereotype is being called into question by Marshall's consideration of the triple struggle for individual autonomy, connectedness, and collective autonomy.

It is not the individual voice that is valorized in the portrait of Estelle's rescue of Primus and of Morlands, but the voice in conversation, the voice on a continuum of other voices. The voice as part of a continuum is also the focus of *Praisesong*, but there the actual words of the heroine's coming to voice are still associated with a single speaker and an audience, even though the speaker is herself multiple and, in a sense, includes the audience in her voice by virtue of their shared legacy of speech. The words are "ordained" by ritual, but they are also the legacy of a single, and singular, person. What stands out in *Daughters,* however, is not one particular act of speech ("It was here that they brought them"); what is valued is the blending of voices: the "intimate, loving palaver" of women friends, a woman and man's "voices melded" in the talk of the free zone.

This valuation is echoed in Marshall's portrait of Ursa's inner life, which she represents as interior discourse, an amalgam of remembered words uttered by other voices, unspoken words Ursa would like to say but does not say, words her friends would be likely to say but say only in Ursa's inner dialogues, and words spoken by a "monitoring voice inside her" (9). Amid this babble of voices, Viney tells Ursa, "you can't hear your own self, your own voice" (112). Marshall manages to convey both how urgent is the necessity for Ursa to find this autonomous voice and how much, on the other hand, even that voice speaks in other voices. What is Ursa's "own voice," anyway? The Creole into which she lapses when she is most moved to anger? The fowl-yard talk she got from Astral? The voice of "Hartford's North End?" The accents of her uncle Grady, distinguishable so clearly in hers?[20] Ursa's "own" voice is itself an amalgam, a superimposition. But what are the implications for women, in their struggle for self-decolonization, if their truest voices are meldings of other voices?

At its most problematic, this issue comes around again to the question with which Paule Marshall's art began, the question of mothers. In Lowell's apartment is something that reminds Ursa of why she became involved with him in the first place: the picture of a mother's voice. This Romare Bearden collage of a mother reading to a child embodies many of the ways in which the mother's voice functions in *Daughters.* That the silent medium of visual art should evoke sound recalls the paradox of Estelle's speech-through-silence: her self-expression in the game of statues; her initiation, through Ursa, of conversations with Justin and Astral; her liberation, from the silence of the margins, of the people's voice. It is also a picture of a woman's voice as an intermediary voice, transmitting one person's thought to another. As the portrayals of Mae and Estelle suggest, this role is not unambiguously positive; it is a traditional woman's role, in which women speak on behalf of others—a version of ventriloquizing. Mae and Estelle, however, unlike Sandy and Primus, are not double but single in their acts of representation, speaking their own most impassioned concerns in the process of melding their voices with those of the people they represent. Their case calls attention to the ways in which Paule Marshall's account of coming to voice here, even more than in her earlier novels, eschews a vision of the self as autonomous by virtue of separateness, in favor of a self most fully articulated—in both senses of the word — in relation. In Ursa's coming-of-age, individual autonomy and the collective autonomy of an oppressed people are versions of the same freedom.

Another important aspect of the mother in Bearden's print is that she speaks, in the present, words written in the past, and her audience is a child — the voice of the future. The mother's voice here, we might assume, nurtures another voice. Thus Ursa's sense of responsibility to speak for Congo Jane and Will Cudjoe, now statues silently imploring her for a voice, is reinforced by Estelle's remembered voice: "*See if you can touch her toes, Ursa-Bea!*" (13). Estelle's bedtime stories of Congo Jane and renditions of Sojourner Truth's great speech "Ain't I a Woman?" ensured her daughter's resistance to silencing. Ursa hears Estelle's voice urging her to reach toward Jane even as she stands before Crowder with the rejected proposal in her hands. The picture on Lowell's wall thus suggests a remedy to one of the greatest dangers the novel portrays, the danger of children being silenced. As in *Praisesong,* the danger is not only metaphorical. When Robeson talks back to the police officer, telling him it's a free country and he has his rights, there is a very real possibility that, as Viney says, "That cracker could have blown my child away. . . . It happens, Ursa! . . . You read about it, you see it on the news" (324). One of Estelle's letters home referred to just such an incident: "To murder a child for *supposedly* talking back to some white shopkeeper! And then to throw his body in a swamp!" (170). Were there no other indications of the concern in *Daughters* for children and their voices, it would be clear simply in the naming of the central child character after a man most famous for his voice — and for the attempts to silence him.

The relation between the mother's voice and that of the children who come after her is complicated. On the one hand, Viney's penchant for outspokenness translates itself into her son's dangerous talk of his "constitutional rights" in a "free country" (323). She wonders whether she did the right thing — whether she shouldn't have raised him in such a way as to expose him to less danger, whether she should have refrained from giving him "that hard-luck name. Look at what they did to the real Robeson. Took away the man's passport. Wouldn't let him sing" (329). On the other hand, Viney herself cannot exercise her voice fully at work, because, like Silla and Ettie, she has her child to support. Ursa, childless, can resign from a lucrative position she finds morally compromising; Viney, as she says, may have similar reservations about her job, but she is not free like Ursa to type out a letter that says she resigns as of this moment. Similarly, Malvern worries about her husband talking about Black Power, because his job supports their children. Malvern berates him loudly in private lest he should speak up too clearly in public. At issue are the compromises that mothers and fathers make in the exercise of their own voices in order to initiate their children's journeys of freedom, and freedom of voice, in a world that deprived the original Robeson of both.

Like the picture of the mother reading to her child, Viney and Robeson are one of the couples the book portrays: "V. Daniels and Son," as their name appears on the sign outside their house. The violation of gender expectations on which the completely serious humor of the nameplate depends points back to Viney's determination to nurture the next generation despite the man-shaped absence. Part of that effort is her nurturing of his relationship with the little girl from the tenement down the street, who is there to watch over Robeson as he sleeps after the trauma of the police station. Viney's concern that class differences not separate them is the reverse of the PM's care for Ursa. Ursa's "twin" has to accost her as a stranger and beggar on the street, and she can only reestablish ties with Justin as an adult by defying the father's injustice in trying to separate them earlier. Estelle was the one who wanted to forge connections, inviting the children in as Viney does.

As these contrasts suggest, the concern in *Daughters* with how to preserve the father's voice from being co-opted is not only paralleled by a concern about how to safeguard children and their voices; the two concerns are in an important sense the same. One consequence of Primus's sellout would be the silencing of the Morlands children in their weekly reenactments of the slave revolt: the transformation of their playground into a "playground" for the rich. Estelle's dispatching of Ursa to speak with Justin and his wife ensures that the children will continue to climb the hill and blow the conch shell, "rallying slaves into soldiers" (384). Here resistance to silencing is resistance to the patriarchy's potential suppression of a future generation's capacity to resist. The mother's voice, however elliptical and marginalized and behind the scenes, works to sustain the next generation's ability to voice resistance, which is their capacity to be free — to be "no more slaves."

It is Primus's destructive doubleness and distance that endanger this capacity. Succumbing like Sandy to the potential for splitting implied in representation, he seems finally to be present neither at the margins nor at the center of power. Instead of being present in two places at once, he and Sandy become absent in two places at once: doubly invisible men. In Ursa, Paule Marshall presents the opposite: the portrait of a successful struggle to make doubleness a source of power. At issue is whether Ursa will be a victim of her distance from both the United States and Triunion or use her presence in both places as the "vital dynamic" (Collier) described in *Praisesong*, whether she will be operated by remote control or use her double perspective as a source of control she herself can direct, whether her doubleness will be a source of "wholeness and unity" or a source of disconnection from herself and others. The potential for disconnection is very real, as when Lowell accuses Ursa of just not being there for him because she is always in Triunion instead. His bitter metaphor of habeas corpus — "Oh, sure. . . . We have the body . . ." (265) — presents a negative version of the first Avatara's visionary distance from the site of her exile, her body there but her mind "long gone with the Ibos." In Avatara's case the distance of mind was a form of resistance to slavery. Here, Lowell implies, it is a form of being colonized — operated "by remote control." Ursa's double-voicedness in their argument over this point seems to confirm his accusation — not only the fact that in her excitement her language breaks in two, but the fact that what she voices silently in her mind is the opposite of what she says aloud.

On the other hand, as the novel nears its climax there is an increasing emphasis on another kind of doubleness: Ursa's propensity for "seeing double" (290), with Midland City superimposed on Triunion and Triunion on Midland City. "[T]here was no separating the landscapes that filled her mind" (297). Here is the paradox of double vision as a source of wholeness and unity. Double vision is a form of psychological splitting, but it is at the same time a *refusal* to separate things. Ursa's vision of "everything superimposed on everything else" (333), in a "series of double exposures" (332), is what reveals to her her father's duplicity. She sees Triunion all the more clearly for Midland City, Primus all the more clearly for Sandy. At the end it is because Ursa sees double that her duplicity can combat patriarchal duplicity. As the audience bursts into speech, Ursa, who instigated that speech, sits silent, playing the double role of supportive-woman-in-the-background and saboteur. But these are in fact a single role. To rescue Primus it is necessary to silence the voice that has run away with his, just as it is necessary, in order to provide Lowell with a "lifeline," to silence him. In both cases, the possessed voice signals the loss of self-possession; sabotaging it is part of the supportive role played by Estelle and Ursa all along. Related to this paradox is the other: it is because Ursa is double that she can be whole.

6

One way to consider the issue of voice in Paule Marshall's novels is to ask what they portray as the causes of silence. One answer is economic pressures, as in the case of Ettie, Silla, Jay, Lowell, and Alberta — characters who wear the mask of silence at work. Another is the pain of intolerable memories of "great wrong" done or suffered, as in Saul's and Merle's silence about the past, and Harriet's moral schizophrenia about her ancestor's relation to Bournehills. Another answer is related especially to mothers. What silences mothers? Avey's dream of Birmingham erases her subsequent dreams, making a numb silence in her memory. In *Daughters* Ursa is accosted on King William Street by the man who speaks up about his poverty, but she is also accosted by a woman who simply uncovers her child silently, so that Ursa can see the sores. The scene is repeated when Mae, "Mother Ryland," uncovers an infant thinking it is too hot, then falls silent in the face of its Saint Vitus dance, and silently covers it again. Another mother's silence: when Ursa is little, Estelle omits from her retellings of Congo Jane's story the fact of her mutilation as a child. All of these are silences in the face of the pain visited on children by what Paule Marshall called in one essay "the present order," which she said "must be swept from center stage" ("Shaping" 108). All of these silences point to the imperative need to give birth, through these children so profoundly threatened by the present order, to something new.

Like Paule Marshall's earlier novels, *Daughters* celebrates women's capacity to give birth to a new order. That capacity is problematized here, however, in a way it has not been before in her work. Images of women's capacity for childbirth are even less straightforward in this novel than in *The Chosen Place*, especially in the scene on the beach in which labor, abortion, miscarriage, and the rescue of a children's play-monument to revolutionary heroes are all superimposed in one act. On the one hand, women's right to choose motherhood is at issue in the juxtaposition of Ursa's legal abortion and Astral's illegal abortion, which has probably left her infertile. The parallel is a sign of the ways in which the criminalizing of abortion, which purports to be about sustaining life and the promise of future generations, is actually about *undermining* women's power to give birth. On the other hand, Ursa's abortion symbolizes a great deal more. She imagines it as incomplete because it involves no pain; the pain finally comes as she separates *herself* from a parent—but from her father, not her mother, with whom this separation forges a new, stronger unity of purpose. The pain is more, however: Ursa's simultaneous miscarriage, abortion, and labor pains on the beach at Government Lands take place on the site of a children's reenactment of the slave revolt. Were it not for her act of separation and birth, these reenactments—and, implicitly, the promise of the next generation—would be lost.

The pain entailed by Ursa's heroine journey also represents what is private and individual and perhaps in conflict with public duty: "No matter how much she's hurting, there's still the main task of the day to be done" (390). Like any mother giving birth, Ursa acts through her pain on behalf of future generations. But again, the image is unstraightforward. For although Ursa's act is heroic, we know that it is not going to give birth to a new order. It is going to preserve the beach at Government Lands. It will preserve the sound of the conch shell. It will preserve the people's capacity to heal themselves in the waters there and, figuratively, their capacity to heal themselves through such revolutionary acts as this one, which is conflated quite specifically with the revolutionary act memorialized in the children's ritual climb, itself reiterated by Ursa. But the reader is all too aware by this point in the novel that these acts have to be repeated and repeated, just as Ursa's scaling of the hill repeats the children's game, repeated every Sunday, which repeats the revolution of Will Cudjoe and Congo Jane. The Sunday ritual, like Jay and Avey's in *Praisesong*, is not only a celebration; it is a necessity, a question of whether a people and their culture will live or die. Were there not such jeopardy, the repetition would not be such a matter of life or death.

There is, too, the sobering fact that Ursa's success in *Daughters* is a fiction — a fact to which the novel itself calls attention through its many forthright allusions to the extrafictional events of contemporary real-world politics: "Bonzo's friend" the White-House "cowboy," the invasion of Grenada, the cutting of funds for mental institutions, the upsurge of homelessness, United States military intimidation of Third World nations during elections. In all of these nonfictional cases, the class interests served by the resort scheme in the fiction won out. At the end of the novel the scheme has failed because of Estelle and Ursa — for the moment. That the resort will not, at least, be located on Government Lands is a small victory in certain ways. Then again, what the victory sustains within the fiction, and what Paule Marshall's fiction itself helps sustain in the real world it mirrors, is the capacity for collective self-healing, which is the same as the capacity for repeating the heroisms of the past, no matter how many times that may be necessary.[21]

"Mother Ryland" speaks of this necessity for repeating: "Maybe he can learn. . . . But if we find he can't learn . . . if we see he just ain't no *use* no kinda way, we'll . . . find us another. . . . And if that one don't do right neither, we'll vote his butt out too, and just keep on till we find us the right one" (299). Mae is not a mother biologically, but her life's work is dedicated to those children, grands and great-grands, on whom she refuses to give up. Sandy himself, she says, is one of the grands. In Patricia Hill Collins's terms (129ff.), Mae is a "community othermother" both in the political senses of the word and in its other sense of just taking care of children physically, as when she takes the cocaine baby into her lap. Such work seems like the labor of Sisyphus. When Ursa comes upon her years after their first encounter, Mae has been to City Hall and left and is right back where she started, without even the equipment that Ursa's foundation purchased for her. She is still sitting in her old office with the same protest on the door: "Sent For You Yesterday, Here You Come Today" (286). Marshall pictures her not as a Sisyphean figure, however, but as a very different figure of repetition, an avatara wearing "the years of her several other lifetimes" (291) as well as the characteristic ruffles and lace that identify her as an incarnation, specifically, of Congo Jane.

7

The question of avatars comes back around to questions of autonomy and connection. No more than any other Paule Marshall novel does *Daughters* represent a unitary self apart from other selves. Ursa's authentic voice is hers alone, but it is made up of many others. Correspondingly, her self-discovery leads her to a "Siamese twin" whose heart beats in her chest. At the end of the novel Ursa, surveying her body and thinking about what is her father's, her mother's, and uniquely her own, is both a couple (a combination of Primus and Estelle) and something else as well — a kind of triunion.

The end of the novel poises on this note of what Ursa elsewhere calls "wholeness and unity" and voices inwardly as her private mantra, "Ke'ram." Characteristically of Paule Marshall, this completely individual word voiced by Ursa in her solitary meditations is also an external voice, the sound of the waves on the beach at Government Lands. It is this voice that her revolutionary silencing and liberation of the father's voice has preserved. The final paragraph of the book pictures Ursa putting herself back together again, restoring her body, voicing the word that is the voice of the healing waters where the people of Morlands come every Sunday to bathe.

During her own early morning visit to these waters on the Sunday of her private revolution, Ursa watches the waves break, leaving foam like Congo Jane's lace. Ursa is alone, but the image makes present Congo Jane and all the other women linked with her: Mae, Astral, Estelle, Viney.[22] Jane's lace hid her physical mutilation by the slave masters, a punishment for stealing pretty things. She stole the lace as part repayment for that mutilation. Ursa's visit to the beach is about loss, recovery, pain, and healing. It uses the events repeated in women's lives — abortion, labor, miscarriage — to represent the collective power of their individual heroine journeys. These journeys are never made alone, just as the heroines' voices are never single or solitary — or even silent, despite their many silencings. Waves break again and again, they are never spent, they come back. Primus wants to take this place away from the people of Morlands. Crowder wanted to take Jane away from Ursa. The avatar Jane, represented metonymically by the lace of the breaking waves, is what Ursa's act rescues — steals back, repossesses in the private act of self-decolonization that decolonizes the "Government" lands.

Her act of separation, her move for freedom, is an act of unity, and not only with all the other women with whom it connects her. Jane's lace hid her mutilation — bound her wound. It also bound the wound of her lover, co-conspirator, consort, friend, fellow revolutionary. At the end of the slave revolt the lace was Will's as well as Jane's, a sign of a bond so close that their very names cannot be spoken separately. Even as Ursa separates herself from Lowell and her father, her visit to Justin signifies a mystical link with these men as co-conspirators, co-revolutionaries. On the beach at Government Lands, the lace, visual sign of the sound of Ke'ram with which the waves break, binds Ursa to Jane and Will, to Primus and Lowell, to Estelle and Astral, to Mae and Viney, and to a perpetually resurgent resistance that unites them all.

Epilogue

> About ten feet below her the waves are quietly exploding with the sound of Ke'ram. They heave themselves onto the shore, there's the soft muffled explosion, the foam spreads like the lace of Jane's shawl, and the wave recedes. Ke'ram. They're breaking and receding with the sound of Ke'ram, saying it for her.
>
> *— Daughters*

It is a long way — thirty years or more — from Max Berman's lake to the beach at Government Lands. Even so, Miss Williams swimming out into the golden water, plunging deep into a voice that is hers and not hers, has much in common with Ursa sitting on the beach at dawn, listening to the waves voicing her private language, "saying it for her." Miss Williams's issues are all there in Ursa's story: the defiance of a white male professor, the act of possession that is an act of self-possession, the woman's voice pitted against an ostensibly more powerful male voice, the interior decolonization that reclaims an exterior place. But what links these pictures most clearly is the way they pose the question of a woman's power in the context of a dialectic between an interior world of the psyche that is nonetheless "profoundly social" and an exterior world of "objective forces" that is simultaneously a psychological terrain. Just as the dynamics of oppressive power-over are simultaneously interior and exterior in the world of Marshall's novels, so the dynamics of resistance require a fusion of internal power-to with a source of such power outside the self. If the drama of imperialism is doubly internal and external, the way the oppressed preserve intact their "energy for change" must likewise fuse the inner and outer — a fusion expressed, especially in *Daughters*, in meldings of voice.

"[M]y way of seeing the world has been so profoundly shaped by my dual experience," Paule Marshall has said. Her own "representative voice" as a realist has from the beginning been informed by her many capacities for "seeing double." Those capacities account, indeed, for the integrity of her representations — the extraordinary fidelity with which she renders character, for example. She is perhaps most famous for her characters, but she should be equally famous for the astuteness of her political vision, which, because it is presented with a clarity and subtlety commensurate with that of her characterization, never betrays or is betrayed by her nuanced renderings of wish, motive, desire, self-doubt, self-revelation. On the contrary, the object of her mimesis itself is the conflation of economic, psychological, and political reality. Her art renders the process whereby the external world works to configure the inner life of the dispossessed. At the same time it renders the ways in which the oppressed resist that configuration, clearing a space, in a political and economic world that works to mold them to the contours of silence, for the journey of freedom.

Notes

Introduction

1. "To be able to use the range of one's voice, to attempt to express the totality of self, is a recurring struggle in the tradition of [Black women] writers," Barbara Christian says (*Black Feminist Criticism* 172).

2. On the dichotomy between agency and oppression in feminist scholarship, see Ellen DuBois et al., 39–40 and 66–67. My thinking about voice, silence, and power in Marshall's works has been especially influenced by all the works of bell hooks, especially *Talking Back: Thinking Feminist, Thinking Black* and *Feminist Theory from Margin to Center.*

3. As Mae Henderson says, "In their works, black women writers have encoded oppression as a discursive dilemma, that is, their works have consistently raised the problem of the black woman's relationship to power and discourse. Silence is an important element of this code" ("Speaking in Tongues" 124).

4. My thinking about this kind of silence has been especially influenced by Carol Cohn's "Sex and Death in the Rational World of Defense Intellectuals," which analyzes in detail one example of coercive, hegemonic discourse.

5. To evoke this theme is to raise the issue of fragmentation and wholeness, a major theme in all of Paule Marshall's work that has recently received its most extensive and definitive treatment in Joyce Pettis's important study, *Toward Wholeness in Paule Marshall's Fiction.* To the extent that my study is concerned with the subject of wholeness—and almost every critical study of Marshall has been concerned with it in some way—it is focused less on wholeness as a theme and more on what might be called a narrative *technique* of wholeness in relation to the double visions implicit in the novel's feminist concerns.

6. Patricia Hill Collins discusses African-American women's "journey from silence to language to action," a "journey toward finding the voice of empowerment" (112): "While the theme of the journey also appears in the work of Black men, African-American women writers and musicians explore this journey toward freedom in ways that are characteristically female" (Thompson-Cager 1989). Black women's journeys, though at times embracing political and social issues, basically take personal and psychological forms and rarely reflect the freedom of movement of Black men who hop 'trains,' 'hit the road,' or in other ways physically travel in order to find that elusive sphere of freedom from racial oppression. Instead, Black women's journeys often involve 'the transformation of

silence into language and action' (Lorde, "Transformation of Silence" 40)" (Collins 105). She is citing Chezia Thompson-Cager, "Ntozake Shange's *Sassafras, Cypress and Indigo*: Resistance and Mythical Women of Power," *NWSA Journal* 1,4 (1989): 589–601, and Audre Lorde, "The Transformation of Silence into Language and Action," in *Sister Outsider* (Trumansberg, N.Y.: Crossing Press, 1984). On the motif of the journey as "an important black aesthetic feature appearing in both oral and written literature," see Carole Boyce Davies (21–22). See also Deborah McDowell on "the black female's journey" and Claudia Tate (xx–xxi), both of whom Davies responds to in her discussion of *Praisesong for the Widow*.

7. Mary Helen Washington calls attention to double-consciousness as "the problem at the heart of *Brown Girl* ("Afterword" 319). "Double vision" and "double-consciousness" are two of the "key terms" in Bernard W. Bell's *The Afro-American Novel and Its Tradition*. His definitions are related to a somewhat broader set of meanings I am evoking here: "*double-consciousness* signifies the biracial and bicultural identities of Afro-Americans . . . and *double vision*, an ambivalent, laughing-to-keep-from-crying perspective toward life as expressed in the use of irony and parody in Afro-American folklore and formal art" (xvi). He cites DuBois's 1897 use of "double-consciousness" as the origin of this "metaphor for the sociopsychological process by which the black American minority responded to the racial and cultural domination of the white American majority," a metaphor "apparently rewritten in 1937 by anthropologist Melville J. Herskovits as socialized ambivalence to explain the existence of conflicting African and European values and behavioral alternatives in postcolonial Haitians. The trope was further developed in 1963 by Ralph Ellison as double vision to describe the ambivalence of modern black Americans toward all people and events" (345). (W. E. B. DuBois, "Strivings of the Negro People," *Atlantic Monthly*, August 1897, pp. 194–89, and "Of Our Spiritual Strivings," *The Souls of Black Folk*, [1903; reprint, Greenwich, Conn.: Crest, 1965], pp. 16–17. Ralph Ellison, "The World and the Jug," *New Leader* 46 [December 9, 1963]: 22–26, and *Shadow and Act* [1964; reprint, New York: Signet, 1966], p. 137.) Ellison's *Shadow and Act* is one of the books Paule Marshall has cited as most influencing her thought as a writer. The meanings inherent in her own use of the term "seeing double" are perhaps most fully suggested in DuBois's use of another term, in his famous description of double-consciousness: "After the Egyptian and Indian, the Greek and Roman, the Teuton and Mongolian, the Negro is a sort of seventh son, born with a veil, and gifted with second-sight in this American world, — a world which yields him no true self-consciousness, but only lets him see himself through the revelation of the other world. It is a peculiar sensation, this double-consciousness, this sense of always looking at one's self through the eyes of others. . . . One ever feels his twoness . . ." (214–15). DuBois speaks of a "longing . . . to merge his double self into a better and truer self" (215), with the implication, in "better," that this doubleness is a negative quality, a lesser condition than what Ursa, clearly beset by "twoness" throughout most of *Daughters*, would call "wholeness and unity" (*Daughters* 40). The term "second-sight," however, with its implications of prescience and prophecy, evokes the full paradox that justifies Bell's description of double-consciousness, socialized ambivalence, and double vision as both the "special burden and blessing of Afro-American identity" (35), and his insistence on not reading them as "a basic personality type or disorder. On the contrary," he says, "they signify both the complex sociopsychological process of acculturation of black Americans—the will to realize their human and civil rights—and the sociocultural

relationship of colonized people of African descent to colonizers of European descent. The shifts in allegiance of black Americans between the values of the white dominant culture and those of the black subculture, in other words, are a normal survival strategy, a healthful self-protective, compensatory response to the oppression and repression fostered by institutionalized racism and economic exploitation" (345). What Marshall seems to me to be studying in such characters as Ursa and Avey, however, is not "shifts in allegiance" but the paradox itself: the relationship between a negative experience of the lack of "wholeness and unity" and the possibility of turning one's doubleness to a "second-sight" that creates unity by holding both worlds in focus at the same time. What I want to suggest is that not only is the *trope* of double vision or double-consciousness at the center of the thematic content of Marshall's works, but that she has developed, with more and more subtlety throughout her career, a *technique of* double vision, a mode of superimposition or double exposure that is her device for representing the simultaneities as the heart of her feminist vision.

8. Most analyses of Marshall have focused in some way on what John McClusky Jr. calls "the interplay of individual and collective history" in her works (333); in Spillers's view "The characters . . . are the part that speaks for the whole, just as the whole is configured in their partialness" (154); Willis identifies Marshall's "great talent as a writer" with "her insightful portrayal of individual characters as they articulate the complex of a community's actions and desires" (54), and Skerrett reads Merle's "community as a symbolic replication of her psychological 'crisis of generativity'" (71). Closest to my emphasis on the *interpenetration* of the social and the psychological, however, is Barbara Christian's view, based on a concept of art similar to that set forth by Angela Davis in the essay from which the epigraph to this chapter comes. Christian describes Marshall's works as "psycho-political images" and sees her as performing the function that makes "persistent creative artists . . . so important to a culture": "they fuse the personal and the social areas that our fragmented world thrusts one against the other," helping us "see the oneness between politics and the individual psyche, oppression and the nature of human history, culture and the individual . . ." (*Black Women Novelists* 135). In these terms, the narrative procedures of superimposition at which I am looking are a formal rendering of the thematic content to which Christian alludes in her picture of the fragmentation of the personal and social—part of the theme of "wholeness" that Joyce Pettis situates at the center of her study of Paule Marshall's examination of race, class, and gender (*Toward Wholeness*).

9. My thinking about self-decolonization and its relationship to decolonized spaces is indebted to Chandra Mohanty ("Porous Borders").

10. See her introduction to "Brooklyn" in *Reena: "Sexual harassment? We didn't even think to use the term back in the early fifties when this story takes place. There were no women's groups on campus to which we could take the problem; no notices on the bulletin boards and in the bathrooms with phone numbers to call for help and advice; no sympathetic ear in administration. There was nowhere to turn, no support system of any kind, as I recall. . . . In my case, I turned down the repeated invitations to visit his place in the country, ignored the look in his eyes and the suggestive play of his white wrinkled hands. . . . Afterwards, to rid myself of the anger I had held in check over the months, I sat down and started writing 'Brooklyn'—really just taking notes for it, because the story didn't assume its present form until some nine years later . . ."* (27).

11. Especially in her interview with DeVeaux and in her 1983 essay "From the Poets in the Kitchen" (*Reena* 3–12.)

Chapter 1: "The Mother's Voice"

1. Related to my description of double vision as a technique in Marshall's work is Willis's discussion of metaphor in *Brown Girl, Brownstones*, which she links to the use of metaphor in African-American women's writing in general and to what she sees as the "allegorical" aspect of "the great majority of modern Third World writing" (20). She argues that texts "whose mode of articulating history is based on metaphor"—the trope best able to embody contradiction by "saying two things at once"—capture "the complex meanings and contradictory relationships generated by capitalism. This is possible because metaphor, based on condensation, delights in defining similarity out of contraries . . ." (21, 22). Willis's view of metaphor is especially akin to my readings of "superimposition" in her example of Selina's flight from Mrs. Benton, as she flees with car horns "bay[ing] behind her" and collapses "like an animal broken by a long hunt." Willis says, "it is as if Marshall suddenly started to tell two stories at once: the harrowing flight of the fugitive slave, pursued by the lights, voices, and baying dogs of the bloodthirsty overseers, and Selina's panic-stricken flight from white bourgeois persecution. In fact, the metaphor allows Marshall to overlap two historical moments, demonstrating that the contradictions born with capitalism's agrarian mode continue to inform urban society" (24). While the particular kind of "overlap" emphasized here points to some of the differences between Willis's interpretation and mine, her description of Marshall "telling two stories at once" is one of the modes of narrative I am describing as "superimposition," and her conclusion that "The combination of condensation and metaphor defines black women's novels as both modernist and historical" (21) is related to my perception that Marshall superimposes realism and allegory. See also Hélène Christol's comment that "Looking inward and outward at the same time was the strategy that [Marshall] constantly adopted in her major works" ("Paule Marshall's Bajan Women" 144).

2. The phrase comes from James's essay "The Art of Fiction" (34), in his discussion of the necessity for the writer of fiction to write from "experience": "It is equally excellent and inconclusive to say that one must write from experience. . . . What kind of experience is intended, and where does it begin and end? Experience is never limited, and it is never complete; it is an immense sensibility, a kind of huge spider-web of the finest silken threads suspended in the chamber of consciousness, and catching every air-borne particle in its tissue. It is the very atmosphere of the mind; and when the mind is imaginative . . . it takes to itself the faintest hints of life, it converts the very pulses of the air into revelations" ("Art of Fiction" 34–35). In her first novel Marshall was clearly writing from "experience," as young writers are always told to do, and the house embodies that experience. The first image of Selina, listening to the silence of the house on the top landing, is in many ways a self-portrait of the writer at work: the fine sensibility in the "chamber of consciousness" that is the brownstone, attuned to the "faintest hints of life" in the old house, "convert[ing] the very pulses of the air into revelations." Calling attention to such phrases as "floor of her mind," Kimberly W. Benston points out that the "linguistic texture" of the novel is "so suffused with psychological uses of architectural images that such syntax becomes the principal controlling device for character delineation" (69).

3. No discussion of the question of multiple voices in the psyche, with regard to African-American women's writing, can fail to be indebted to Mae Henderson's "Speaking in Tongues: Dialogics, Dialectics, and the Black Woman Writer's Literary Tradition." Of particular relevance here is Henderson's emphasis on the

"interlocutory, or dialogic, character" of "black women's writing," "reflecting not only a relationship with the 'other(s),' but an internal dialogue with the plural aspects of self that constitute the matrix of black female subjectivity" (118). Using Bakhtin's view of consciousness as, in Henderson's summary, "a kind of 'inner speech' reflecting 'the outer word' in a process that links the psyche, language, and social interaction" (118), she says, "If the psyche functions as an internalization of heterogeneous social voices, black women's speech/writing becomes at once a dialogue between self and society and between self and psyche" (119). In African-American women writers, she concludes, "One discovers . . . a kind of internal dialogue reflecting an *intrasubjective* engagement with the *intersubjective* aspects of self, a dialectic neither repressing difference nor, for that matter, privileging identity, but rather expressing engagement with the social aspects of self . . ." (137) — a formulation that complements Angela Davis's insistence on "the intensely social character" of the "interior" life. Henderson's discussion is focused on the "heteroglossia" of the African-American woman writer herself, but her formulations apply especially well to Marshall's representations of Selina's inner world as it is allegorized in the brownstone, echoing with voices in so many different shades and accents. Henderson's discussion of the writer's own heteroglossia is even more relevant when one considers the obviously autobiographical quality of this first novel, whose protagonist begins as a young poet reciting her verse aloud as she wanders the halls and rooms of this house full of multiple voices.

4. As Sabine Bröck says, "this spatial image with its double implications works as the perfect metaphor for the ambivalence of Silla's character" ("Transcending" 85).

5. "Alma from Latin *almus*, 'nourishing', i.e., the soul. Her castle is an allegory of the body, the mortal part of man," with representations of the mouth (a porch), beard (a wandering vine), moustache (ivy), nose (portcullis), mouth (barbican), porter (tongue), and so on (Thomas P. Roche's notes pp. 1126–27). Entering by this route, the knight, Guyon, first encounters "a jolly yeoman" named Appetite. His tour includes the lungs, stomach, and anus; eventually he ascends to the turret (the brain).

> Therein were diverse roomes, and diverse stages,
> But three the chiefest, and of greatest powre,
> In which there dwelt three honorable sages,
> The wisest men, I weene, that liued in their ages. (2.9.47)

These are three of the "senses of the mind" (Roche 1128) in the persons of Phantastes (akin to Imagination), Eumnestes (Memory), and Anamnestes (The Reminder: a "young helper" of the old man Memory) (Roche 1128). Their rooms, and their placement in relation to each other (e.g., all three rooms are at the top of the house, but Phantastes' room is in the front in keeping with his "sharpe foresight"; Memory is "hindmost"), are described in details that describe the nature and importance of each quality being allegorized and its relationship to the other qualities.

6. Mary Helen Washington says, "The relationship between Silla and Selina Boyce is so full of mystery, passion, and conflict that it may well be the most complex treatment of the mother-daughter bond in contemporary American literature. Marshall writes the mother figure into the entire novel, resisting the temptation to make the daughter's life preeminent, to make the daughter's victory contingent on the rejection of the mother's world or on her elimination

from the narrative. Silla and Selina are so embedded in each other's lives that Selina can only come to know herself by acknowledging that connection and by respecting that part of herself which is like her mother" ("I Sign My Mother's Name" 157). Washington provides an invaluable discussion of the link between this complex relationship and the relationship of Paule Marshall and her own mother.

7. Missy Dehn Kubitschek points out that Miss Mary embodies "The results of identifying with the oppressor," and that Mary has herself "entered the fantasy which eight-year-old Selina creates when imagining herself as one of the whites who originally lived in the Boyces' brownstone.... [Miss Mary] identifies with and takes pride in her employer's family rather than her own" (49).

8. For a discussion of the psychomachia as a basic "pattern" of allegory, see Fletcher (151–63).

9. Indeed, as Leseur points out, this silence is "The first intimation of Selina's perception of" the mother herself (120).

10. As Mary Helen Washington says, "Selina calls her 'the mother,' not 'my mother,' reinforcing [the] sense of Silla's dominance and power. Silla is *the* mother much as someone might be called *the* president" ("Afterword" 313).

11. "... a mere cog in the deathworks of industrial machinery," as Benston describes Silla (69). The complexity of the representation of Silla's power here is part of the attack on "the myth of the matriarchy" to which Dorothy L. Denniston has called attention in this novel. She sees this attack first emerging in Marshall's work in a passage from "Reena": "They condemn us . . . without taking history into account. We are still, most of us, the black woman who had to be almost frighteningly strong in order for us all to survive" (*Reena* 86). Denniston distinguishes between "an indomitable spirit," as evidenced in Silla, and power: "But an indomitable spirit is not to be equated with indisputable power—strength, perhaps, but not power" (43).

12. Barbara Christian (*Black Women Novelists*) provides an excellent discussion of the complex ways in which Silla and Deighton are "intertwined in their defeat of each other" (97): "Perhaps such a sensibility as Deighton's demands another kind of sensibility to keep it warm and comfortable, just as a sensibility that is essentially practical is deadening without the touch of magic. Perhaps Silla and Deighton at one time shared so much of the same sensibility that the one in having to become solely practical is enraged, while the other in being only magical is razed by guilt" (99). For a discussion of the dialectical function of the differences between Deighton and Silla, see Keith E. Byerman, who explains why, "in order to survive, either Deighton or Silla must destroy the other, which means, of course, destroying a vital part of the self" (141). For Deighton,

Success is pleasure, dreams, freedom. For Silla. . . . Success is defined as the acceptance of responsibility, of limitation. . . . Deighton requires the reality principle that Silla represents in order to give nurture and substance to his being while he dreams. . . . The very envisioning of a realm of freedom is premised on control of the realm of necessity. . . . On the other hand, Silla is dehumanized by her rejection of Deighton. . . . It is only Deighton's passion that humanizes her. . . . while the two definitions of success are symbiotic, they are also mutually destructive. For Silla, to accept Deighton means to question the self-reification necessary to achieve her own ends; it means to step outside the security of community values; it means to renounce the positive identity and power gained through struggle. For Deighton, acceptance of Silla's definition of success means death, since it would require entrance into that realm where his failure is guaranteed. (141)

Byerman sees Deighton's "ritual of excess" as a "final act of self-assertion," "his ultimate refusal to turn dreams into objects of exchange," which "is also a ceremony of death, for it is apparent that the dreamer cannot survive in this world" (142).

13. Hélène Christol discusses the relationship between work and "sex roles and gender" in *Brown Girl* from a different perspective that sees "the definitions of man and woman" as running "counter to Silla's and Deighton's personalities" ("Black Woman's Burden" 157). There are, however, important differences between gender roles as the Barbadian community conceives of them and as the surrounding white culture conceives of them, and even within the community, gender roles are inflected by class. These differences help to account for the way in which something for which Silla has worked so hard, the successful assimilation of Ina, who will belong to a higher socioeconomic class than her mother, produces an ideal of womanhood so alien to Silla's own enactment of womanhood in the brownstone and in the Barbadian community.

14. She cites Cellestine Ware's *Woman Power: The Movement for Women's Liberation* (New York: Tower, 1970).

15. See Part 1, "Toward a Feminist Poetics," of *The Madwoman in the Attic.* Another interesting aspect of Silla's rebellion here is noted by Deborah Schneider: "As a fictional character Silla Boyce bears little resemblance to Nora in Ibsen's feminist classic, *A Doll's House,* but it is interesting to note that her crime is also the forging of a man's signature for money to do what she considers to be in her husband's best interests" (71).

16. Trudier Harris describes Silla as being in "a state of the blues," but without "a sustained means of expressing it, either artistically or otherwise" ("No Outlet for the Blues" 58). The word "sustained" is particularly interesting in terms of Marshall's representation of Silla as a kind of artist. Silla's verbal art is something she uses often but sporadically, as a temporary outlet (the metaphor of the gun comes to mind) rather than a "sustained" act that can sustain liberation, which is what Selina's art promises to become. Likewise, her writing is focused on one particular obsession, so that although she sustains it, in one sense, over a long period of time, it is not capable in turn of sustaining *her* psychologically, except in a very temporary way that dissipates with Deighton's dissipation of the money.

17. Relevant here is Ebele Eko's description of Selina rebelling against her mother "not as [a mother] but as [a representative] of societal authority and expectation" (141).

18. Simone de Beauvoir described it perfectly in her discussion of woman's role as "Other" in man's drama of transcendence and immanence. Compared to flowers, streams, trees, the sea, woman in this drama plays Nature, which man possesses by possessing her. But because nature implies mortality she must also — in her perfect artifice of makeup, coiffure, and dress that deny her own mortal nature — embody man's fantasy of immortality.

19. In response to Sylvia Baer's question, "I want to know how you were able to hold onto your vision and to your voice," Marshall said, "I think credit for that has to be given to a group of women from my childhood, whom I talk about every opportunity I get — just four or five ordinary-looking immigrant women from a tiny island in the West Indies that nobody had ever heard of."

20. As Linda Pannill says, "Commentators have called this novel a *Bildungs-*

roman, but it is more: a *Künstlerroman*, an artist-heroine fiction. A recent scholarly study, *A Portrait of the Artist as a Young Woman*, states that there are *no* Black women artist-apprenticeship novels! Paule Marshall has written one, however, and her work as a whole has been concerned with the shaping of creativity in individual women and in communities, an energy often represented by dance" (63). Susan Stanford Friedman also discusses *Brown Girl* as an "autobiographical *kunstler-roman*" (50–51).

21. He was of course only one of her heroes: "When I was a teenager, I was influenced by all kinds of writers, from Emile Zola to Zane Grey. Then I went through a very heavy Thomas Mann and Joseph Conrad period. . . . I was also influenced by Richard Wright, to a lesser degree. Of course there was Paul Lawrence Dunbar. Women writers like Zora Neale Hurston and Dorothy West I didn't discover until later on" (DeVeaux 35).

22. As Collier points out, "for Selina . . . to dream of being white is essentially to reject the community of the oppressed and to long—futilely—to be part of the oppressor," a dynamic that "has been a vital factor in the perpetuation of oppression" (299). Thus the rejection of that dream issues logically in an embracing of "the community of the oppressed."

23. For a different reading of this scene, see Marie H. Buncombe, who looks at Selina's sense of unity from another angle: "To Selina, the cost of attaining the American dream was far too dear. She gradually came to realize that her victories of going to college and living in a Brooklyn brownstone . . . were really small ones, for she was still a black girl in a white world that denied her humanity and refused to accept her blackness as anything but a badge of inferiority. Nothing could change that fact. She gradually learned that the materialistic triumphs of the aspiring black middle class did not separate her in any appreciable way from her hairdresser, who had been violated by white men in the South many years before, or the whores and pimps on Fulton Street in Brooklyn" (18).

24. Laura Niesen de Abruna has seen "the positive and empowering connections between women" (88)—the survival of women characters "by forming a bond, a 'mirroring' relationship with other women" (87)—as a crucial aspect of works by Caribbean women writers, whose "strength . . . is their concern with relational interaction" (90). In Mrs. Benton's case, she describes the failure of such a potential for mirroring: "Although Selina might expect the image of her hope and youth to be reflected in the woman's regard, the white woman's pale eyes reflect only one thing—that Selina is black and must be made to feel inferior. 'Those eyes were a well-lighted mirror. . . .' This racism obviates any reciprocity between Selina and the older woman" (92).

25. Susan Stanford Friedman links this scene to Sheila Rowbotham's image of "The prevailing social order" as "a great and resplendent hall of mirrors" (*Woman's Consciousness, Man's World* [London: Penguin, 1973], 27, quoted in Friedman 38), the mirrors being "the reflecting surface of cultural representation into which a woman stares to form an identity" (38). In the scene of the "false self in the window," Friedman says, Selina "tries to shatter the alienating image in the cultural mirror" but cannot do so "until she can learn to respect the Bajan community she despised. . . . The illusion that she was a single individual who could make her way alone in the white world nearly destroyed Selina. The lesson of the mirror is the lesson of collective identity, in both its alienating and transformative aspects" (51).

26. On the significance of Selina's new, "larger view of her mother," see Gloria

Wade-Gayles (10) and Rosalie Riegle Troester. Both see Selina as realizing that, in Troester's words, "she *is* her mother in some deep and eternal sense" (13).

27. Marshall's revisioning of the Gothic here explains in terms of internalized oppression the ambivalent masochism that often infuses Gothic pursuits.

28. As Elwanda D. Ingram says, Selina must "free herself from her immediate environment" to fulfill her "quest in search of 'peace, love, a clearer vision, a place' (308)" (Ingram 26). My reading of the escape from the brownstone's interior at the end has been influenced by Hanna Nowak's reading of Marshall's heroines as journeying toward a "wild zone": a term "Elaine Showalter borrows from the anthropologists Shirley and Edwin Ardener . . . to designate a special women's sphere outside the dominant male culture" (70). See also Sabine Bröck's discussion of place and placelessness in Marshall, especially her discussion of the ending: "Silla and Selina's ideas of how and where a black woman can find a space of her own in white society collide in their argument about the Brownstone, the image of which has dominated the entire novel: ' . . . I'm not interested in houses!' [Selina's] scream burst the room and soared up to the main hall.' . . . Selina's painful efforts to find out *what* she wants then culminate in these musings: 'What was at the center?. . . . Peace, perhaps, as fleeting as that was, and the things that shaped it: love, a clearer vision, a *place*' " (Bröck, "Transcending" 84; Bröck's emphasis). Bröck's view of the brownstone as central to the issue of where Black women can find "space" points to yet another example of the conflation of social/political and psychological issues in the novel, because while the house is Selina's mind as well as Silla's, its role as Bröck describes it situates the space it encompasses as profoundly social as well.

29. "Movement is freedom in Paule Marshall's work, and Selina is a dancer, an artist-heroine. . . . Appropriately for a book full of purposeful movement, *Brown Girl, Brownstones* ends with an articulate gesture" (Pannill 65).

Chapter 2: Losses and Recognitions

1. For a different but related view of the conjunction of setting and psychology in this novel, see Joyce Pettis's discussion of the way in which the characters' "personal problems personify and embody the troubled, public history of the setting" ("Talk" 111). As she says, "Marshall's technique of intertwining public and private histories of a place and its people reaches panoramic dimensions in *The Chosen Place*" ("Talk" 111).

The only critics who describe the novel in terms of allegory are Marcia Keizs, who is referring to plot rather than landscape when she terms the novel "an allegory of Western civilization" (74), and Jean Carey Bond, who describes *The Chosen Place* as an "allegorical novel" that "succeeds nobly" but "also fails monumentally" (76). The success and failure seem in this review to be equated with the novel's realism and its allegory, respectively, the latter being seen in terms of "symbolic chords" struck "with too heavy a hand" (77). (Thomas Lask's review, in contrast, described Marshall as "never didactic, never god or preacher" [31].) The appearance of allegory in a narrative is indeed often announced by a certain transparency, the hint of one-to-one equations of sign and signified that has tended to disconcert many critics since Coleridge's famous designation of allegory as produced by a lower faculty of the creative mind. I would see this transparency as a signal, an opening, an invitation to read in a certain way rather than a one-dimensional barrier thrown up across the path of the imaginative reader who must thereafter resent what appeared to be a dead-end. The post-Romantic loss of feeling in much mainstream Western criticism for the multidimensional potential of allegory as social/political criticism as well as its capacity for psychological subtlety and nuance should not lead readers to draw back from one of the most interesting aspects of Marshall's work.

Portions of this chapter appeared first as an article in *Callaloo* 16.1 (Winter 1993): "Women, Silence, and History in *The Chosen Place, the Timeless People*."

2. See Marcia Keizs's description of Marshall's vision as "at once personal and political" (71), and Marshall's comments in an interview with Omolara Ogundipe-Leslie:

> PM: . . . I would like to see it described as a Third World novel, because it is set in a mythical island in the West Indies. Readers spend an awful lot of time trying to identify the place rather than seeing its larger meaning; the fact that it makes a statement about what is happening in the Third World in general.
> OO-L: Politically and psychologically?
> PM: Yes.

See also Marshall's identification of one of her two central themes as "the importance of truly confronting the past, both in personal and historical terms" ("Shaping the World of My Art" 110–11).

3. As Marshall said the women in this novel were intended to do (DeVeaux 126).

4. As Sascha Talmor points out, its "worth for the world" is that "it produces sugar canes. . . . Bourneville [sic] here clearly stands as a symbol for all those places in the world whose importance for the world is in terms of their product" (126).

5. As Marlow's ship penetrates into the jungle, Carroll points out, the whites on board perceive the Africans dancing on shore as a kaleidoscope of rolling eyes, whirling limbs, clapping hands — disembodied parts of human beings, not real people. "And it is this absence of other people which declares the writer's intention. He is using Africa as a symbol, a backcloth onto which his characters can project their inner doubts, their sense of alienation" (3).

6. Marshall's treatment of issues of labor did not, before Joyce Pettis's study, receive much of the attention it should command. "The threat posed to the psyche in the world of work" is a special focus of Pettis's discussion of "symbols of capitalism" in Marshall's fiction (*Toward Wholeness* 8, 85–94). "The residues of enslavement and of colonialism in *The Chosen Place*," she says, "are offered with the perspective of an insider who understands the interplay between power and labor" (*Toward Wholeness* 30).

7. Barbara Christian says that, "the development of the novel consists of the characters' recognition of themselves because of their unwitting confrontation with its dominant character, the Chosen Place: Bournehills" (*Black Women Novelists* 105).

8. As Peter Nazareth says, although Merle talks garrulously and compulsively, her "honesty, genuineness and historical awareness cut through what the others are saying as a scythe cutting through burnt-out grass" (116–17). And as Bell Gale Chevigny says, Merle "gives full voice to the hysteria of our times without being destroyed or surrendering to illusion" (31).

9. Joyce Pettis presents the fullest analysis of the multiple functions of Merle's

talk: "Merle uses talk to divert, subvert, and mystify; to conceal her 'self,' or to attack her enemies; and she uses it with ingenuity and cleverness to mask her mental fragility and vulnerability. In short, talk becomes Merle's defensive artifice, and she is conscious of its contrivance as an intensive barrier against others' perceptions of her loss of psychological equilibrium. In a very positive way, talk binds Merle's badly fractured 'self' and sustains her. As importantly, talk becomes the means through which she initiates self-healing and potential wholeness" ("Talk" 110). Relevant in particular to my discussion of double exposures in the novel is Pettis's discussion of Marshall's appropriation of the "public dimension" of Black discourse "to a private mode, simultaneously privileging the Black oral tradition and situating talk as integral to the subjective domain of women" ("Talk" 109). She says, "[B]efore Merle may initiate self-healing and restore her talk to agreeably normal levels, she must confront and reconcile her personal history and, in doing so, dissolve the disruptive dichotomies of public and private" ("Talk" 115).

10. A quite literal representation of this superimposition occurs in *Praisesong for the Widow*, where Jerome's face is portrayed as both black and white, the "pale outline" of a "pallid" stranger "superimposed" on his face "as in a double exposure" (131).

11. "The repetition and crisscrossing of patterns of domination across the Americas and the world is the major emphasis in the novel . . ." (Coser 56).

12. Marshall said in "Shaping the World of My Art" that the Black writer's task is "two-fold: on one hand to make use of the rich body of folk and historical material that is there; and on the other to interpret that past in heroic terms . . ." (108). Marcia Keizs sees the novel as one in which "Mrs. Marshall emerges fully into the realm of politics and history, attempting to render them on an epic scale" (73–74). Linda Pannill likewise describes it as "a novel of epic ambitions" (68). In addition to referring to the classical epic, of course, Vereson's name suggests the hero of the Christian epic, the "Son of Man."

13. Cf. Hélène Christol's discussion of Silla's work in the kitchen: "traditional domestic chores, which are usually trivialized, but which Marshall presents as moments of insight and of cultural identity" ("Black Woman's Burden" 156).

14. As John McClusky says, "the interplay of individual and collective history" has been one of Marshall's consistent themes (333). Of the same theme, Hortense Spillers says, "The characters . . . are the part that speaks for the whole, just as the whole is configured in their partialness" (154). Susan Willis defines Marshall's "great talent as a writer" as "her insightful portrayal of individual characters as they articulate the complex of a community's actions and desires" (54). And Joseph T. Skerrett, who sees "Marshall's portrait of Merle as both richly psychological and richly social" (69), reads Merle's "community as a symbolic replication of her psychological 'crisis of generativity' " (71). As Eugenia Collier says, in *The Chosen Place* "the divided self — both the individual and the collective self — finds wholeness" (307). Her study traces through Marshall's works the progression "from the divided individual self to the self-made whole through merging with the community" (295). The most extensive study of wholeness as a theme in this and all of Marshall's work is by Joyce Pettis, who links the question of wholeness specifically to issues of gender, race, and class (*Toward Wholeness*).

15. As Winifred L. Stoelting says, her catatonia is "symbolic of the helplessness of her people" (71).

16. Patricia Hill Collins points out that silence is not necessarily submission in a certain tradition of Black women's resistance. She quotes Marita Bonner, from

1925: "So—being a woman—you can wait. You must sit quietly. . . . Not wasting strength in enervating gestures as if two hundred years of bonds and whips had really tricked you into nervous uncertainty. But quiet; quiet. Like Buddha—who brown like I am—sat entirely at ease, entirely sure of himself; motionless and knowing. . . . Motionless on the outside. But inside?" (quoted from "On Being Young—A Woman—and Colored," in *Frye Street and Environs: The Collected Works of Marita Bonner*, ed. Joyce Flynn and Joyce Occomy Stricklin [Boston: Beacon, 1987], 3–8; quoted from p. 7).

17. For an illuminating discussion of the many significances of carnival in the extended Caribbean and related significances in the novel, see Stelamaris Coser (39–48 and 57). Of particular interest is Coser's statement that in this novel "costumes and parades are strategically used to address central issues of our time: the relations among races, ethnicities, genders, and classes; between the colonizer and the colonized; and between the hegemonic and the popular cultures" (57).

18. "Marshall organizes the deterioration of Harriet's character by showing that she is both victim and oppressor" (Christian, *Black Women Novelists* 126).

19. On the question of homosexuality in this novel, see Spillers (172–73), who attempts to refute Judith Fetterley's idea that the novel is homophobic, and Kubitschek (52–53), who sees the "rejection of lesbianism" in the first two novels as homophobic but places *Praisesong* as "a lesbian novel" (only if lesbian means woman-centered rather than referring "to an expressed physical, sexual relationship"). In contrast, Coser sees Marshall's work, including *The Chosen Place*, as being "willing to examine homosexuality as a viable alternative for both sexes" (169).

20. See Barbara Christian's discussion of the "specifically masculine" quality of the race (*Black Women Novelists* 119) and her comments on the gender issues involved in the encounter between Vere and his girl (118–19).

21. As Leela Kapai points out, Harriet's "death seems to be a symbolic end of all that white America stands for . . ." (54).

22. See Marshall's comments on this novel in "Shaping the World of My Art": "In it there is a conscious attempt to project the view of the future to which I am personally committed. Stated simply it is a view, a vision if you will, which sees the rise through revolutionary struggle of the darker peoples of the world and, as a necessary corollary, the decline and eclipse of America and the West. The two phenomena, the emergence of the oppressed and the fall of the powerful, I mention together because to my mind one is not really possible without the other; i.e., for the new world of African, Asian and Afro-American dimensions to come into being, the present world order which Fanon has described as 'swaying between atomic and spiritual disintegration' must be swept from center stage" (108). The quotation from Fanon, in particular, is a good description of what Marshall depicts in Harriet.

23. For a different but interestingly related reading of Vere as an "epic hero," see Wilson Harris's discussion of Vere in the context of versions of the "rainbow/phallic bridge" myth involving "an abortive expedition in which the 'epic hero' clings to an end of the broken phallus or bridge" (10). Especially suggestive in the context of double exposures associated with Vere's death is Harris's description of "the 'magical corpse' that the immersed hero may wear when he is pulled out of the sea. . . . Though apparently inanimate, he is subtly alive—a portion of his harlequin body is consumed by the culture or the people that have drawn him up. . . . The essence of such a 'magical corpse' is virtually, I think, an

unbearable phenomenon of the mystery of grace that links birth and death, deity and humanity . . ." (11). Though such figures are "rare in so-called realist fictions" (11), he says, "the 'phallic/rainbow' bridge may be implied . . . as a symbolic arc ridden by Vere, an Icarus-Anancy figure. . . . He builds a racing car of precarious technology that symbolises his *ad hoc* wings. That blind dream of conquest ends in disaster, but the relics of Icarus-Anancy's death and fall may be read as a spectral watershed or gateway between the kingdom of the living dead and the rebirth of innovative living (present and future) . . ." (12).

24. For other readings of Harriet's suicide, see Coser (53–54): "In her self-sacrifice, she finally rejects the history of violent domination and oppression in which she and her family participated. She also escapes her own contradictions . . ." (54), and Pettis's description of Harriet as "arriv[ing] at an impasse between the personal and historical" (*Toward Wholeness* 3).

25. Trudier Harris's discussion of Cuffee's inspiration for Merle's ability to "regain her psychological health" ("Three Black Women Writers" 66) helps explain why it should be the carnival, in particular, that catalyzes her psychological integration.

26. Cf. Pettis's discussion of the way in which Merle's achievement of wholeness depends on "dissolv[ing] the disruptive dichotomies of public and private" ("Talk" 115).

27. Marshall mentions her early interest in Conrad in "Shaping the World of My Art" (105) and her interview with DeVeaux (135). In the interview with Ogundipe-Leslie, she says, "I also admired Joseph Conrad during my adolescence. Again for this marvelous use of language. I found *Heart of Darkness* valuable because the theme is that man is complex, and until you begin to deal with all the dimensions of his personality, the sort of dark underbelly of the human personality, you are not dealing with him in his full dimension. I find that there is a reluctance, an inability on the part of white writers sometimes to acknowledge the multifaceted nature of the human personality. And one of the things that I am always trying to do as a writer is to suggest how complex and sometimes contradictory human nature is. So Conrad was also helpful" (30).

28. For Marshall's observations on the necessity "for black people to effect this spiritual return" to Africa, see Marshall and Condé's "Return of a Native Daughter" (52–53) and Marshall's "Shaping the World of My Art" (106–7). In addition, Bröck's discussion of the struggle "to create a space for women to move" in *Brown Girl* and *Praisesong* is relevant to Merle's final journey ("Transcending" 80), as is Nowak's placing of the journey in the context of "the acquisition of an imaginary free space needed for female self-assertion" (77).

Chapter 3: Voice, Spirit, Materiality

1. For this reason I would agree with Carole Boyce Davies's statement that Avey's journey is "as much an internal, personal journey inside herself as it is a journey outside herself, dealing equally with the social and political as with the psychological" ("Black Woman's Journey" 19).

2. "Marshall's entire opus focuses on the consciousness of black people as they remember, retain, develop their sense of spiritual/sensual integrity and individual selves, against the materialism that characterizes American societies" (Christian, "Ritualistic Process," in *Black Feminist Criticism* 149). Christian points out that "Central to African ritual is the concept that the body and spirit are one" (156);

she examines the relationship between body and mind in Avey's "ritualistic process" toward "spiritual/sensual integrity" (149). She says, "Marshall demonstrates . . . how a visceral understanding of their history and rituals can help black people transcend their displacement and retain their wholeness" (149). See also Barbara Frey Waxman on the novel as charting "a journey toward integration of body and spirit" (94), and Angelita Reyes on the importance for this novel of the lack of "distinct boundaries" in African thought "between the sacred and profane. . . . African peoples consider all reality as potentially sacred. Furthermore, other worlds exist, but *in* this world" (185). Geraldine Smith-Wright's discussion of ghosts in the novel is interestingly related to this issue of other worlds existing "in" this world (159–65).

3. As Keith A. Sandiford says, "Marshall does not suggest that the move [to North White Plains] per se, with its attendant increase in affluence and comfort, represents some unpardonable moral transgression. Instead of facile platitudes of anti-middle-class rhetoric, she frames a nondogmatic discourse that acknowledges the complex interplay of legitimate human aspirations and the nature of the cultural institutions that engender and propel those aspirations" (382). See also Sabine Bröck ("Transcending" 88) and Angelita Reyes, who emphasizes that Marshall understands "the importance of economic security for all Americans. But values need to be reappropriated in terms of equitable economic achievement rather than in terms of modern El Dorados" (201). As Joyce Pettis puts it, "Black women as writers critique the valuation of material possessions above character and morality, but they also recognize deliberate designs that thwart or restrict economic prosperity for African Americans yet also make prosperity more appealing" (*Toward Wholeness* 115).

4. In my use of this term throughout this chapter I am thinking of Patricia Williams's final chapter in *The Alchemy of Race and Rights*, "On Being the Object of Property," which presents in intricate relation the economic, legal, spiritual, and psychological effects of the legacy of slavery.

5. Almost every study of the novel discusses the spiritual journey back to Africa in some way. As Emmanuel S. Nelson says, "Her final participation in the ritualized Big Drum ceremony with the islanders signals Avey's spiritual homecoming. Avey's forging of a healing renewal of her sense of self is made possible only after she sheds her Euro-American values, reconnects with the Afrocentric world-view of great-aunt Cuney, and spiritually awakens to Pan-African possibilities. Marshall's message is clear: the ancestral connections among the heirs of the Middle Passage cannot be and should not be ignored in contemporary constructions of Black identity in the Western hemisphere" (55). Velma Pollard points in particular to the importance of Marshall's inclusion of "the Caribbean, Anglophone and Francophone" in her treatment of "The African connection" (296), and Stelamaris Coser makes "the various ways in which [Toni Morrison's, Paule Marshall's, and Gayl Jones's] storytelling constructs inter-American bridges" the focal point of her study of those writers. On the particular significance of the Caribbean in Avey's journey see also Gay Wilentz (9–10). On Marshall's view of the importance of the journey to Africa, see Marshall and Condé's "Return of a Native Daughter."

6. Her inspiration here is the passage from Toni Morrison's *Beloved* in which "Sixo describes his love for Thirty-Mile Woman, declaring, 'She is a friend of mind. She gather me, man. The pieces I am, she gather them and give them back to me in all the right order . . .'" (hooks and West 19). The specific context in *Breaking Bread*, relationships between African-American women and men, is ap-

plicable to Marshall's portrait of Avey and Jay, but the image of re-membering also applies more broadly to Marshall's whole vision of African-American community.

7. A central aspect of the connection between the theme of individual and collective self-integration in *Praisesong* and the theme of recapturing the past is revealed in Joyce Pettis's statement that "in this novel, Marshall not only makes visible the abstract notion of spiritual wholeness but also develops its contiguous relationship to Afrocentricity" (*Toward Wholeness* 107). This relationship provides the connection between spiritual wholeness and historical re-membering.

8. The world of work experienced by African Americans as Marshall portrays it in all her novels, but especially in her portrait of Jay, is the world of mandatory self-suppression that domestic worker "Ella Surrey" (the name is itself a masking device) described to John Gwaltney: "We have always been the best actors in the world. . . . I think that we are much more clever than they are because we know that we have to play the game. We've always had to live two lives — one for them and one for ourselves" (Gwaltney 238, 240). Collins quotes Surrey's comment and discusses the implications of this necessity for self-concealment in African-American women in particular (91–93).

9. As Patricia Williams says, in our culture especially, "possessions become the description of who we are and the reflection of our worth" (124).

10. See also Willis: "The influence of capitalism as a lived experience, particularly as it shapes the middle class, is most evident in Marshall's descriptions of domestic space and — not surprisingly — women's bodies" (78).

11. On the debate as to whether Foucault's concept of docile bodies is useful to feminism, see Lois McNay, *Foucault and Feminism* (Boston: Northeastern University Press, 1993).

12. Critics who have discussed race, class, and gender most specifically in this novel are Joyce Pettis and Giulia Scarpa. Especially relevant to my view of the interpenetration of the social and psychological in the novel is Scarpa's reading of Jay and Avey's "decline" in terms of a "social dynamic . . . internalized and transformed into an interpersonal dynamic," a process that deprives the social dynamic "of its actual broader meaning" (98). Scarpa also makes an important point about gender, race, and class in the dream of Aunt Cuney: "Significantly, it is only in the form of a nightmare that we see Avey performing the gender role by which middle-class values define womanhood as the reflection of man's wealth and societal accomplishments" (101).

13. "In all of Marshall's novels, the transformation out of bourgeois encumbrances and values is enacted physically on the bodies of her female characters" (Willis 80).

14. See for example *Black Skin, White Masks* and *The Wretched of the Earth*.

15. For the most extended analysis of this psychic fragmentation, see Pettis (*Toward Wholeness*).

16. Williams is punning in a much more complicated way than I am here, and her immediate context — a discussion of racism that alludes back to the discussion of internalized racism I cited earlier (Williams 62) — is so different that I will quote it here to avoid misrepresenting her insight. Speaking of the 1986 assault by white youths on three Black men in Howard Beach, she says,

> Another scenario of the distancing of the self from responsibility for racism is the inventing of some vast wilderness of others . . . against which the self must barricade itself. . . . Not only do such attitudes set up angry, excluding bound-

aries, but they imply that the *failure* to protect and avenge is a bad policy, bad statesmanship, an embarrassment. . . . The need to avenge becomes a separate issue of protocol, of etiquette — not a loss of a piece of the self, which is the real cost of real tragedies, but a loss of self-regard. By "self-regard" I don't mean self-concept, as in self-esteem; I mean, again, that view of the self which is attained when the self steps outside to regard and evaluate the self; in which the self is watched by an imaginary other, a projection of the opinions of real others . . . in which refusal of the designated other to be dominated is felt as a personal assault. Thus the failure to avenge is treated as a loss of self-regard; it is used as a psychological metaphor for whatever trauma or original assault constituted the real loss to the self. (66)

17. Citing Alice Walker's "historical view of black women," Mary Helen Washington says, "the price assimilated women have to pay for their acceptance is the negation of their racial identity and the separation from the sustenance that such an identity could afford them" ("Teaching Black-Eyed Susans" 214). Avey fits into the second cycle of Alice Walker's "personal historical view of black women" as recounted by Washington (212). She describes assimilated women as victims "not of physical violence" like most women in the first cycle of "suspended" women, "but of a kind of a psychic violence that alienates them from their roots and cuts them off from real contact with their own people and also from a part of themselves" (213).

18. Christian says that "ritual is at the novel's core" ("Ritualistic Process" 150), and Eugenia Collier discusses the use of ritual as "A major technique" (295).

19. Willis looks at a similar transformation in the other, but clearly related, context of Silla's and Harriet's "calculated brand of betrayal," which entails regarding their husbands as objects. She says that their betrayal "speaks for a transformation in human relationships that occurs under capitalism and transforms human beings into objects capable of being perceived as obstructions to progress" (77).

20. Cf. Henry Louis Gates Jr.'s discussion of perfectibility (*Black Literature and Literary Theory* 5–10), which Linda Wells makes central to her reading of *Praisesong*: "To answer the question 'what shall I give my children,' some African American parents would shape an answer in favor of materialism, teaching their children the work ethic and the model of success epitomized in the American dream. To achieve success the children must perfect themselves by white standards because the white power structure determines who will have access to material well-being. Henry Louis Gates, Jr. analyzes the problem of adhering to this theory of perfectibility, whereby blacks internalize a sense of themselves as defective and seek to perfect themselves by white values and standards" (46). The question "What Shall I Give My Children" is from the Gwendolyn Brooks poem that, as Wells says, reverberates through the novel. Suzanne Stutman points out that the reference "establishes the sense of anguish and frustration faced by the mother who seeks to give to her children a sense of worth and self-esteem in a society which automatically disenfranchises them" (58).

21. I borrow bell hooks' term "coming to voice" from *Talking Back* (12 and throughout).

22. On the same theme, see Abena P. Busia ("Words Whispered" 17ff.)

23. She cites his limp and ragged clothes, his literal position at the crossroads, and his role as trickster (312); one could point also to the fluidity of his shape and gender and the oracular incomprehensibility to Avey of his strange pronounce-

ments. On Lebert Joseph as Legba, see also Busia ("What Is Your Nation?" 204–5), Velma Pollard (289), Angelita Reyes (190), and Gay Wilentz (14–15).

24. Cited by Collier.

25. As Henry Louis Gates Jr. says, "The most fundamental absolute of the Yoruba is that there exist, simultaneously, three stages of existence: the past, the present, and the unborn. Esu represents these stages, and makes their simultaneous existence possible, 'without any contradiction,' precisely because he is the principle of discourse both as messenger and as the god of communication" (*Signifying Monkey* 37).

26. Fred Lee Hord quotes this passage in his discussion of colonialism in *Reconstructing Memory*. Although he does not discuss Marshall, *Praisesong* would fit well into his "pedagogical model of black literary criticism rooted both in Third World and African-American colonial theories of literature, as well as in the African-American literary tradition of consciousness raising and collectivity" (xi). In particular, *Praisesong* is a good illustration of his thesis that "the history of African-American literature and literary criticism can be read as consonant with" the "collective-consciousness-raising purposes of literature in a colonial situation — as outlined by Cabral, Fanon, and Memmi . . ." (25, 24).

27. "The boat is compelled to rock violently because, just like Avey/Avatara, it is crossing a rough channel where two opposing currents clash" (Coser 64).

28. As Willis says, "The purge represents a symbolic break from bourgeois consumption . . ." (62).

29. John McCluskey Jr. refers to this "necessary physical purging — a 'middle passage' of the spirit?" (332). On purging in the novel in general, see Ann Armstrong Scarboro (30–31 and passim).

30. As Willis says, "Avey's return to the past . . . is no mere psychic journey, but one graphically etched on the physical senses. . . . Throughout the novel, the history of slavery is recorded as a physical memory . . ." (64).

31. See also Joyce Pettis's discussion of the function of labor, under capitalism, in producing a self-alienation in which women such as Silla are separated "from a sense of meaning other than physical survival" (*Toward Wholeness* 109).

32. A number of critics have analyzed these techniques. Karla F. C. Holloway's discussion of the novel involves various forms of these conjunctions or superimpositions, for example in her statement that Avey's memory of her childhood illness is "a moment when a metaphysical disturbance substantiates the physical" (88), or her comment that "The shifting back and forth between various dimensions of the past and the distorted dimensions of Avey's present eventually enables the narrative to sublimate successfully the distinctions between them" (188). Wilentz makes a point especially relevant to the technique of double exposure as it is related to the theme of the African diaspora: "In the course of the novel, Cuney not only appears as Avey's ancestor, she also acts as a presence for the reader, so that we are constantly super-imposing Tatem and the African-American experience over the Afro-Caribbean scene" (13). Reyes's point that the praisesong as genre "is both a sacred and profane modality" is also relevant here (185).

33. On *Praisesong* as a novel of aging, see Waxman, who points out that "Readers who accompany Avey on her rejuvenating journey must critically examine their own feelings about aging women as they observe the complex interactions of age, gender, race, and middle-class status in Marshall's novel" (94). See also Lucy Wilson, whose picture of aging as a process of "exile" is especially suggestive in the context of my argument (189).

34. On the significance of the name, see Busia ("What Is Your Nation?" 210) and Bowen (55).

35. On the many other aspects of the title, see especially Reyes (185) and Busia ("What is Your Nation?" 198). Busia points out that praisesongs, "a particular kind of traditional heroic poem," are sometimes "sung to mark social transition. Sung as a part of rites of passage, they mark the upward movement of a person from one group to the next" (198). In this sense what Marshall's praisesong for Avey celebrates is a spiritual ascent that reverses the "downward slide" of her life with Jerome. Reyes emphasizes the fact that the genre of the praisesong in African oral literature "is both a sacred and profane modality" (185), and she ties it to the interweaving of "sacred forces . . . into the quotidian life of the community" in African philosophy and religion (185).

36. On the full significance of Avey's "choice to become a teller" (Holloway 134), see Karla Holloway's argument that "the mythologies in black women writers' texts are self-*reflexive* and their history is the history of orature — the primal mythic source" (100). Holloway's discussion throughout *Moorings and Metaphors* illuminates the rich complexity of the many ways in which the question of voice is integrally a part of the question of re-membering: "Through the narrative activity of revision and recursion," she says, "texts of African-American women writers reinforce the ritualized behaviors of cultural memory, insisting on the relationship between the preserved (or recovered) myth, the creativity of women's language, and the place of necromancy in the voiced text" (140). One of Holloway's central terms is "(re)membrance," a term she uses in a sense intimately related to the meanings my allusions to bell hooks's meditations on re-membering are intended to evoke. Her focus can be seen in her thesis that "far from being a coincidental selection of metaphor, the ancestral presence in contemporary African-American women's writing reconstructs an imaginative, cultural (re)-membrance of a dimension of West African spirituality, and . . . the spiritual place of this subjective figuration is fixed into the structures of the text's language" (2).

37. Busia points out that in Marion "The saving internal self becomes truly interiorized, and the daughter born becomes her mother's salvation. That which is healing about Halsey Street lies dormant in the child then conceived" ("Words Whispered" 12).

38. See Joseph Campbell's account of the hero journey across the threshold (30, 245–56).

39. The move from Brooklyn took place "some twelve years" after the night on Halsey Street (112).

40. The time between her departure from the cruise ship and her departure from Carriacou. She arrives in Grenada one day, spends the night in the hotel, goes the next day to Carriacou, stays two nights (the second night being the ceremony of the Big Drum), and leaves the next day.

41. As McCluskey says, "the myth of Ibo Landing" is "a narrative of resistance, of return as profound resistance and not simple flight" (333).

42. From *Midnight Birds* (New York: Anchor, 1980) xv, quoted in Collins (106).

Chapter 4: Conflations of Discourse

1. My understanding of signifying comes from Gates, *The Signifying Monkey*. In view of some current controversies surrounding African-American women writ-

ers' treatment of gender and race, it would be useful, although beyond the scope of this chapter, to compare Gates's account of Ishmael Reed's signifying on *Invisible Man* with Marshall's signifying on the same novel (*Signifying Monkey* 217–38).

2. An ironic nickname, as Marshall says, "an empty symbol of power and authority in a country that still takes its orders from America and the West" (Dance 4).

3. The term "lesbian continuum" is from Adrienne Rich's influential essay "Compulsory Heterosexuality" (156ff).

4. A real-life counterpart of Ursa and Viney's conversations on this issue are the two transcripts of conversations among a group of African American women in 1979 on the topic of "the scarcity of available males" that Gloria I. Joseph records in *Common Differences* (219–29), citing statistics from the Black Think Tank that among African-American urban college-educated women from nineteen to forty-four years old there are 154 females for every 100 males. She lists incarceration, drugs, war casualties, interracial marriages, and homosexuality as factors.

5. As Truth said, "There is a great stir about colored men getting their rights, but not a word about the colored women; and if colored men get their rights, and not colored women theirs, you see the colored men will be masters over the women, and it will be just as bad as it was before" (Loewenberg and Bogin 238). African-American feminists were of course divided on the particular question Truth was addressing here, the question of whether the fight for woman suffrage should come after the fight for universal manhood suffrage that would enfranchise African-American men. Frances Ellen Watkins Harper, for example, took a different position. See Paula Giddings (64–68).

6. Furthermore, as Ann duCille points out, for those "standing at an intersection — particularly at such a suddenly busy, three-way intersection," there is "likelihood of being run over by oncoming traffic" (593).

7. Marshall has identified one meaning of Ursa's abortion as the expulsion of the "incubus" of her father's domination (Dance 10).

8. "One significant consequence of spiritual wholeness, *Daughters* suggests, is a vision that resists self-absorption to embrace collective definition" (Pettis, *Toward Wholeness* 137).

9. See for example her description of "The conflict between self and other" as "the central moral problem for women" (70–71), which can be solved only through the development of an "ethic of care" that sees self and other as interdependent (74). It is the dilemma of "the conflict between compassion and autonomy, between virtue and power," she says, "which the feminine voice struggles to resolve in its effort to reclaim the self and to solve the moral problem in such a way that no one is hurt" (71).

10. Among the numerous discussions of this double struggle are bell hooks ("Confronting Sexism in Black Life: The Struggle Continues"), Audre Lorde ("Sexism: An American Disease in Blackface" in *Common Differences*), and Barbara Smith (Introduction to *Home Girls*).

11. Significantly, this time was the era of the Black Power movement. In *Black Looks*, bell hooks comments on "the phallocentric idealization of masculinity" in George Jackson and Amiri Baraka at that time and cites Davis in particular as confronting Jackson on this issue (98–99). For Davis's own comments on the sexism of the Black Power movement, see her review of Elaine Brown's *A Taste of Power: A Black Woman's Story* ("The Making of a Revolutionary").

12. In "Reconstructing Black Masculinity" (*Black Looks* 87–113), bell hooks makes a somewhat more complicated argument that acknowledges the African

gender hierarchies in the traditions slavery brought to this country but also implicates white gender ideologies in the specific shaping of free Black men's desire to assume the role of Black patriarch.

13. On Dante's Beatrice, for example, see Gayatri Chakravorty Spivak ("Finding Feminist Readings: Dante-Yeats").

14. As Paule Marshall has emphasized in an interview: "Let me point out, though, that the action taken by Ursa at Estelle's orders is designed, not to defeat the PM, but rather to restore him to his original commitment and values" (Dance 20).

15. See Lorde, Smith, and Norton cited earlier, as well as bell hooks's many analyses of this dynamic.

16. To cite only one example, Eleanor Holmes Norton wrote in 1970, "If some [black women] have been forced into roles as providers or, out of the insecurity associated with being a black woman alone, have dared not develop independence, the result is not that black women are today liberated women. For they have been 'liberated' only from love, from family life, from meaningful work, and just as often from the basic comforts and necessities of an ordinary existence. There is neither power nor satisfaction in such a 'matriarchy.' There is only the bitter knowledge that one is a victim. . . . To allow the white oppressor to share the burden of his responsibility with the black woman is madness" (399). See also Barbara Smith's introduction to *Home Girls* and Paula Giddings's chapter on the Moynihan report in *When and Where I Enter* (325–35).

17. Paula Giddings cites the effect the report had even on many African Americans, as in the *Ebony* article that concluded, "The immediate goal of Negro women today should be the establishment of a strong family unit in which the father is the dominant person" (329). See also Patricia Hill Collins (75), Barbara Smith (xxvi–xxvii), and bell hooks (*Black Looks*), whose comments are especially relevant here. Growing up in a segregated black community in the South, hooks saw many different versions of Black manhood, she says, but the interpretations to which she was exposed at an elite white college viewed Black men as monolithic: "Learning about the matriarchy myth and white culture's notion that black men were emasculated, I was shocked" (*Black Looks* 88).

18. We know that she did not merely send the prospectus but that she delivered it in person, and that the people who speak up from Primus's audience know something not recorded in the prospectus—that Primus has invested in the scheme himself. Only Ursa could have conveyed this information, by speaking to whomever she went to meet.

19. On Primus's colonization see Pettis, who cites Fanon: "the colonized man is an envious man" (*Toward Wholeness* 64).

20. Such questions evoke the discussions of interior voices in Mae Henderson.

21. Kevin Quashie's theory of the relationships among healing, rememory, and re-performance in African-American literature will contribute an important basis for future considerations of the kinds of relationship at issue here. See a preliminary version in his M.A. thesis, "Reperformance as Voice Trope and Healing Imperative in Toni Morrison's Works."

22. As Pettis says, in her revolutionary act, Ursa "achieves emotional liberation, which connects her with the spirit of community and the legacy of female political resistance" (*Toward Wholeness* 70).

Works Cited

Allen, Paula Gunn. *The Sacred Hoop: Recovering the Feminine in American Indian Traditions.* Boston: Beacon, 1986.

Anzaldúa, Gloria, ed. *Making Face, Making Soul, Haciendo Caras: Creative and Critical Perspectives by Women of Color.* San Francisco: Aunt Lute Foundation Books, 1990.

Baer, Sylvia. "Holding onto the Vision: Sylvia Baer Interviews Paule Marshall." *Women's Review of Books* 8.10–11 (July 1991).

Baldwin, James. *The Fire Next Time.* 1962. Reprint New York: Vintage, 1993.

Bell, Bernard W. *The Afro-American Novel and Its Tradition.* Amherst: University of Massachusetts Press, 1987.

Benston, Kimberly W. "Architectural Imagery and Unity in Paule Marshall's *Brown Girl, Brownstones.*" *Negro American Literature Forum* 9.3 (Fall 1975): 67–70.

Bond, Jean Carey. "Allegorical Novel by Talented Storyteller." Review of *The Chosen Place, the Timeless People. Freedomways* (First Quarter 1970): 76–78.

Bordo, Susan R. "The Body and the Reproduction of Femininity: A Feminist Appropriation of Foucault." In *Gender/Body/Knowledge: Feminist Reconstructions of Being and Knowing,* ed. Alison M. Jaggar and Susan R. Bordo, 13–33. New Brunswick, N.J.: Rutgers University Press, 1989.

Bowen, Sandra E. Critique of Linda Wells, " 'What Shall I Give My Children?' The Role of the Mentor in Gloria Naylor's *The Women of Brewster Place* and Paule Marshall's *Praisesong for the Widow.*" *Explorations in Ethnic Studies* 13.2 (July 1990): 52–56.

Brewer, Rose M. "Theorizing Race, Class and Gender: The New Scholarship of Black Feminist Intellectuals and Black Women's Labor." In *Theorizing Black Feminisms: The Visionary Pragmatism of Black Women,* ed. Stanlie M. James and Abena P.A. Busia, 13–30. London and New York: Routledge, 1993.

Bröck, Sabine. " 'Talk as a Form of Action': An Interview with Paule Marshall, September 1982." In *History and Tradition in Afro-American Culture,* 194–206. Vol. 1 of *Schriftenreihe des Zentrums für Nordamerika-Forschung, U. of Frankfurt.* Frankfurt and New York: Campus, 1984.

———. "Transcending the 'Loophole of Retreat': Paule Marshall's Placing of Female Generations." *Callaloo* 10.1 (Winter 1987): 79–90.

Buncombe, Marie H. "From Harlem to Brooklyn: The New York Scene in the Fiction of Meriwether, Petry, and Marshall." *MAWA Review: Quarterly Publication of the Middle Atlantic Writers Association* 1.1 (1982): 16–19.

Busia, Abena P. "What Is Your Nation? Reconnecting Africa and Her Diaspora Through Paule Marshall's *Praisesong for the Widow.*" In *Changing Our Own Words: Essays on Criticism, Theory, and Writing by Black Women,* ed. Cheryl A. Wall, 196–211. New Brunswick, N.J.: Rutgers University Press, 1989.

——. "Words Whispered over Voids: A Context for Black Women's Rebellious Voices in the Novel of the African Diaspora." In *Black Feminist Criticism and Critical Theory,* ed. Joe Weixlmann and Houston A. Baker Jr., 1–41. Studies in Black American Literature 3. Greenwood, Fl.: Penkevill, 1988.

Byerman, Keith E. "Gender, Culture, and Identity in Paule Marshall's *Brown Girl, Brownstones.*" In *Redefining Autobiography in Twentieth-Century Women's Fiction: An Essay Collection,* 135–47. Garland Reference Library of the Humanities, vol. 1386. New York: Garland, 1991.

Campbell, Joseph. *The Hero with a Thousand Faces.* 1949. Cleveland: Meridian-World, 1969.

Carroll, David. *Chinua Achebe.* 2nd ed. New York: St. Martin's Press, 1980.

Chevigny, Bell Gale. Review of *The Chosen Place, the Timeless People. Village Voice,* October 8, 1970, 6, 30–31.

Chopin, Kate. *The Awakening.* 1899. Reprinted in *The Norton Anthology of Literature by Women: The Tradition in English,* ed. Sandra Gilbert and Susan Gubar, 993–1102, New York: Norton, 1985.

Christian, Barbara. *Black Feminist Criticism: Perspectives on Black Women Writers.* New York: Pergamon, 1985.

——. *Black Women Novelists: The Development of a Tradition, 1892–1976.* Contributions in Afro-American and African Studies 52. Westport, Conn.: Greenwood, 1980.

——. "Ritualistic Process and the Structure of Paule Marshall's *Praisesong for the Widow.*" *Callaloo* 6.2 (18) (Spring–Summer 1983): 21–84. Reprinted in *Black Feminist Criticism,* 149–58.

Christol, Hélène. " 'The Black Woman's Burden': Black Women and Work in *The Street* (Ann Petry) and *Brown Girl, Brownstones* (Paule Marshall)." In *Les États-Unis: Images du travail et des loisirs,* ed. Groupe de Recherche et d'Études Nord-Américaines, 145–158. *Actes du Colloque des 3, 4, et 5 Mars 1989.* Aix-en-Provence: Publications/Diffusion Université de Provence, 1989. 145–58.

——. "Paule Marshall's Bajan Women in *Brown Girl, Brownstones.*" In *Women and War: The Changing Status of American Women from the 1930s to the 1950s,* ed. Maria Diedrich and Dorothea Fischer Hornung, 141–53. New York: Berg, 1990.

Cohn, Carol. "Sex and Death in the Rational World of Defense Intellectuals." In *Feminist Theory in Practice and Process,* ed. Micheline R. Malson, Jean F. O'Barr, Sarah Westphal-Wihl, and Mary Wyer, 107–38. Chicago: University of Chicago Press, 1986.

Collier, Eugenia. "The Closing of the Circle: Movement from Division to Wholeness in Paule Marshall's Fiction." In *Black Women Writers (1950–1980): A Critical Evaluation,* ed. Mari Evans, 295–315. New York: Anchor, 1984.

Collins, Patricia Hill. *Black Feminist Thought: Knowledge, Consciousness, and the Politics of Empowerment.* Perspectives on Gender 2. London: HarperCollins, 1990.

Combahee River Collective. "The Combahee River Collective Statement." 1978. Reprinted in *Home Girls: A Black Feminist Anthology,* ed. Barbara Smith, 272–82. New York: Kitchen Table: Women of Color Press, 1983.

Coser, Stelamaris. *Bridging the Americas: The Literature of Paule Marshall, Toni Morrison, and Gayl Jones.* Philadelphia: Temple University Press, 1994.

Dance, Daryl Cumber. "An Interview with Paule Marshall." June 14, 1991. *Southern Review* 28.1 (Winter 1992): 1–20.

Davies, Carole Boyce. "Black Woman's Journey into Self: A Womanist Reading of Paule Marshall's *Praisesong for the Widow*." *Matatu* 1.1 (1987): 19–34.

Davis, Angela. "The Making of a Revolutionary." Review of Elaine Brown's *A Taste of Power: A Black Woman's Story*." *Women's Review of Books* 10.9 (June 1993): 1, 3–4.

———. "Reflections on the Black Woman's Role in the Community of Slaves." *Black Scholar* 3 (December 1971): 3–15. Expanded version printed as "The Legacy of Slavery: Standards for a New Womanhood," in *Women, Race, and Class*, 3–29. New York: Vintage, 1981.

———. *Women, Culture, and Politics*. New York: Vintage, 1989.

de Abruna, Laura Niesen. "Twentieth-Century Women Writers from the English-Speaking Caribbean." In *Caribbean Women Writers: Essays from the First International Conference*, ed. Selwyn R. Cudjoe, 86–97. Wellesley, Mass.: Calaloux, 1990.

de Beauvoir, Simone. *The Second Sex*. Paris, 1949. Trans. H. M. Parshley. New York: Knopf, 1952. Reprint New York: Vintage, 1989.

DeLamotte, Eugenia. *Perils of the Night: A Feminist Study of Nineteenth-Century Gothic*. New York: Oxford, 1990.

———. "Women, Silence, and History in *The Chosen Place, the Timeless People*." *Callaloo* 16.1 (Winter 1993): 227–42.

Denniston, Dorothy L. "Early Short Fiction by Paule Marshall." *Callaloo* 6.2 (18) (Spring–Summer 1983): 31–45.

DeVeaux, Alexis. "Paule Marshall — In Celebration of Our Triumph." Interview in *Essence* (May 1979): 70–71, 96–98, 123–35.

DuBois, Ellen Carol, Gail Paradise Kelly, Elizabeth Lapovsky Kennedy, Carolyn W. Korsmeyer, and Lillian S. Robinson, eds. *Feminist Scholarship: Kindling in the Groves of Academe*. Urbana and Chicago: University of Illinois Press, 1987.

DuBois, W.E.B. *The Souls of Black Folk*. 1903. Reprinted in *Three Negro Classics*, ed. John Hope Franklin, 207–389. New York: Avon, 1965.

duCille, Ann. "The Occult of True Black Womanhood: Critical Demeanor and Black Feminist Studies." *Signs* 19.3 (Spring 1994): 591–629.

Edel, Leon. *The Life of Henry James*. Vol. 1. 1953. Reprint. Harmondsworth: Penguin, 1977.

Eko, Ebele. "Beyond the Myth of Confrontation: A Comparative Study of African and African-American Female Protagonists." *Ariel: A Review of International English Literature* 17.4 (October 1986): 139–52.

Ellison, Ralph. *Invisible Man*. 1947. Reprint New York: Vintage, 1952.

Erickson, Peter. "Hard Work: Paule Marshall's *Daughters*." *Callaloo* 16.1 (Winter 1993): 268–71.

Evans, Mari, ed. *Black Women Writers (1950–1980): A Critical Evaluation*. New York: Anchor, 1984.

Fanon, Frantz. *Black Skin, White Masks*. Paris, 1952. Reprint New York: Grove, 1967.

———. *The Wretched of the Earth*. Paris, 1961. Reprint New York: Grove, 1963.

Fauset, Jessie. *There Is Confusion*. New York: Boni and Liveright, 1924.

Fletcher, Angus. *Allegory: The Theory of a Symbolic Mode*. Ithaca, N.Y., and London: Cornell University Press, 1964.

Flexner, Eleanor. *Century of Struggle: The Woman's Rights Movement in the United States*. Cambridge, Mass.: Belknap Press of Harvard University Press, 1975.

Friedman, Susan Stanford. "Women's Autobiographical Selves: Theory and Practice." In *The Private Self: Theory and Practice of Women's Autobiographical Writings*, ed. Shari Benstock, 34–62. Chapel Hill: University of North Carolina Press, 1988.

Gates, Henry Louis, Jr. *Black Literature and Literary Theory*. New York: Methuen, 1983.

———. *The Signifying Monkey: A Theory of African-American Literary Criticism*. New York: Oxford, 1988.

———, ed. *Reading Black, Reading Feminist: A Critical Anthology*. New York: Meridian, 1990.

Giddings, Paula. *When and Where I Enter: The Impact of Black Women on Race and Sex in America*. New York: Bantam, 1984.

Gilbert, Sandra, and Susan Gubar. *The Madwoman in the Attic: The Woman Writer and the Nineteenth-Century Literary Imagination*. New Haven, Conn., and London: Yale University Press, 1979.

Gilligan, Carol. *In a Different Voice: Psychological Theory and Women's Development*. Cambridge, Mass.: Harvard University Press, 1982.

Gomez, Jewelle L. "I Lost It at the Movies." In *Making Face, Making Soul, Hacienda Caras*, ed. Gloria Anzaldúa, 203–6. San Francisco: Aunt Lute Foundation Books, 1990.

Gwaltney, John Langston. *Drylongso: A Self-Portrait of Black America*. New York: Vintage, 1980.

Harris, Trudier. "No Outlet for the Blues: Silla Boyce's Plight in *Brown Girl, Brownstones*." *Callaloo* 6, 2 (18) (Spring–Summer 1983): 57–67.

———. "Three Black Women Writers and Humanism: A Folk Perspective." In *Black American Literature and Humanism*, ed. R. Baxter Miller, 50–74. Lexington: University Press of Kentucky, 1981.

Harris, Wilson. "Metaphor and Myth." In *Myth and Metaphor*, ed. Robert Sellick, 1–14. Adelaide: Centre for Research in the New Literatures in English, 1982.

Henderson, Mae Gwendolyn. "Speaking in Tongues: Dialogics, Dialectics, and the Black Woman Writer's Literary Tradition." In *Reading Black, Reading Feminist*, ed. Henry Louis Gates Jr., 116–142. New York: Meridian, 1990.

Holloway, Karla F. C. *Moorings and Metaphors: Figures of Culture and Gender in Black Women's Literature*. New Brunswick, N.J.: Rutgers University Press, 1992.

hooks, bell. *Black Looks: Race and Representation*. Boston: South End, 1992.

———. "Confronting Sexism in Black Life: The Struggle Continues." *Z Magazine* (October 1993): 36–39.

———. *Feminist Theory from Margin to Center*. Boston: South End Press, 1984.

———. *Talking Back: Thinking Feminist, Thinking Black*. Boston: South End Press, 1989.

hooks, bell and Cornel West. *Breaking Bread: Insurgent Black Intellectual Life*. Boston: South End, 1991.

Hord, Fred Lee. *Reconstructing Memory: Black Literary Criticism*. Chicago: Third World Press, 1991.

Hull, Gloria T., Patricia Bell Scott, and Barbara Smith, eds. *All the Women Are White, All the Blacks Are Men, But Some of Us Are Brave: Black Women's Studies*. New York: Feminist Press, 1982.

Hurston, Zora Neale. *Their Eyes Were Watching God*. 1937. Reprint Urbana, Chicago, London: University of Illinois Press, 1978.

Ingram, Elwanda D. "Selina and Reena: Paule Marshall's Assertive Black Women."

MAWA Review: Quarterly Publication of the Middle Atlantic Writers Association 2.1 (1986): 25–27.

James, Henry. "The Art of Fiction." 1884. Reprinted in *Theory of Fiction: Henry James*, ed. James E. Miller Jr., 28–44. Lincoln: University of Nebraska Press, 1972.

Joseph, Gloria I. and Jill Lewis. *Common Differences: Conflicts in Black and White Feminist Perspectives*. Boston: South End, 1981.

Kapai, Leela. "Dominant Themes and Technique in Paule Marshall's Fiction." *CLA Journal* 16.1 (September 1972): 49–59.

Keizs, Marcia. "Themes and Style in the Works of Paule Marshall." *Negro American Literature Forum* 9.3 (Fall 1975): 67, 71–76.

King, Deborah K. "Multiple Jeopardy, Multiple Consciousness: The Context of a Black Feminist Ideology." *Signs* 14.1 (Autumn 1988). Reprinted in *Black Women in America: Social Science Perspectives*, ed. Micheline R. Malson, Elisabeth Mudimbe-Boyi, Jean F. O'Barr, and Mary Wyer, 265–95. Chicago and London: University of Chicago Press, 1990.

Kubitschek, Missy Dehn. "Paule Marshall's Women on Quest." *Black American Literature Forum* 21.1–2 (Spring–Summer 1987): 43–60.

Lask, Thomas. "Promise and Fulfillment." Review of *The Chosen Place, the Timeless People*. *New York Times*, November 8, 1969, 31.

Lerner, Gerda. "Reconceptualizing Differences Among Women." *Journal of Women's History* (Winter 1990): 106–22.

Leseur, Geta J. "*Brown Girl, Brownstones* as a Novel of Development." *Obsidian II: Black Literature in Review* 1, 3 (Winter 1986): 119–29.

Lessing, Doris. *The Summer Before the Dark*. London: Cape, 1973.

Loewenberg, Bert James and Ruth Bogin, eds. *Black Women in Nineteenth-Century American Life: Their Words, Their Thoughts, Their Feelings*. University Park and London: Pennsylvania State University Press, 1976.

Lorde, Audre. "The Transformation of Silence into Language and Action." *Sinister Wisdom* 6 (1978). Reprinted in *Sister Outsider: Essays and Speeches by Audre Lorde*, 40–44. Crossing Press Feminist Series. Freedom, Calif.: Crossing Press, 1984.

———. "Uses of the Erotic: The Erotic as Power." *Black Scholar* 9, 7 (1978). Reprinted in *Sister Outsider: Essays and Speeches by Audre Lorde*, 53–59. Crossing Press Feminist Series. Freedom, Calif.: Crossing Press, 1984.

Marshall, Paule. "Brooklyn." 1961. Reprinted in *Reena and Other Stories*, 27–48. Old Westbury, N.Y.: Feminist Press, 1983.

———. *Brown Girl, Brownstones*. 1959. New York: Feminist Press, 1981.

———. *The Chosen Place, the Timeless People*. 1969. New York: Vintage, 1984.

———. *Daughters*. New York: Athenaeum, 1991.

———. "The Negro Woman in Literature." *Freedomways* 4 (First Quarter 1966): 20–25.

———. *Praisesong for the Widow*. New York: Dutton, 1984.

———. *Reena and Other Stories*, 27–48. Old Westbury, N.Y.: Feminist Press, 1983.

———. "Shaping the World of My Art." *New Letters* 40.1 (October 1973): 97–112.

Marshall, Paule and Maryse Condé. "Return of a Native Daughter: An Interview with Paule Marshall and Maryse Condé." Trans. John Williams. *SAGE: A Scholarly Journal on Black Women* 3.2 (Fall 1986): 52–53.

McCluskey, John, Jr. "And Called Every Generation Blessed: Theme, Setting, and Ritual in the Works of Paule Marshall." In *Black Women Writers (1950–1980): A Critical Evaluation*, ed. Mari Evans, 316–34. New York: Doubleday, 1984.

McDowell, Deborah. "New Directions for Black Feminist Criticism." *Black American Literature Forum* (Winter 1980): 153–59.

Minnich, Elizabeth Kamark. *Transforming Knowledge.* Philadelphia: Temple University Press, 1990.

Mohanty, Chandra. "Porous Borders: Anti-Racist Feminist Education in the New/Old World Order." Lecture at Duke University, March 1, 1994.

Moraga, Cherríe. *Loving in the War Years: Lo que nunca pasó por sus labios.* Boston: South End Press, 1983.

Nazareth, Peter. "Paule Marshall's Timeless People." *New Letters* 40.1 (October 1973): 113–31.

Ndebele, Njabulo. *Fools and Other Stories.* Johannesburg, 1983. New York: Readers International, 1986.

Nelson, Emmanuel. "Black America and the Anglophone Afro-Caribbean Literary Consciousness." *Journal of American Culture* 12.4 (Winter 1989): 53–58.

Norton, Eleanor Holmes. "For Sadie and Maude." In *Sisterhood Is Powerful: An Anthology of Writing from the Women's Liberation Movement,* ed. Robin Morgan, 397–403. New York: Random House, 1970.

Nowak, Hanna. "The Wild Zone in Paule Marshall's Fiction." In *Für eine offene Literaturwissenschaft: Erkundungen und Eroprobungen am Beispiel US-amerikanischer Texte/Opening Up Literary Criticism: Essays on American Prose and Poetry,* ed. Leo Truchlar, 69–87. Salzburg: Neugebauer, 1986.

Ogundipe-Leslie, Omolara. " 'Re-creating Ourselves All Over the World': Interview with Paule Marshall." Interview, January 28, 1977. Intro. by Carole Boyce Davies. *Matatu: Journal for African Culture and Society.* 3.6 (1989): 25–38.

Pannill, Linda. "From the 'Wordshop': The Fiction of Paule Marshall." *MELUS: The Journal of the Society for the Study of the Multi-Ethnic Literature of the United States* 12.2 (Summer 1985): 63–73.

Pettis, Joyce. " 'Talk' as Defensive Artifice: Merle Kinbona in *The Chosen Place, the Timeless People.*" *African American Review* 26.1 (1992): 109–17.

———. *Toward Wholeness in Paule Marshall's Fiction.* Charlottesville and London: University Press of Virginia, 1995.

Pollard, Velma. "Cultural Connections in Paule Marshall's *Praisesong for the Widow.*" *World Literature Written in English* 25.2 (Autumn 1985): 285–98.

Quashie, Kevin. "Reperformance as Voice Trope and Healing Imperative in Toni Morrison's Works." Unpublished M.A. thesis. Department of English, Arizona State University, 1997.

Reyes, Angelita. "Politics and Metaphors of Materialism in Paule Marshall's *Praisesong for the Widow* and Toni Morrison's *Tar Baby.*" In *Politics and the Muse: Studies in the Politics of Recent American Literature,* ed. Adam J. Sorkin, 179–205. Bowling Green, Oh.: Popular Press, 1989.

Rich, Adrienne. "Compulsory Heterosexuality and Lesbian Existence." In *The Signs Reader: Women, Gender and Scholarship,* ed. Elizabeth Abel and Emily K. Abel. Chicago: University of Chicago Press, 1983. 139–68.

Sanchez, Sonia. Interview by Claudia Tate. In *Black Women Writers at Work,* ed. Claudia Tate, 132–48. New York: Continuum, 1990.

Sandiford, Keith A. "Paule Marshall's *Praisesong for the Widow*: The Reluctant Heiress, or Whose Life Is It Anyway?" *Black American Literature Forum* 20.4 (Winter 1986): 371–92.

Sandoval, Chela. "Feminism and Racism: A Report on the 1981 National Women's Studies Association Conference." In *Making Face, Making Soul, Haciendo*

Caras, ed. Gloria Anzaldúa, 55–71. San Francisco: Aunt Lute Foundation Books, 1990.

Scarboro, Ann Armstrong. "The Healing Process: A Paradigm for Self-Renewal in Paule Marshall's *Praisesong for the Widow* and Camara Laye's *Le Regard du roi.*" *MLS* 19.1 (Winter 1989): 28–36.

Scarpa, Giulia. " 'Couldn't They Have Done Differently?' Caught in the Web of Race, Gender, and Class: Paule Marshall's *Praisesong for the Widow.*" *World Literature Written in English* 29.2 (1989): 94–104.

Schneider, Deborah. "A Search for Selfhood: Paule Marshall's *Brown Girl, Brownstones.*" In *The Afro-American Novel Since 1960,* ed. Peter Bruck and Wolfgang Karrer, 53–73. Amsterdam: Gruner, 1982.

Segrest, Mab. *My Mama's Dead Squirrel: Lesbian Essays on Southern Culture.* Ithaca, N.Y.: Firebrand, 1985.

Skerrett, Joseph T., Jr. "Paule Marshall and the Crisis of Middle Years: *The Chosen Place, the Timeless People.*" *Callaloo* 6.2 (Spring–Summer 1983): 68–73.

Smith, Barbara, ed. *Home Girls: A Black Feminist Anthology.* New York: Kitchen Table: Women of Color Press, 1983.

Smith-Wright, Geraldine. "In Spite of the Klan: Ghosts in the Fiction of Black Women Writers." In *Haunting the House of Fiction: Feminist Perspectives on Ghost Stories by American Women,* 142–165. Knoxville: University of Tennesee Press, 1991.

Spenser, Edmund. *The Faerie Queene.* 1596. Reprint Harmondsworth: Penguin, 1978.

Spillers, Hortense J. "Chosen Place, Timeless People: Some Figurations on the New World." In *Conjuring: Black Women, Fiction, and Literary Tradition,* ed. Marjorie Pryse and Hortense J. Spillers, 151–75. Bloomington: Indiana University Press, 1985.

Spivak, Gayatri Chakravorty. "Finding Feminist Readings: Dante-Yeats." In *In Other Worlds: Essays in Cultural Politics,* 15–29. Routledge: New York and London, 1988.

Stoelting, Winifred L. "Time Past and Time Present: The Search for Viable Links in *The Chosen Place, the Timeless People* by Paule Marshall." *CLA Journal* 16.1 (September 1972): 60–71.

Stutman, Suzanne. Critique of Linda Wells, " 'What Shall I Give My Children?' The Role of the Mentor in Gloria Naylor's *The Women of Brewster Place* and Paule Marshall's *Praisesong for the Widow.*" *Explorations in Ethnic Studies* 13.2 (July 1990): 58–60.

Talmor, Sascha. "Merle of Bournehills." Review article. *Durham University Journal* 80.1 (December 1987): 125–28.

Tate, Claudia, ed. *Black Women Writers at Work.* New York: Continuum, 1990.

Troester, Rosalie Riegle. "Turbulence and Tenderness: Mothers, Daughters, and 'Othermothers' in Paule Marshall's *Brown Girl, Brownstones.*" *SAGE: A Scholarly Journal on Black Women* 1.2 (Fall 1984): 13–16.

Wade-Gayles, Gloria. "The Truths of Our Mothers' Lives: Mother-Daughter Relationships in Black Women's Fiction." *SAGE: A Scholarly Journal on Black Women* 1.2 (Fall 1984): 8–12.

Washington, Mary Helen. "Afterword." 1981. In Paule Marshall, *Brown Girl, Brownstones,* 311–325. New York: Feminist Press, 1981.

———. "I Sign My Mother's Name: Alice Walker, Dorothy West, Paule Marshall." In *Mothering the Mind: Twelve Studies of Writers and Their Silent Partners,* ed. Ruth Perry and Martine Watson, 143–63. New York: Holmes and Meier, 1984.

————. "Teaching *Black-Eyed Susans*: An Approach to the Study of Black Women Writers." *Black American Literature Forum* 2 (1977): 20–24. Reprinted in *All the Women Are White, All the Blacks Are Men, but Some of Us Are Brave: Black Women's Studies*, ed. Gloria T. Hull, Patricia Bell Scott, and Barbara Smith, 208–17. New York: Feminist Press, 1982.

Waxman, Barbara Frey. "The Widow's Journey to Self and Roots: Aging and Society in Paule Marshall's *Praisesong for the Widow*." *Frontiers: A Journal of Women Studies* 9.3 (1987): 94–99.

Wells, Linda. " 'What Shall I Give My Children?' The Role of the Mentor in Gloria Naylor's *The Women of Brewster Place* and Paule Marshall's *Praisesong for the Widow*." *Explorations in Ethnic Studies* 13.2 (July 1990): 41–51.

West, Cornel. *Prophesy Deliverance: An Afro-American Revolutionary Christianity*. Philadelphia: Westminster Press, 1982.

Wilentz, Gay. "Towards a Spiritual Middle Passage Back: Paule Marshall's Diasporic Vision in *Praisesong for the Widow*." *Obsidian II : Black Literature in Review* 5.3 (Winter 1990): 1–21.

Williams, Patricia J. *The Alchemy of Race and Rights: Diary of a Law Professor.* Cambridge, Mass.: Harvard University Press, 1991.

Willis, Susan. *Specifying: Black Women Writing the American Experience*. Madison: University of Wisconsin Press, 1987.

Wilson, Lucy. "Aging and Ageism in Paule Marshall's *Praisesong for the Widow* and Beryl Gilroy's *Frangipani House*." *Journal of Caribbean Studies* 7.2–3 (1990): 189–99.

Index